DATE			

Behaviourism
and the Limits of
Scientific Method

International Library of Philosophy and Scientific Method

Editor: Ted Honderich

A Catalogue of books already published in the
International Library of Philosophy and Scientific Method
will be found at the end of this volume

Behaviourism and the Limits of Scientific Method

Brian D. Mackenzie

Lecturer in Psychology
The University of Tasmania

HUMANITIES PRESS

ATLANTIC HIGHLANDS, N.J.

First published in the United States of America
in 1977 by Humanities Press Inc.
Atlantic Highlands, N.J. 07716
Copyright © Brian D. Mackenzie 1977
No part of this book may be reproduced in
any form without permission from the
publisher, except for the quotation of brief
passages in criticism

Library of Congress Cataloging in Publication Data

Mackenzie, Brian D
    Behaviourism and the Limits of Scientific Method
    (International library of philosophy and scientific method)
    Includes bibliographical references.
    1. Behaviourism. I. Title. II. Series.
BF199.M22   1976   150'.19'43   76-16278
ISBN 0-391-00620-7

Printed in Great Britain

For Lynne

CONTENTS

Contents

PREFACE

Perhaps this is the most important book ever written. One stands for an instant blinded with a great hope.

From a review of John B. Watson's *Behaviorism* (New York: People's Institute Publishing Co., 1924), quoted in R. S. Woodworth, *Contemporary Schools of Psychology* (New York: Ronald Press, 1931, p. 97).

Not for an instant but for fifty years, psychologists were blinded with the great hope that they could make psychology a genuine and successful science if only they would follow a number of clear-cut rules. Chief among these rules were the elimination of consciousness as the subject matter of psychology on the one hand, and the rigorous use of scientific method on the other; the history of behaviourism is the history of the attempt to treat these two rules as one. This book is a study of those rules and of that hope.

This is not, however, a history of behaviourism. It treats the founding of behaviourism in considerable detail and traces the evolution of the behaviourist uses of scientific method, but says little about the rise and fall of any behaviourist theories or about the experiments and the controversies associated with those theories. It deals instead with what was common to the various theories, that is, with their common background in pre-behaviourist experimental psychology and with their reliance on various techniques for ensuring objectivity and scientific validity; Chapter I presents the case for considering these, rather than any theories or findings, as definitive of behaviourism. The aim is to show where the behaviourists got their great hope, how it took the particular form it did, and why it was incapable of being realized.

Where the behaviourists got their great hope and how it became particularized are questions that belong mainly to the history of psychology; why the hope could not be realized is a question that belongs mainly to the philosophy of science. This book tries to answer both kinds of question; psychologists who read it, therefore, may find that it contains more philosophy than they like, while philosophers may find that it has too much psychology. The overlap cannot be helped, however. The main question is why behaviourism failed as a scientific movement, and that question demands both psychological and philosophical material in its answer. Behaviourism was more deeply and explicitly involved with philosophy – philosophy of science, that is – than most scientific movements are. To understand behaviourism's career, it is necessary to understand both why it became involved with the philosophy of science and why that involvement failed, eventually, to do it any good. It is certain that answers to the question of why behaviourism failed are of interest to all those of us, whether philosophers or psychologists, who are still concerned to develop a psychology that is in some meaningful sense scientific. The answers proposed in this book have some consequences for any future attempt to 'construct' a scientific psychology by following any rules of procedure. They may also have some implications for the understanding of the history of science in general. For these reasons, the alternation of historical and philosophical analysis is presented without apology.

Chapter I, accordingly, is mostly psychological; it introduces the problem of accounting for the career of behaviourism and begins the analysis of the movement. On the basis of a brief review of the characteristics of behaviourist research it concludes, fairly unexceptionally, that behaviourism must be understood in methodological rather than substantive terms; what was central to behaviourism was a set of general methodological principles for doing research, rather than any theories or discoveries. Along the way, this chapter attempts to make it clear why a Kuhnian analysis of paradigms and normal science is inapplicable to behaviourism. Chapter II is more philosophical. It deals with methodological approaches to science in general and contrasts them with substantive or content-orientated ones; the contrast can often be expressed as one between 'positivist' and 'realist' orientations. A positivist orientation, it is suggested, is most appropriate when the focus of scientific interest is on the terms and concepts of a scientific theory as such (the 'context of reconstruction'), while a realist orientation is most appropriate when the focus of interest is on the events which the theory attempts to explain (the 'context of construction'). Chapter III is again psychological, analysing the circumstances that led to the founding of behaviourism and to its acquiring a positivist orientation. Those circumstances stemmed from the difficulties in doing animal behaviour research along the introspective model which dominated American comparative psychology at the turn of the century. The repudiation of introspection and of consciousness in comparative psychology was an appropriate response to these difficulties. The extension of this response to the rest of experimental psychology was not so clearly appropriate, however, and owed its success largely to adventitious factors associated with the collapse of Newtonian theory in the physical sciences. The adventitious success of this response determined the subsequent positivist orientation of behaviourism throughout its career. Chapter IV emphasises psychological and philosophical material by turns. It begins by tracing the gradual transformation of behaviourism's positivism from its unsystematic and unreflective state in early or classical behaviourism to its explicit and sophisticated state in neobehaviourism. It then builds on the analysis of Chapter II, to show that a positivist orientation is bound to be unsuccessful when implemented in the context of construction, in which neobehaviourism operated; the reason is that methodological rules, or decision procedures, cannot be applied satisfactorily to many of the kinds of problem that arise in the course of scientific research. Those problems require the kind of commitment characteristic of a realist orientation, in which faith, luck and hunches are sometimes given more weight than the rules of inference. These conclusions are then illustrated by the characteristics of some neobehaviourist research. Chapter V concludes the study with the judgment that the main systematic contribution of behaviourism to psychology is its practical demonstration of the untenability of the methodological principles on which it was founded; as a consolation, however, it suggests that behaviourism's unsystematic contributions, to do with training psychologists in ways of seeing, are greater than have been appreciated.

A book is always the product of many hands. I am indebted to John Beloff, Chris Brand, Professor R. S. Peters, and James Alexander

Preface

for a critical reading of an earlier version of the manuscript. John
Beloff, indeed, did far more, and was a constant source of encouragement and helpful criticism. Paul Agutter, Lawrence Brisk-
man, and Robert Young helped thrash out many of the problems
that arose along the way. Patricia Dovadola typed the manuscript in
its various versions, and was eternally co-operative in meeting all the
real and illusory deadlines. The Psychology Department of Simon
Fraser University generously provided office and library facilities
during the spring and summer of 1973. The work on which this
book is based was carried out while I held a Canada Council
Fellowship at the University of Edinburgh. The Canada Council and
the University of Tasmania both provided financial assistance with
typing and preparation of the manuscript. To all of these, my very
sincere thanks. But most of all, my wife, Lynne Mackenzie, provided
the kind of indispensable critical stimulation that can come only
from a long and productive period of intellectual partnership. The
dedication of this book is the barest expression of my debt to her.

I

INTRODUCTION

1 THE PROBLEM

The psychological movement called behaviourism is still of great importance to psychology, even although it has lost most of its influence. It is important because it was the most sustained attempt ever made to construct a science of psychology through the use of detailed and explicit rules of procedure, because these rules were the outcome of the most sophisticated and rigorous analyses of the logic of science ever made, and because both the attempt and the movement were ultimately failures. The failure was almost total, even although behaviourism seemed to have every possible advantage. Behaviourism was based largely on an aggressively objective approach to the problems of psychology; it won the allegiance of the majority of psychologists and logicians who came into close contact with it; it continued to attract new adherents and to develop new methods of investigation throughout the forty to fifty years in which it dominated psychology; most important, it provided the basis for a truly enormous amount of careful and sophisticated research; but despite all of this, it never managed to produce a significant body of lasting scientific knowledge comparable to what can be found in many other less well endowed sciences. This lack of large-scale results has taken its toll of the movement. Partly as a result of this lack, behaviourism's grand theories have almost all been abandoned, many of the movement's ablest figures have come out against it, its support from logicians and philosophers has evaporated, and the mainstream American psychological journals are eagerly publishing articles on

1

imagery and the nature of consciousness.[1] All of these trends index the decline of behaviourism's influence. Only in some applied fields, such as certain parts of clinical psychology (which will be briefly discussed in the last chapter), does behaviourism retain anything of its old eminence.

Why did behaviourism fail in its attempts to construct a viable scientific psychology, and what does it matter now? The rest of this book will try to answer the first of these questions. We may try now to give a brief answer to the second.

Behaviourism was many things to many people, but one of the main things it was was an attempt to be rigorously scientific in the practice of psychology. Behaviourists did everything they could to ensure that their movement would be a genuinely scientific one, and yet that movement was a failure. Since many of us still have the goal of developing a psychology that is in some meaningful sense scientific, it is important for us to know what relation behaviourism's scientific aspirations had to its failure. Did behaviourism fail despite its efforts to be scientific or, in some sense, because of them?

The latter possibility is not as absurd as it might seem. There are a number of ways in which behaviourism's 'scientificness' might have been implicated in its failure. Did behaviourism fail because psychology cannot, by its very nature, be a science? Or was the conception of science pursued by the behaviourists an erroneous conception, not really characteristic of science at all? Or was that conception appropriate only to some sciences, such as physics, and inappropriate to others, such as psychology? That is, are there perhaps fundamental differences between what can count as a science of the physical world and what can count as a science of mind or behaviour, with behaviourism ignoring these differences to its peril? Or then again, did behaviourism perhaps not fail at all, but achieve all that could reasonably be expected of it before it was replaced by a successor? These are all more or less open questions and, especially given psychology's present uncertainty, worthy of consideration. It may not be possible to give a final answer to all of them, but it is clear that if one or another of the possibilities they suggest should turn out to be the case, it would have very significant implications for what we can expect psychology to be like, and to amount to, in the future.

This book will try to answer some of these questions, but a simple yes or no to any of them will not be offered, nor would such a simple answer do much to explain what it was about behaviourism that led to its failure. That explanation will require an analysis of what is involved in scientific inquiry at the most general level, and of how the pattern of inquiry found in behaviourism contrasts with the usual one.

2 THE SCIENTIFIC FOUNDATIONS OF BEHAVIOURISM

Paradigms

It has become common in recent years to assert that behaviourism displayed the pattern of scientific development described by Kuhn in his *Structure of Scientific Revolutions.*[2] Behaviourism, that is, was based on a 'paradigm' that defined the dimensions of psychological practice. This paradigm was 'articulated' by means of the theories and experiments involved in behaviourist 'normal science'. Eventually the behaviourist paradigm encountered a large number of 'anomalies' which provoked the current 'crisis' in psychological research. The crisis will be resolved through a 'scientific revolution' when a new paradigm replaces the faltering behaviourist one.

The popularity of Kuhn's account in psychology is easy to understand. If a Kuhnian analysis can successfully be applied to psychology, then it will do much to explain the rise and fall of behaviourism and to make psychology's current transitional state comprehensible. Such an analysis can also be very comforting. It serves in a way to legitimate the dominance of behaviourism and its later decline because the same pattern of dominance and decline is also characteristic of the physical sciences – and it gives some assurance that psychology's present uncertainty will disappear when a new paradigm emerges, as the analysis promises it will.

Whether a Kuhnian analysis can be applied to psychology or not hinges on the notion of a paradigm. If behaviourism was based on a paradigm, then the rest of Kuhn's analysis follows; otherwise, it does not. Now, there are certainly some senses of this notoriously vague concept in which behaviourism can be said to have had one or more paradigms. In his later writings Kuhn[3] identifies paradigms with the intra-group communication patterns of small or medium-sized groups of scientists sharing common interests. Groups are defined as people who write to each other on professional matters, who are on each other's mailing lists for prepublication reports of research, etc.; their 'paradigm' is whatever common concern holds them together. It is certain that behaviourism had its share of paradigms of this sort, but it is equally certain that that fact throws little light on the character of the movement as a whole.

The concept of a paradigm is not without ambiguities in Kuhn's original treatise,[4] but a basic or root sense of the term can be pinned down without difficulty. Paradigms are 'universally recognized scientific achievements that for a time provide model problems and solutions to a community of practitioners'.[5] These exemplary achievements provide models for all aspects of scientific inquiry: 'I mean to suggest that some accepted examples of actual scientific practice – examples which include law, theory, application, and instrumentation together – provide models from which spring particular coherent traditions of scientific research.'[6] The specific character of the paradigm is emphasized, just as it is in the (Shorter Oxford) dictionary definition of a paradigm as an example or exemplar. Thus, 'the concrete scientific achievement, as a locus of professional commitment, [is] prior to the various concepts, laws, theories, and points of view that may be abstracted from it'.[7] While Kuhn goes on in his treatise to use the concept of a paradigm in a variety of other related ways, the subsequent uses are all derived from this original meaning and are all compatible with it.

Now, it is clear that behaviourism never had a paradigm in this sense. That is, it was not based on a scientific achievement of demonstrated and continuing substantive significance for psychology, which could be 'articulated' through related experiments and theories in a 'coherent tradition of scientific research'. This point has been well made by Heidbreder: behaviourists, like all other psychologists,[8]

> have produced no achievement which, in the manner of Newton's in physics and Darwin's in biology, has given psychology a conceptual scheme with reference to which, over a considerable period of time, all or nearly all of its available knowledge could be integrated, its ongoing research directed and to some degree co-ordinated, and its workers united into a single group sharing, despite diverse interests and specialized practices, a common outlook on their common domain.

4

Paradigms do not have to be as all-embracing as Newton's or Darwin's to give rise to coherent traditions of scientific research, of course. But they have to be sufficiently all-embracing to provide models for research, and resultant agreement on fundamentals, for all the members of an (often redefined) group of practitioners in a scientific discipline. The achievements to which various groups of behaviourists referred never, as we shall see, had this much of an all-embracing character.[9] Behaviourism clearly produced a redefined group of practitioners, but they did not share commitment to any concrete scientific achievement. What they shared was a dissatisfaction with the way that psychology was being done by those who dominated the field, and a hope that a new way of doing things would bring important and scientifically respectable results.

Methodological Objectivism

There are three publications or researches that can be taken jointly as the foundation of behaviourism: Thorndike's early animal researches, Pavlov's (and Bechterev's) investigations of the conditioned reflex, and Watson's polemical article, 'Psychology as the behaviorist views it'. This is not to say that these three provided a complete basis for behaviourism, but that in so far as behaviourism was founded on specific achievements in psychology, these were the ones. The first two provided the models for almost all behaviourist experimentation on learning – the models of instrumental (Thorndikian, operant) conditioning and classical (Pavlovian, respondent) conditioning. The last signalled the start of behaviourism as a self-conscious movement. None of these three, however, constituted a major and substantive scientific achievement, at least not for behaviourism.

The qualification, 'at least not for behaviourism', is fundamental. Both Thorndike's and Pavlov's early researches were addressed to important questions in their respective fields and made some progress in answering them. Thorndike[10] attempted to demonstrate that, in learning to escape from puzzle boxes, his subject animals acquired their responses solely on a basis of trial and error. He advanced the major hypothesis that all learning might conform to the pattern displayed by his experimental animals, that is, that all learning might proceed by trial and error without any effective exercise of insight or conscious reflection. In proposing this hypothesis, he was setting

5

himself explicitly in opposition to the broadly cognitive hypothesis of Romanes[11] and Lloyd Morgan.[12] His use of puzzle boxes was a relevant and useful method of experimentation precisely because of the new light which it was able to throw on the contentious issue he was investigating.

However, Thorndike's major hypothesis and the evidence on which it was based – which might indeed have constituted a paradigm – did not constitute an agreed-upon basis for behaviourism. On the contrary, it was the source of one of the most intensive theoretical controversies for behaviourism. Lashley, Krechevsky, and Tolman (to cite some of the major figures only) maintained that some sort of insight or hypothesis testing or central representation – these terms defined objectively, of course – had to be attributed to organisms in a learning situation in order to account for their learning. Their position was almost the precise opposite of Thorndike's and was much the same position that Thorndike had been attempting to discredit in its earlier less objective formulations by Romanes and Lloyd Morgan. In contrast, Watson, Guthrie, Hull, and Skinner agreed that no such attribution of insight, etc., was necessary or relevant to an account of the learning process. They disagreed among themselves otherwise, and Watson and Guthrie, at least, insisted that 'trial and error' could no more serve as a first approximation to a description of what went on in learning than could 'insight'. In short, behaviourist psychologists as a group never agreed on acceptance of Thorndike's results and his systematic hypotheses as the basis for their subsequent practice. What they did agree on, and almost all that they agreed on, was that Thorndike's use of puzzle boxes was a good way to answer questions about animal behaviour. They agreed that it was a good way, not because Thorndike's experimental technique was finely suited to the problems which he was investigating, but because it was a reliable and objective method for the study of behaviour. This agreement on the worth of Thorndike's method persisted despite the fact that use of the method never had the slightest success in bringing about any agreement on the answers themselves.

The case with Pavlov is similar but even more pointed, for the theory and the problems to which Pavlov's method was connected never made a major entry to behaviourist psychology at all. Originally, the conditioned reflex was discovered and used by Pavlov in the study of digestive processes. Its properties were sufficiently remarkable that Pavlov and his co-workers began to give it very serious consideration in its own right, and came to use it as the basis for study of higher nervous activity.[13] The conditioned reflex was not treated by them as a tool, separate from the problems which it was used to investigate, but as the unit of their subject matter, that is, as a fundamental manifestation of nervous excitation. As a result, for Russian workers use of the conditioned reflex was inseparable from Pavlov's theory of nervous excitation and inhibition. This coalescence of Pavlovian theory and method, each dependent on and supporting the other, has continued to be typical of Russian psychology, in which a vigorous theoretical and experimental programme is still extending Pavlovian theory to cover more and more aspects of human behaviour. It is thus likely that a Kuhnian analysis could be profitably applied to the development of Russian psychology after Pavlov, for Pavlov's early work would seem to constitute a paradigm, and subsequent Russian psychology has certainly been based on it.[14]

By contrast, in behaviourist psychology, the only acknowledged and enduring merit of the conditioned reflex, which was nevertheless sufficient to lead to its widespread experimental use, was that it was an objective method for the study of behaviour. The Pavlovian theory of cortical excitation was regarded by most American psychologists, and continues to be regarded, as either preposterous or, at best, ill-founded. As with Thorndike's method of animal experimentation, the conditioned reflex received general approval predicated almost solely upon its objectivity, and hardly at all upon its unique appropriateness for answering certain specific questions asked in certain specific ways. The use and extension of Pavlov's method of classical conditioning, like the use and extension of Thorndike's method of instrumental conditioning, has been piecemeal, general, and not closely related to any specific theoretical framework.

Finally, Watson's polemic[15] was not intended to advance seriously any specific hypotheses, nor even primarily to advance any specific methods as appropriate for the study of current problems. Rather, its intent was to stipulate that psychology could and should be exclusively the objective study of observable behaviour, to maintain that a certain *class* of methods – those which were objective or which abjured any form of mentalism – were the appropriate ones for studying such behaviour, and to argue that psychology as so conceived and practised would become a successful scientific enterprise.

In summary, two of the founding achievements of behaviourism had considerable substantive significance in their own context, but in the form in which they were incorporated into behaviourism they were shorn of their content and adopted solely for their methodological import, that is, for their objectivity. The third, Watson's polemic, made little in the way of substantive claims at all but merely advanced the cause of objectivity in general. Thus, none of these three achievements answered any major questions – for behaviourism – or solved any long-standing problems in psychology – for behaviourism. Instead, they were taken by behaviourist psychologists to proclaim that human and animal functioning *could* be understood in a particular way (the way of objective experimentation), and to promise that the use of a properly objective methodology *would* make psychology into a genuine science. It is for this reason that Thorndike's and Pavlov's results were never of principal importance; instead it was their techniques, and the methodological principles abstracted from their techniques, that were valued and that became central. The revolution that produced behaviourism was a methodological, or even a meta-methodological, revolution.

The foundation of behaviourism may thus be characterized at least in part as methodological objectivism, that is, as the pursuit of objectivity through the exclusive employment of methods which were themselves known to be objective. This pursuit of and emphasis on objectivity undoubtedly filled a need that was felt in American psychology at the time. As Boring explains it, 'Psychology was all ready for behaviorism . . . the times were ripe for more objectivity in psychology, and Watson was the agent of the times.'[16]

But just what is this touchstone of 'objectivity' by which experimental techniques were assessed? Why, when it was discovered in them, did it lead to their adoption without regard to the theoretical context in which they were developed and embedded? These may seem like odd questions; surely 'objectivity', in a minimal sense that implies an elimination of bias and a concern with observable events, whatever they might be, is basic to any scientific enterprise. And perhaps it is, but this minimal sense of 'objectivity' does not differentiate behaviourism from Wundtian introspective psychology. In this minimal sense, involving standardized experimental methods, replicability of results, etc., the introspective

8

method of Wundt and Titchener also was, or was at least intended to be, thoroughly objective.

The introspective method was judged to be unreliable, of course, since results obtained with it were not always replicable at different laboratories; and this unreliability was cited as justification for rejecting it. Equally, the desire to use methods that had high inter-experimenter reliability was a factor in the adoption of Pavlov's and Thorndike's methods. However, the question of the objectivity of these methods was not resolved by considering the question of their reliability; if anything the converse was true. Watson made it quite clear in all of his polemical writings that the introspective method was unreliable because of the crippling flaws inherent in it from the beginning. The lack of objectivity in that method was not simply discovered as a consequence of its unreliability; rather, its unreliability might have been predicted in advance because of its lack of objectivity. Again, when Watson first advocated use of the conditioned reflex for the study of behaviour[17] that method had been used in a few preliminary studies in Watson's own laboratory, but otherwise had received almost no trials or applications outside of Russian laboratories, the literature from which was almost inaccessible. It thus had not been shown to have precisely that inter-experimenter reliability, the absence of which was supposedly the justification for rejecting introspection. The objectivity of the Pavlovian-Bechterevian methods, nevertheless, provided a sufficient guarantee that they would be reliable, and made experimental confirmation of their reliability not really necessary.[18]

Obviously, therefore, the objectivity which behaviourism required, and which it found in the methods of Thorndike and Pavlov, was something other than or additional to the objectivity that was intended to be (even if it was not sufficiently) characteristic of Wundt's method. The additional element lay, in the first instance, simply in *the rejection in principle of any concern with mental events,* on the basis that these were, by their very (alleged) nature, impossible to investigate objectively. The failure of the introspective method was due simply to the fact that it was attempting to investigate something that could not be investigated. Thus, Watson characterized introspection and its downfall as follows:[19]

[Wundt] grew up in the midst of a dualistic philosophy of the most pronounced type. He could not see his way clear to a solution of the mind-body problem. His psychology, which has reigned supreme to the present day, is necessarily a compromise. He substituted the term *consciousness* for the term soul. Consciousness is not quite so unobservable as soul. We observe it by peeking in suddenly and catching it unawares as it were (*introspection*). . . . In 1912 the objective psychologists or behaviorists reached the conclusion that they could no longer be content to work with Wundt's formulations. They felt that the 30 odd barren years since the establishment of Wundt's laboratory had proved conclusively that the so-called introspective psychology of Germany was founded upon wrong hypotheses – that no psychology which included the religious mind-body problem could ever arrive at verifiable conclusions.

Both claims are brought out clearly in this quotation: Wundt's programme was scientifically sterile from the beginning, and its sterility was a result of its concentration on mind and consciousness.

The objectivity which behaviourism sought was thus one which from the beginning excluded the mental from science, and did so independent of purely evidential considerations. This *a priori* character of the exclusion of the mental is sufficiently indicated both by the explanation given to the failure of introspection and by the reception afforded Pavlov's method. The demonstration is reinforced, furthermore, by consideration of the specific issues which, more than anything else, are taken to have sparked off the behaviourist decision to repudiate introspection in general as both unreliable and untenable.

The most important of these issues was the 'imageless thought' controversy raging between Wundt and Titchener on the one side, and a loose group of psychologists centred at Wurzburg on the other. This controversy, over whether or not thought could in principle be reduced to trains of images, occasioned a large amount of contradictory research and polemic on both sides. The dispute was never resolved altogether, although the Wurzburgers had somewhat the better of it. The dominant reaction to the controversy among American psychologists, at least those not involved in it, was that if the introspective method could not even begin to settle so apparently basic a question as to whether or not thought is made of images, then what good was it? The answer seemed plainly to be, not much. Boring writes that shortly before behaviourism was launched,

'Watson had just seen introspection fail at Wurzburg – that is what most Americans in 1910 thought had happened there.'[20]

However, the introspective method used at Wurzburg was very different from the one used in Wundt's laboratory; the two were related to quite different theories of mind. That the results obtained with the two methods were not identical was no more a methodological failure of introspection than the inability to obtain many responses equally well with both classical and instrumental conditioning is a methodological failure of behaviourism. Furthermore, the Wurzburg results were not merely the (possibly artifactual) product of a single laboratory. The imageless thought hypothesis was independently confirmed by Binet in France, Bovet in Switzerland, and Woodworth in America. The findings from Titchener's laboratory, against imageless thought, might however have been artifactual in this sense, as they were never independently confirmed at another laboratory (Wundt never performed any Wurzburg-type experiments).[21]

This is not to underplay the importance of the imageless thought controversy. The dispute between the Wundtians and the Wurzburgers was a very major theoretical and experimental problem for both of them, and had it been resolved would probably have led to a serious modification of one or both methods and theories. But the dispute did not constitute a methodological failure generally of all introspective methods, at least not for introspectionists, including those who were uncommitted in the controversy. It could be seen as a general failure only by those who were already prepared to repudiate introspection on other grounds. The two introspectionist methods could be treated as equivalent, and their divergent results attributed to the unreliability of introspection in general, only by treating the differences between the two methods as insignificant; and that in turn could be done only by contrasting both methods indifferently with an already favoured alternative conception of scientific observation in which introspection of any sort is excluded from the beginning. In short, interpretation of the imageless thought controversy as showing the unreliability of 'the' introspective method, or of all of them, was possible only within a framework which was already more narrowly objectivist or proto-behaviourist.

If the rejection of consciousness as a focus of research and study was not strictly forced by the unreliability of introspection, neither can it be seen, today at least, as an extreme but inevitable reaction to a rigid introspectionist orthodoxy, as the only way in which 'objective' (non-introspective) methods could gain any hearing at all. Students sometimes gain the impression that the behaviourist revolution was necessary in order to establish non-introspective methods as permissible and appropriate in psychology; and they are not totally corrected of their error if they read Watson's own statements on the subject. In fact there was a wide diversity of methods in use in experimental psychology – particularly but not solely in human experimental psychology – before 1913; introspective and non-introspective methods of investigation were employed, side by side and independently, with greater flexibility and tolerance than has been characteristic of psychology since that date. Woodworth observes that before the founding of behaviourism in 1913:[22]

> there had been a large amount of objective experimental work by those who were interested in what I have been calling the psychology of performance. Watson alludes to some of it . . . when he speaks of experimental pedagogy, the psychology of tests, etc. He leaves the impression that all such objective work was very recent, as well as being partially vitiated by introspection. Tests, completely objective and free from introspection, go back to Galton in about 1880. Objective study of the learning process was active in the nineties, and may be dated back to Ebbinghaus's celebrated study of memory in 1885, a purely objective study. But even Galton and Ebbinghaus are not entitled to rank as the originators of objective psychology, for still further back we find the purely objective beginnings of work on reaction time; and much of the work on sense perception, carried on by the method of impression, can perfectly well be considered as an objective study of an individual's accuracy of observation. Thus the objective method was in use from the very beginnings of experimental psychology, and the amount of research carried on by this method, up to 1900 or 1912, was very large indeed. As we saw before, psychology was not at all limited in practice to the study of experience. The study of performance was in full swing, and even those psychologists who made great use of introspection, like Müller and Külpe, used it largely for the light it threw on performance.

During this period there were, of course, a great number of

Introduction

experiments carried out with introspective methods that might better have been conducted with non-introspective ones. The point is merely that non-introspective methods were firmly enough established in psychology that there was little in the way of entrenched social forces that could have been expected to prevent their further systematic use.

Again, therefore, behaviourism's initial rejection of the mental and exclusive concentration on 'objective' methods cannot legitimately be justified, as they are often said to be, by reference to the state of introspective psychology of the time – as being of demonstrated scientific worthlessness or as exercising an oppressive scientific hegemony. The behaviourist stance was taken largely in self-conscious opposition to introspective psychology, of course, but not in response to the very real inadequacies of the latter in dealing with its own subject matter. Instead, the factors responsible for the emergence of behaviourism – consisting mainly in the ill-considered association of introspective and comparative psychology – were, as we shall see in Chapter III, unrelated to most of the career of introspective psychology, and totally unrelated to the problems introspective psychology was facing at the time.

The negative characterization of behaviourism's brand of objectivity, that it was in principle anti-mentalistic, is an obvious and familiar point, even a trivial one. What is not so trivial is the demonstration that the 'principles' involved, and the grounds for the adoption of an anti-mentalism, were *a priori* ones; or at least ones not in any way called for by experimental evidence. To sum up the point once more: 'objective psychologists' rejected introspection *because* they were anti-mentalistic; they did not *become* anti-mentalistic on the basis of having had to reject introspection.

The converse of the rejection of mentalism, and the affirmative side of behaviourism's quest for objectivity, was the acceptance of a loose 'physicalism'. Behaviourism's methodological objectivism was of a sort that related the methods and scope of psychology to those characteristic of the natural sciences. Wundt's distinction (accepted with modifications by Titchener) between 'mediate experience' and 'immediate experience' as the basis for demarcation between physics and psychology was to be abolished. The same logical methods, observational techniques, standards of evidence, and criteria of validity were to apply to psychology as to physics. Hence, the kinds of thing that psychology was to study were to be at the most general

13

level the same kinds of thing as physics studied – bodies in motion.
Applying this precept to psychology dictated a restriction of concern
to publicly observable behaviour. Thus, that behaviour alone is the
proper subject matter for psychology was indicated by the example
of successful sciences as well as by the example of what was defined
as an unsuccessful one, Wundtian introspective psychology.

The insistence that the canons of science for psychology were to
be the same as (and where necessary taken over from) those of the
natural sciences was a feature of behaviourism from the beginning.
As Watson put it, the behaviourists[23]

> decided either to give up psychology or else to make it a
> natural science. They saw their brother-scientists making
> progress in medicine, in chemistry, in physics. Every new
> discovery in those fields was of prime importance; every new
> element isolated in one laboratory could be isolated in some
> other laboratory; each new element was immediately taken up
> in the warp and woof of science as a whole. One need only
> mention wireless, radium, insulin, thyroxin, to verify this.
> Elements so isolated and methods so formulated immediately
> began to function in human achievement. . . . The behaviorist
> asks: Why don't we make what we can *observe* the real field of
> psychology? Let us limit ourselves to things that can be
> observed, and formulate laws concerning only those things. . . .
> You will find, then, the behaviorist working like any other
> scientist. His sole object is to gather facts about behavior – verify
> his data – subject them both to logic and to mathematics (the
> tools of every scientist). . . . It may never make a pretense of
> being a *system*. Indeed systems in every scientific field are out of
> date. We collect our facts from observation. Now and then we
> select a group of facts and draw certain general conclusions
> about them. In a few years as new experimental data are
> gathered by better methods, even these tentative general
> conclusions have to be modified. Every scientific field, zoology,
> physiology, chemistry and physics, is more or less in a state of
> flux. Experimental technique, the accumulation of facts by that
> technique, occasional tentative consolidation of these facts into
> a theory or an hypothesis describe our procedure in science.
> Judged upon this basis, behaviorism is a true natural science.

The tendency toward self-assimilation into the natural sciences remained much the same as behaviourism developed. Weiss[24] went farther even than Watson, in a surprisingly sophisticated attempt to show that both the methods and the content of psychology could be formulated in terms appropriate to atomic physics. Avoiding Weiss' reductionism, Skinner was the first psychologist to concern himself with recasting psychology along Bridgman's operationist principles.[25] Hull chose detailed cases from the history of physics and astronomy to provide examples of how science should be carried out.[26]

The adoption of a natural-science based orientation in behaviourism was itself, strictly speaking, *a priori*, just as was the rejection of mentalism; although the former provided much of the basis for the latter. The rejection of mentalism was justified by appeal to the practices of physics, but the appropriateness of these practices for psychology had by no means been demonstrated when they were first advocated. However, the general validity of basing psychology in some way on the natural sciences, and particularly on physics, was an assumption that had rarely been questioned in any kind of psychology which had claims to being scientific. Behaviourism, in searching for a lead from the natural sciences, was at least in this respect only following a respected tradition.

The Contentual Pluralism of Behaviourist Research

The foundation of behaviourism, then, was an anti-mentalist methodological objectivism adopted largely on *a priori* grounds. Just what these grounds were will be discussed in detail in the following chapters, but they have already been alluded to. The first involved the tendency endemic to psychology at least since Locke, to attempt to base psychology on the methods and models of the physical sciences; the coming of behaviourism was marked by a new turn in this long-standing trend. The second was an entirely legitimate dissatisfaction with the way in which introspective psychology had become involved with comparative psychology, a dissatisfaction that might have led quite reasonably to a separation of the two.

It remains to consider the character of the research based on the objectivist foundation of behaviourism. That foundation, again, was *a priori* methodological, and quite unspecific. The faith in the power of an objective methodology was not closely tied to any concrete achievement in psychology, nor even to a particular set of methods. The faith was a general one, repeatedly affirmed on the basis of the promise which it issued for future success, and justified by appeal to other 'objective' sciences which were already successful. Keeping the faith, therefore, was fully compatible with the development of numerous diverse formulations of the scope, methods, and theoretical orientation most appropriate to psychology, with the different viewpoints connected by little more than their anti-mentalism and their pursuit of objectivity. And indeed, in just such a way did behaviourism develop. What was most vigorously 'articulated' in behaviourist research was this very objectivism, through the development of a multiplicity of methods and models for investigating behaviour in the newly objective manner.

There were two factors which were responsible for the limited amount of cohesiveness which did exist in behaviourist research and theory. The first was the agreement on objectivism itself, an objectivism which had as its central tenet the repudiation of unobservable internal agents or substances. It implied, therefore, at the very least a severe distrust of alleged internal influences on behaviour. An exception could be made for physiological internal factors, since these were both physical and, in consequence, observable in principle. Even so, the fact that physiological factors were usually not observable in practice precluded any agreement on the value of mentioning them in psychological theories. Physiological references were admissible in behaviourist theories, but were not crucial. Other internal factors received considerably shorter shrift. Instincts, desires, expectations, affects, etc., had little credibility unless they were reduced entirely to either physiological or behavioural measures.

The other factor accounting for some cohesiveness in behaviourist research was its continuity with pre-behaviourist animal psychology. That psychology, in both Britain and America, was based largely on Darwinian evolutionary theory, and was concerned with the adaptive capacities of behaviour as a reaction to changing external circumstances (see Chapter III). While behaviourism gradually cast off almost all traces of a Darwinian orientation, the tradition of experimentation on animal learning was sufficiently well developed to continue as viable. Indeed, it was in the context of this tradition that the demand for greater objectivity emerged. This continuity was initally responsible for the behaviourist preoccupation with problems of learning; and conversely, experimentation on learning was the context most suited to the newly defined or refined requirements of objectivity.

Within the limitations produced by these two factors, which were not very restrictive at least as far as the content of theories was concerned, behaviourist theories developed in wide divergence and often in basic conflict with each other. Watson's original programme was mechanistic, elementaristic, associationistic, peripheralistic, environmentalistic – and correspondingly anti-teleological, anti-purposive, anti-nativist, and anti-emergent. None of these features received full assent from later behaviourists.

Tolman's reintroduction of purpose into behaviourism took place only six years after Watson began promoting conditioning principles.[27] In his fuller theory, Tolman[28] continued to abjure mentalism as such, but made free use of cognitive concepts such as expectancy. In doing so, he repudiated elementarism by insisting on the primacy and irreducibility of molar behaviour, and minimized the implication of associationistic and mechanistic linkages between stimuli and responses by stressing the organism's selective control over its environment. Tolman's student Krechevsky continued in a similar vein, hypothesizing hypotheses in rats.[29] The theoretical concepts of Tolman and Krechevsky were not formally mentalistic ones, despite their appearance, because they were intended strictly as intervening variables, with no significance or existence apart from that which they openly displayed in behaviour. Nevertheless, or rather as a result, emphasis on such concepts made a break with the mechanistic features of Watson's programme inevitable.

Watson's rather ambiguous peripheralism was shown to be wholly untenable by Cannon in his *The Wisdom of the Body*,[30] a work which gave the conception of homeostatic mechanisms a wide currency among psychologists, and thereby reintroduced the inside of the body into psychology in the same year in which many felt that Tolman had reintroduced the mind. Hull made a detailed attempt to ground all of his major theoretical postulates in physiological (and often homeostatic) mechanisms,[31] an attempt later shelved by his student and colleague Spence.[32] Spence also hedged his bets, at least, with regard to the question of anti-emergentism, particularly as related to human language behaviour.[33]

Hull also accepted, with reservations, Tolman's emphasis on the molar characteristics of behaviour, and postulated mechanisms to account for the teleological and purposive features of behaviour. (These, however, did not constitute an admission of purpose as such, but were rather an attempt at translation of 'subjective' concepts into mechanistic 'objective' ones.) In addition, Hull postulated a fairly long list of inborn drives, including drives for hunger, thirst, maternal behaviour, air, pain avoidance, maintenance of body temperature, defecation, urination, rest, sleep, and activity, and judged that additional ones might well prove necessary.[34] While not all of these drives played a major part in Hull's theory, the inclusion of all of them served to weaken the force of his presumed anti-nativism and environmentalism. His activity drive, in particular, foreshadowed the curiosity and exploratory drives which, because of their implications for behavioural autonomy, later became a major embarrassment to drive-reduction varieties of behaviourism.

Elementarism, environmentalism, 'mechanicism',[35] and the rest: the significance of these features was not just that they were included in Watson's position, but that they continued to be central to the popular (and even the professional) stereotype of behaviourism. The significance of their modification of tacit dismissal by later behaviourists was not just that it happened, but (*a*) that it happened relatively easily, with no agonizing reappraisals concerning their validity, and (*b*) that different behaviourist psychologists chose altogether different theoretical features to retain, change, drop, or newly invent. Specific content was no more a defining characteristic of behaviourism's theories than it was of behaviourism's foundation.

Nevertheless, most of the major figures associated with behaviourism – Guthrie, Hull, Krechevsky, Lashley, Miller, Skinner, Spence, etc. – continued to regard themselves as behaviourists, and justifiably felt that there was a definite continuity and cohesiveness in behaviourist research. The existence of this continuity and cohesiveness has confirmed some writers in their judgment that behaviourism had what Kuhn calls a normal-scientific tradition. However, the cohesiveness was not of this sort. Behaviourists shared a common conception of (and faith in) objectivity, an emphasis on problems of learning, and a willingness to investigate these problems with human and animal subjects indifferently; the cohesiveness of behaviourist research consisted entirely in these elements. Behaviourists did not share any common views on what is learned, how it is learned, or what class of theoretical conceptions (e.g., teleological, mechanistic) were most appropriate to account for the learning. The contrast between what behaviourists shared and what they did not share clearly serves to distinguish behaviourist research from a normal scientific tradition, as follows.

Normal science, as Kuhn describes it, is such that it can be almost entirely cumulative. It consists in building up the body of science by accretion, by adding more and more bits to what is regarded as the common store of knowledge. While different normal scientists may disagree on particular theoretical matters, they agree on what they regard as fundamental and background matters. The issues on which they agree comprise the bulk of what they see as their science, and are always their starting point in conducting further research.

By contrast, behaviourism never included an agreed-upon body of background knowledge in this sense. The various behaviourist theories each commenced with definitions of the subject matter of psychology, with statements of the classes of problems to be considered, and with an indication of how these problems were going to be approached. The whole theoretical framework had to be constructed from the ground up for the purpose of putting forward each major theory. As a result, the theories advanced by different behaviourist psychologists were not merely different, they were also – for their proponents, who comprise the context in which it matters – fundamentally different.

While behaviourist theories of learning had some common ground, as described above, it was not their similarities that served as the basis for experimentation and theoretical development, but their differences. The answers to questions such as: What is learned (responses, S-R associations, expectations, relationships)? How is it learned (reinforcement, contiguity, confirmation)? What if anything is reinforcement (drive reduction, tissue need satisfaction, change in the stimulus array, a particular kind of stimulus, a particular kind of response)? These and a number of other contentious issues defined the principal differences between the major behaviourist theories. They also determined the course and direction of most behaviourist research. Each theory had answers to these questions, and a major part of the theoretical and experimental work performed by the proponents of each theory constituted an attempt to show that their theory's answers were right and that a competing theory's answers were wrong. The attempt to do in a rival, or to avoid being done in, was often the principal factor behind the introduction of new apparatus (e.g., the Lashley jumping stand), the demonstration of new experimental phenomena (e.g., sensory preconditioning, the reward value of saccharin), and modifications to existing theory (e.g., Hull's r_G, Tolman's 'motor pattern' learning). None of this is characteristic of normal science.

It is certainly true, nevertheless, that many behaviourists performed minute and intricate experiments specifically in order to fill in the details in an accepted theoretical schema, and hence acted in a way unquestionably typical of normal science. The way in which they did this, however, reveals differences from paradigm-based normal science that are as instructive as the similarities. The context in which any behaviourist psychologists could work in this way, and the background which they could take as established, were specific to the particular theoretical tradition within behaviourism (e.g., Hullian or Tolmanian) with which they were affiliated; they were not ones shared by all or even by most behaviourists. There was something like normal science going on in behaviourist psychology, but it was Hullian normal science, Tolmanian normal science, Guthrian and Skinnerian normal science – all of them different – and not simply behaviourist normal science. Similarly, there was something like a paradigm directing research in each of these mini-traditions, but it was a Hullian paradigm, a Tolmanian paradigm, etc., and not simply a behaviourist paradigm.

The difference is an important one. Since each group of behaviourist practitioners – whom we may loosely designate as a school – had to build up their science from its theoretical foundations, and spent much of their scientific energy in inter-school rivalry, the practice of behaviourist psychology never became genuinely cumulative. No theory was able to progress with any degree of scientific certainty very far beyond its particular laboratory base. Each was prevented from doing so, first by the existence of the others as serious rivals and hence as foci of attention; and also by the consideration that made the multiplicity of schools possible, that is, the absence of a major scientific achievement that they could or would jointly accept as providing the basis on which to build their theories. Instead, each theory, consistent with Kuhn's description of a pre-paradigm school, handled a certain class of problems particularly well. Tolman's theory was most suited to accounting for the determinants of behaviour at a choice point; Hull's to relating response strength to drive level and to the interrelationships between drives in a single-response experimental situation; Guthrie's to accounting for changes in behaviour as a function of arbitrary changes in the stimulus array; Skinner's to controlling the detailed topography of isolated responses of any desired degree of complexity.

Extensions of the theories were often directed toward accommodating some of the phenomena emphasized by a competing theory; one of the most intensively pursued behaviourist achievements, the extension of Hullian theory to cover transposition behaviour (emphasized previously by Tolman), was of this sort. This kind of extension was appropriate to the competitive scientific climate of the times, but made problem selection a relatively *ad hoc* procedure. More general extensions of theory to complex human behaviour – the ostensible goal of most behaviourist theories – were typically not genuine extensions of theory at all, but schematic applications, often resting heavily on analogy, of existing theoretical concepts to the description of social situations. As Koch[36] points out, such 'extensions', far from being based on the judgment that the limited theories were sufficiently developed to deal with extra-laboratory behaviour, were rather prodded by the realization that such theories in their laboratory context had made no significant progress in approaching real situations. As a result, the later extensions to real-life situations arising from fully matured behaviourist theories[37] have been as programmatic as were the recognizably premature but optimistic earlier ones.[38]

In short, the plurality of schools, and the resulting necessity for each to address much of its research to the others, established a situation in which long-range, uni-directional, cumulative development was impossible. Behaviourism as a whole never possessed the unanimity of outlook necessary for the practice of normal science, and the individual schools within behaviourism were never sufficiently free of serious external challenges to devote themselves without distractions to articulation of their various theoretical positions. Their attempts to generalize their positions outside of their laboratory context were, in the absence of a developed scientific tradition sufficiently viable to provide detailed empirical foundations for them, bound always to be premature.

3 CONCLUSION

The preliminary account of behaviourism sketched in this chapter has been developed largely through contrast with the Kuhnian analysis of psychology which has become increasingly popular in recent years. This procedure is convenient for expository purposes and is also appropriate, since the differences between the Kuhnian view and the one sketched here are important. However, placing emphasis on the differences between the two may serve to conceal the extent of their agreement, and it is necessary to put both into perspective.

All recent attempts to understand the scientific career of behaviourism assume the truth of the following statements. Behaviourism has been a dominant but diffuse movement in (mainly) American experimental psychology for at least the past fifty to sixty years. Since about 1950 it has been confronted with a growing number of conceptual, methodological, and empirical difficulties. Attempts to meet these difficulties have not been altogether successful, and have resulted mainly in the boundaries of the movement growing even more blurred than formerly. These unresolved difficulties have been instrumental in bringing about a rejection of behaviourism on a scale which by now could be described as revolutionary.

If there is room for disagreement, it is over the interpretation of these events, based on different analyses of the foundations of behaviourism. The view taken here is that while experimental psychology is undergoing a revolution, it is not a Kuhnian revolution. A Kuhnian interpretation cannot profitably be applied to the career of behaviourism; behaviourism was not based on a paradigm, and consequently did not have the means to settle what were taken to be fundamental substantive issues in the way necessary for the practice of paradigm-based normal science.

This difference in interpretation is, however, only of narrowly academic interest unless it leads to different predictions or recommendations for post-behaviourist psychology. And, as we shall see, the difference does make a difference in precisely that way. Some of the writers favouring a Kuhnian analysis of behaviourism have tended to define 'paradigms' in methodological terms, rather than in terms of the 'concrete scientific achievements' emphasized by Kuhn. None of these writers has made critical mention of what, it will be argued, was the fundamental methodological error of behaviourism, its adoption of a position of methodological objectivism. To the extent that an extreme emphasis on methodology, codified in the term 'methodological objectivism', was an error, those writers who interpret Kuhnian paradigms in methodological terms may be continuing the error. Methodological objectivism and Kuhnian paradigms are incompatible, not as alternative interpretative schemas for the rational reconstruction of science, but, assuming that both kinds of reconstruction have some validity, as bases for practice within a science.

This last point deserves to be clarified. Mention was made previously of what could loosely be called competing schools within behaviourism. This plurality of schools did not arise without good reason. It was closely linked, as indicated, to the absence of a paradigm that could function effectively for all of behaviourism. To generalize the point beyond Kuhnian paradigms as such (as will be done throughout the rest of this work), it was linked to the absence of any kind of defining contentual base for behaviourism. Furthermore, *this absence of a defining content in behaviourism was quite intentional.* There were, as we have seen, scientific achievements that might have provided the basis for behaviourist research in such a way that that research would have exhibited the Kuhnian pattern. Either Thorndike's researches or Pavlov's, or a combination of them, were likely candidates for a paradigm in this sense.

However, it was no part of – it was incompatible with – the objectivist and aggressively scientific programme of behaviourism to go any farther than rigorous logic required in accepting a shared commitment either to a concrete achievement or to a specific set of systematic hypotheses. Any shared commitment of *that* sort would violate what behaviourists did share, which was their conception of science. What united behaviourists was their conviction that the methodology of science, rather than its content, was what constituted an activity specifically as scientific; and that methodological principles provided a sufficient basis on which to build scientific systems. Commitment to a theory or to a point of view was at the very most an individual matter. Commitment to the procedures of science was the main shared characteristic of the group. The behaviourists came to agree, that is, that a set of decision procedures for evaluating research, appropriate to all sciences indifferently, was the principal requirement for the constitution of a science; that with these decision procedures determined the content of scientific theories would be self-correcting; and that once their science possessed these it would as a result acquire continually increasing systematic validity as it continued to develop; *and in all this they were wrong.* Why they were wrong, that is, why their conception of science was such that its implementation could not fulfil their aims, is the subject of the following chapters.

II

POSITIVISM, REALISM, AND
BEHAVIOURIST
PSYCHOLOGY

As we have seen, behaviourism consisted largely in an attempt to base psychology on the practices of the physical sciences. As such, there is nothing very new in this attempt; for centuries, it has been quite typical for psychologists and mental philosophers to try in one way or another to base their discipline on the practices of physics and related sciences. The trend toward not merely relating the two but explicitly basing psychology on physics has been a strong, even a dominant one, since the beginnings of modern science in the seventeenth century. Hobbes[1] and Gassendi[2] began implementing the trend in its modern and systematic form by making thorough analyses of perception, cognition, and memory as purely material processes, thereby translating the mind into a physical system operating according to the principles of Galilean dynamics. The rather crude materialism of their theories seemed inappropriate, and even unscientific, on grounds which were more epistemological than metaphysical. It was, accordingly, decisively eliminated by Locke, who declined to 'meddle with the physical consideration of mind; or trouble myself to examine wherein its essence consists'[3] and substituted for an avowed materialism an autonomously mental atomism, explicitly analogous to Newton's physical atomism. It is with Locke, in fact, that mental elements, separate from but having properties derived from those of physical atoms or particles, may be said to have become influential in modern (i.e., post-Renaissance) psychology. Hume, somewhat later, declared on the title page of his *Treatise of Human Nature* that it was 'an attempt to introduce the experimental method of reasoning into moral subjects',[4] and characterized association as a 'gentle force' analogous to gravity. Hartley, in turn, initially based his theory of association on some of Newton's own speculations on the vibratory action of the nervous system. James and John Stuart Mill represented association after the pattern of chemical theory in their respective times; Wundt extended the chemical analogy and made it the basis for a general analysis of mental events, while Bain tried to model his theoretical statements on recent advances in physiology.[5]

Examples could be further multiplied. The point which they establish is that the content of psychological theories, particularly in traditions continuous with that of British empiricism, has in large measure consisted in the analogical application of principles and concepts derived from the most popular current physical theories.

It was not in this way, however, that behaviourism was based on the practices of the physical sciences. It is, of course, true that behaviourist psychology has borrowed some of its concepts and models from other sciences. As mentioned in the last chapter, Weiss attempted a reduction, equally logical and theoretical, of psychology to atomic physics. Perhaps the best current example of borrowed concepts is that of cybernetic and information-processing models of perception and cognition. The practice of borrowing models has never been applied systematically within behaviourism, however, and has never been a central characteristic of the movement. Instead, what was explicitly taken as the basis of behaviourism, and what thus marked a new or relatively new turn in psychology's scientistic history, was a strict commitment to scientific *method*, with relatively little prior commitment to particular types of scientific theories. This emphasis on scientific method shows clearly in the examples given previously: Watson's emphasis on observation and verification, logic and mathematics ('the tools of every scientist'); Skinner's early interest in operationism; Hull's search for a methodological paradigm in Galileo's astronomical theories, etc.

An emphasis on scientific method, as abstracted from the practices and methodological analyses of the physical sciences, was, if not altogether new in psychology, at least new in the extent of its systematic application and in its clear demarcation from concern with physical theories. The adoption of both the observational procedures and the logic of physics, without any corresponding systematic adoption of the theories of physics, was unprecedented. Wundt, and

25

following him Titchener, attempted in their theory construction to mirror the logical procedures of the physical sciences, but they also adopted a conceptual scheme based on that of chemistry, while they made a sharp distinction between the observational procedures appropriate to such sciences and those appropriate to psychology.

Even to say, however, that behaviourism consisted largely in the adoption of a rigorous scientific method is insufficient to characterize it, for the conception of scientific method adopted within behaviourism was only one of many possible ones. It is not hard, nonetheless, to specify the kind of conception that was implemented. That conception was purportedly based on the dominant practices of then contemporary science. It was of course hard-headedly empiricist, and correspondingly anti-rationalist and anti-intuitionist. It was indifferently inductivist and deductivist, encompassing both procedures without strain. All of these features of scientific method, behaviourism shared with various forms of introspective psychology. What differentiated it was, again, the refusal to give any consideration to any entities or processes which were not directly and publicly observable, a refusal that was explicitly implemented as a methodological maxim. Behaviourism, in short, adopted – and in large measure defined itself by adopting – a conception of scientific method that required a strong commitment to observation and strictly logical analysis, a rejection of all concern with unobservables of any sort, and a corresponding unwillingness to extrapolate beyond observables in the systematic interpretation of data. In Chapter III it will be shown how this conception was initially developed piecemeal in behaviourist and immediately pre-behaviourist psychology. Considered as a systematic conception, as it eventually came to be considered within behaviourism, it was one which had close affinities with the methodological programme announced by Karl Pearson in his *The Grammar of Science*,[6] and also, with some reservations, with that put forward by Ernst Mach in his *The Science of Mechanics*[7] – a conception of science, that is, that can generally be described as a positivist one.

The implication of positivism enables the discussion to become more specific. To speak of behaviourism as founded on a positivist methodological orientation toward the practice of psychology is to make a descriptive generalization about the movement, just as it was to speak of the movement as founded on a position of methodological objectivism. The present one is, furthermore, a

26

generalization that would have been agreed to by many prominent behaviourists during the movement's heyday.[8] But in this case, more is involved than simple description; it is a description with explanatory power. A central theme of this book is that the label 'positivism' denotes a recognizable natural family of approaches to science, and that much of the career of behaviourism, its successes and failures alike, is interpretable specifically through an analysis of the implications and consequences of adopting such an approach within psychology. The career of behaviourism is thus intimately bound up with the potentialities and limitations of a positivist orientation toward science. It follows that it is impossible fully to understand the former without also having some understanding of the latter.

In modern times, both in science and in the philosophy of science, the terms 'positivism' and 'logical positivism' usually refer to the verifiability criterion and other techniques, or decision procedures, which have been developed and used for the rigorous evaluation and testing of scientific statements, hypotheses, and theories. Indeed, it is not too much to say that the systematic use of such procedures identifies and characterizes the implementation of a positivist orientation in modern science. Strict use of such decision procedures was, furthermore, characteristic of much of behaviourism, and was explicitly relied upon to ensure the scientific cast of mature behaviourist theorizing. A major part of the examination of positivism will, accordingly, involve an analysis of the viability and effectiveness of these procedures. Adherence to such explicit decision procedures is not, however, all there is to positivism. Rather, such adherence defines the way in which a positivist orientation has most recently been implemented, in behaviourism as elsewhere, just as it was previously implemented mainly through the repudiation of unobservables as such – again, in behaviourism as elsewhere (e.g., by Mach and Pearson). But however a positivist orientation is implemented in science, it has certain general functions which it usually performs. Analysis of the role of positivism in behaviourism thus requires prior identification of what these general functions are.

The remainder of the present chapter will therefore discuss the general character and significance of positivism as an orientation toward science, considering it in as informal a manner as possible. Chapter III will consider how positivism initially became associated with behaviourism, and Chapter IV will present a slightly more

27

technical review of the decision procedures characteristic of both modern logical positivism and neobehaviourism.

1 POSITIVISM AND REALISM AS CONTRASTING ORIENTATIONS TOWARD SCIENCE

For a beginning, positivism is certainly a tough-minded attitude toward science and philosophy. It rejects all or most metaphysics as sterile and advocates the restriction of scientific attention to publicly observable data. Beyond these basics, however, there is some ambiguity as to just what positivism is and where it comes from. In one sense, positivism originated with Auguste Comte, who coined the term and made it the basis for his mildly scientistic social philosophy. In another sense, quite opposed to Comte's, positivism is a very general and very ancient way, common at least since the time of the astronomer Ptolemy, of being cautious about claims of scientific validity or, in general, about the truth of supposedly factual statements. In a third sense, most familiar today, positivism is a kind of technical philosophical analysis for distinguishing between meaningful and nonsensical statements. It is therefore at least slightly arbitrary just what we choose to call 'positivism'.

It will become clear, however, that attempts to define positivism as a proposed answer to any classic philosophical problems – to define it in terms of some philosophical content – lead to serious problems. Such attempts are often enough made, and one of the best of them is that by Kolakowski.[9] To highlight the problems involved in such an attempt, and through them to throw some light on the functions of positivism, it is worth looking briefly at Kolakowski's analysis.

Kolakowski characterizes positivism in terms of four maxims or rules which he states are generally typical of positivist thought; these are phenomenalism, nominalism, the fact-value distinction, and the unity of scientific method, the first two being the most important. The rule of phenomenalism states that 'there is no real difference between "essence" and "phenomenon" '.[10] Anything that cannot be manifest in a purely phenomenal way, such as the Kantian *ding an sich* or the scholastic essences, has no place in scientific thought. Kolakowski states:[11]

According to positivism, the distinction between essences and phenomena should be eliminated from science on the ground that it is misleading. We are entitled to record only that which is actually manifested in experience; opinions concerning occult entities of which experienced things are supposedly the manifestations are untrustworthy. Disagreements over questions that go beyond the domain of experience are purely verbal in character.

The rule of nominalism states that 'we may not assume that any insight formulated in general terms can have any real referents other than individual concrete objects'.[12] There is no such thing – or we should not assume that there is any such thing – as mankind over and above all individual persons; the inverse square law does not apply (or should not be considered to apply) except between specific, particular bodies, etc.[13]

> A system ordering our experiences must be such that it does not introduce into experience more entities than are obtained in experience. But since it inevitably uses abstractions among its means it must also be such that we do not forget that these abstractions are no more or less than means, human creations that serve to organize experience but that are not entitled to lay claim to any separate existence.

The fact-value distinction is the traditional one, according to which facts and values (is's and ought's) never imply each other. The last rule, asserting the unity of scientific method, 'expresses the belief that the methods for acquiring valid knowledge, and the main stages for elaborating experience through theoretical reflection, are essentially the same in all spheres of experience'.[14]

These four rules or maxims certainly convey the flavour of much identifiably positivist thought. However, the problem that arises in attempting to maintain that positivism *consists* in these is that many figures whom we should want to call positivists have not adhered to some of them, while many whom we should not want to call positivists, have. Kolakowski recognizes the problem; Galileo, Descartes, and Leibniz, for instance,[15]

> shared the positivist conviction that interpretation of the world in terms of unseen faculties or forces, inaccessible to empirical investigation, is absurd. . . . Though he clung to the concept of substance, Descartes tried to characterize it in such a way that it

lost its old mysteriousness; matter, or extended substance, is nothing but extension, and the soul, or thinking substance, is nothing but thinking. There is no 'nature' hidden behind the actually observed qualities of things, reference to which accounts for anything whatsoever.... Although Descartes did not carry this position to its ultimate consequences, and was not perfectly consistent in asserting it, it certainly is in line with the positivist programme.

However, Descartes' position is similar to that of recognizably positivist thought only in the one, certainly important, respect that both involve an attempt to demystify metaphysical concepts. What is more important than this similarity is that the methods and the reasons for doing so have practically nothing in common in the two positions. Descartes, like Galileo and Leibniz, was a realist, a rationalist, and at least half a Platonist. All three attempted to intuit non-phenomenal reality of some sort, had little faith in empirical investigations unless guided by independent intuitions of the truth, and shared with identifiably positivist thought little more than a distaste for the obscurantism of the later scholastics. But if this distaste is expressed as a denial of 'essences' which lie behind and support phenomena – if it is described without the qualification that the 'essences' thus abjured were not identical with non-phenomenal reality in general but were rather the focal point of one particular sterile system of metaphysics – then it does indeed seem to mark these highly metaphysical thinkers as strangely sympathetic to the central phenomenalistic tenet of positivism.

Kolakowski attempts to minimize the paradoxical consequences of considering Descartes as a positivist by suggesting that he was only partly a positivist:[16]

Thus, if mere denial of non-phenomenal 'essences' sufficed to earn a thinker the title 'positivist', Descartes (like Leibniz) would be a fully-fledged representative of the tradition. But because, at least in the light of the development of positivism in the last two centuries, this criterion can hardly be considered sufficient, Descartes can be called a positivist only with serious reservations.

The reservations concern the distinction between analytic and synthetic statements, or necessary and contingent truths, according to their source, the form of their validity, and their informational content about the world. Descartes' positivist credentials are weakened because he did not observe this distinction and attempted to apply necessary truths in characterizing the world as it actually exists. But this facet of Descartes' thought was of crucial epistemological significance to him. More than a reservation concerning the extent of his adherence to positivism, it constituted a complete repudiation of the phenomenalist assimilation of phenomena and essences (in a general sense), as well as a complete rejection of any need for empirical verification. Descartes, again, was 'anti-essentialist' only if the concept of 'essence' is restricted to its technical use in scholastic philosophy. In so far as essences refer generally to the reality that is separate from and supportive of phenomena, he was clearly an essentialist.

Thus, Descartes' 'denial of non-phenomenal essences' did not constitute a denial of non-phenomenal reality or of its availability to scientific investigation, and it is consequently difficult to credit him as a positivist. A precisely opposite difficulty in the characterization of positivism can be found in the early twentieth-century movement in the philosophy of science known as conventionalism, whose adherents often did believe in non-phenomenal essences – and often scholastic ones at that – but were, as scientists, positivists nonetheless. Conventionalism is clearly in the historical mainstream of positivist thought. It was in part an outgrowth and extension of Mach's positivism, and had a major influence on the development of logical positivism.[17] However, the leading exponents of conventionalism – Poincaré, Duhem, and LeRoy in France, Dingler in Germany – were neither phenomenalists nor nominalists. Poincaré and Duhem were both scholastic philosophers in the neothomist tradition. LeRoy was a popularizer of Bergson's theories of intuition and direct contemplation of reality. Dingler was a philosopher in the German voluntaristic tradition of Fichte and Schopenhauer, according to which our conception of nature (some would say nature itself) is an untrammelled creative act of the will. These philosophers were all transcendentalist in their conception of reality; what made them positivists was their analyses of the methodology and epistemology of science, which, on principle, they kept entirely separate from their philosophizing about reality.

Adherence to positions such as phenomenalism and nominalism clearly does not suffice, therefore, as a characterization of positivism.[18] It is instead necessary to consider the relationship between science and the real world, in the conceptions of some of these thinkers, to clarify what it is that makes Poincaré and Duhem positivists but Descartes and Leibniz something else.

The distinction between these two pairs of philosophers lies in the different status which they accorded to their scientific theories. Descartes and Leibniz believed that their theories were true or, at worst, false. That is, for them the validity and worth of their theories consisted in their accord with reality; since reality was partly phenomenal and partly non-phenomenal, any valid theory had likewise to incorporate phenomenal and non-phenomenal references. Poincaré and Duhem, on the other hand, maintained their theories – and all scientific theories – were neither true nor false, but merely more or less useful. For them, the validity and worth of their theories consisted solely in their accord with the observed events in their domain. The corpuscles and monads with which Descartes and Leibniz filled the universe were considered to be real; the space, time, mass, and gravitation with which Poincaré and Duhem filled the universe were assumed to be irreducibly hypothetical. Since these entities, forces, etc., are merely hypothetical, they can whenever they outlive their usefulness be replaced with other hypotheses, without such replacement necessitating any basic change in our conception of reality. Regardless of the nature of reality – and Poincaré and Duhem fully agreed with Descartes and Leibniz that much of reality is not phenomenal – science is necessarily restricted to phenomena. Science, for the conventionalists, does not give access to a trans-empirical realm of essences, things in themselves, or reality, and this is a genuine limitation of science. This trans-empirical realm was of great importance to the conventionalists, as it was historically for many other positivists, but it was not the realm of science. Science deals only with the observable; and for the conventionalists even that was not absolute and fixed, but was in large part a product of previous experience, expectations, 'knowledge', etc.; and as a result science delivers only the useful or workable.

This distinction between conventionalists such as Poincaré and Duhem and rationalists such as Descartes and Leibniz can be extended to cover positivists and non-positivists in general. Mach's positivism was not the handmaiden to theology that Duhem's sometimes seemed to be. Mach had no interest in metaphysics of any sort, and was concerned only to guarantee the empirical character of science. To this end he made searching criticisms of scientific concepts which were assumed to have universal applicability, such as space and time in Newtonian mechanics. Mach maintained that there was no way in which such universal concepts could have empirical significance, that they should therefore be considered inadmissible in science, and that their unwarranted extension to universal status was largely responsible for the (then) current crisis in physical explanation. All these scientific concepts are founded in our observations, Mach insisted, and as a result they cannot validly be extended beyond the reach of observation. For Mach, the function of scientific theories – their only possible function – is to provide the most economical arrangement and classification of our observations.[19]

In opposition to Mach we may place Planck—and this opposition was a real one at the time. If Mach's positivism was not in the service of the transcendent, neither was Planck's rejection of it. Unlike Descartes and Leibniz, Planck made no claims in favour of a rationalist theory of knowledge or of a reality that had any transcendent characteristics. With those philosophers however, and even more forcefully, Planck insisted that the goal of science was to uncover the truth about nature, and he allowed no hedgings about the status of the truth thus sought. In particular, he stressed that any lesser goal such as Mach's principle of economy of description of observed phenomena failed to account for scientific activity as it was actually practised. In a paper published in 1909 Planck stated:[20]

When the great masters of exact investigation of nature gave their ideas to science, when Nicholas Copernicus removed the earth from the center of the universe, when Johannes Kepler formulated the laws named after him, when Isaac Newton discovered gravitation . . . – the series could be long continued – surely, economical points of view were the very last thing to steel these men in their struggle against traditional opinions and dominating authorities. No, it was their unshakeable belief – whether resting on an artistic, or on a religious basis – in the reality of their world picture. In view of these certainly incontestable facts, one cannot reject the surmise that, if the Mach principle of economy were really to be put at the center of the theory of knowledge, the trains of thought of such leading spirits would be disturbed, the flight of their imagination crippled, and consequently the progress of science perhaps fatefully hindered.

The distinction between Descartes, Leibniz, and Planck on the one hand, and Poincaré, Duhem, and Mach on the other, can best be summed up as a distinction between positivism and realism, and this opposition between the two orientations towards science serves to characterize them. The most fundamental characteristic of positivism in science on this view is a refusal to ascribe realistic significance to a scientific theory. Positivism in general, that is, consists not in any proposed answers to classic philosophical questions, but in the refusal to consider the questions at all. More precisely therefore, positivism as an orientation toward science consists fundamentally in a systematic suspension of judgment, or a denial of the possibility or meaningfulness of judgment, concerning the absolute truth or falsity of a scientific theory. Scientific theories are neither true nor false – truth and falsity are judgments not applicable to them – but only useful or useless, economical or uneconomical. Hypothesized entities and forces are neither real (existent) nor unreal (nonexistent), but only and inescapably provisional. Thus, any judgments about whether a theory is true or false, or about whether it represents reality or not, are barred as a matter of principle from being relevant to the assessment of the theory. The truth or falsity of a theory is not available as a criterion for judging it, and the judgment that a theory is true thus adds nothing to its empirical content.

There are almost incontestable logical reasons for this suspension or abjuration of judgment. Any such judgment goes beyond any observations which can provide empirical support for the theory, and to that extent is not even in principle confirmable or disconfirmable by reference to such observations. If reality consists in anything other than what we can or do observe, then our observations cannot reveal that reality to us, or even reveal the fact that it so consists. Conversely, if reality does not consist in anything other than what we can or do observe, then our observations cannot reveal that fact to us either. As a result, the questions of what reality consists in, and what it is like, are questions which empirical data cannot be used in any way to answer; any answer to such questions is empirically meaningless. It follows that the questions are not ones that have any place in science.

The systematic suspension or abjuration of judgment can also be characterized, therefore, as a repudiation of all empirically unverifiable or 'metaphysical' statements or questions in science. It constitutes, as such, a general form of the verifiability criterion associated with logical positivism. The verifiability criterion asserts, in its simplest formulation, that the meaning of a statement is identical with or is given by the operations and observations that would constitute its verification. The intended consequence of this criterion is that synthetic statements (statements purporting to give some factual information about the world) can be considered to have factual meaning only if they can be empirically verified. All others are categorized as meaningless and metaphysical.[21] The verifiability criterion has, through its vigorous promulgation, been sufficiently influential that lack of empirical verifiability has come to be accepted almost as a defining characteristic of metaphysical statements. Its influence has not been sufficient, it is true, to secure general agreement that all such statements are 'meaningless' in a broad sense. Still, the criterion has been accepted as sufficient at least to demonstrate that scientific theories can and should have nothing to do with metaphysics.

The field is thereby left open, however, for metaphysical – that is, non-empirical, non-scientific – theories to claim access to a higher kind of truth than that available to scientific theories. The access of such theories to a higher truth cannot be strictly denied on scientific grounds, so long as their proponents are careful not to incorporate any empirically meaningful statements into their theories. This restriction is one which some philosophers have found themselves able to meet, and the resulting opportunity for a complementary relationship between positivism and non-empirical or metaphysical philosophy has been a source of considerable ambiguity within positivist philosophy, one that at times has occasioned severe discomfort. Some positivist philosophers, such as Poincaré and Duhem, have promoted positivist analyses as a means for clear demarcation between science and metaphysics, a demarcation salutary to the progress of both. Others, such as Mach, have disdained any interest in metaphysics at all, and wished merely to get on with their science. Still others, and particularly the logical positivists of the Vienna Circle, were vigorously opposed to any sort of rapprochement between science and metaphysics; they took it as their aim to effect the complete banishment of metaphysics, or at least the demonstration that metaphysics could have none other than poetic or emotional significance.

In all fairness, however, it must be said that this aim of the logical positivists was a failure from the outset. For on their own principles, there was no way that the verifiability criterion – the touchstone for distinguishing between meaningful and meaningless statements – could have any other than stipulative significance. This property of the verifiability criterion – that it was itself, strictly speaking, empirically meaningless – was a formal embarrassment to logical positivism from the beginning, although not one that was worried about unduly. A statement that could not be empirically verified could be called meaningless only by restricting the domain of meaningful statements to those which were empirically verifiable, and this restriction could not itself be justified on empirical grounds. The verifiability criterion of *meaning* thus reduces immediately to, at best, a criterion of *demarcation* between empirical science and everything else, particularly between science and metaphysics. This purely demarcative function of the verifiability criterion was sufficiently obvious at the time it was introduced that, despite the hostility of logical positivism to metaphysics, many metaphysicians welcomed the movement with open arms. It seemed to them that logical positivism would safeguard the status of metaphysics as much as that of science. Phillip Frank, one of the earliest members of the Vienna Circle and a particular opponent of scholastic philosophy, bleakly instantiates this trend:[22]

> The French Catholic philosopher J. Maritain, at the Thomistic Congress in Rome in the summer of 1936, characterized as a great service that was essential also for Catholic philosophy the fact that the aim of the Vienna Circle and of the whole movement of logical empiricism was 'to disontologize science'.

Thus, from the point of view of the metaphysicians, logical positivism provided a demonstration that scientists had no business encroaching on their territory, which included all questions concerning ultimate reality. Where empirical data are relevant they cannot, indeed, be transcended, but for the most important questions they are not always relevant and must then quite properly be ignored.

Realism, as the general alternative to positivism, has only rarely received any systematic formulation as such. In general, it can be defined as the implicit or explicit conviction that scientific inquiry is capable of revealing the truth about the world, or about that part of it being studied. It carries also the accompanying conviction, as expressed in the quotation from Planck, that this truth cannot be assigned limits corresponding to the limitations of the experimental procedures employed in its determination. The truth that is sought by science always has a wider domain of applicability than that of the experiments utilized in the search; typically, the truths sought are universal ones. In relation to any specific scientific theory, it is both meaningful and important from a realist viewpoint to ask whether the theory is true or false. Unequivocally answering this question, however, necessitates going beyond the available empirical evidence, and going beyond it in a direction in which, as was shown above, future empirical evidence cannot strictly follow. Thus, the maintaining of the truth or falsity of a scientific theory within a realist orientation necessarily involves affirming the theory to an extent greater than can ever possibly be strictly warrantable on the basis of empirical evidence and logic.

Nevertheless, the truth that, on a realist account of science, is revealed by scientific investigations, is not necessarily thought of as being wholly trans-phenomenal; but neither is it wholly phenomenal either, in the sense of being identified with phenomena. More representative would seem to be the often implicit belief that while appearances can be deceiving, they can also, with proper selection and control, be revealing.[23] The unanalysed or uninterpreted phenomena of everyday life are insufficient to provide the truth about the world, because these phenomena are the final perceptible result of a long causal chain beginning with the complicated interacting forces which constitute those components or aspects of physical reality that are operative in one form or another in our immediate vicinity. These forces are themselves, however, at least in principle open to discovery, even in their most general form. They can be distinguished, separated, identified, and understood – but only through careful investigation, control, and measurement, or in short, through the sophisticated and careful practice of science.

The fundamental differences between a realist and a positivist orientation toward science thus lies in this choice of whether or not to ascribe realistic significance to a theory, that is, in the willingness or unwillingness to judge on the basis of empirical data that a theory is true (rather than economical, useful, or well-corroborated) or false (rather than uneconomical, useless, or discorroborated). This difference in the toleration of conclusions which go beyond the strict warrant of any possible data is reflected in the differing attitudes toward scientific method. On a positivist conception of science, it is the methodology of scientific research – the logical, observational, and experimental procedures of a field of inquiry – that constitutes an activity as scientific. Neither the form nor the content of scientific theories can themselves exercise this function. Thus, a given string of words may comprise a metaphysical or a scientific statement, depending entirely on what procedures are used to justify it. This emphasis on the methodology of science is not of course an all-or-nothing matter, rigidly separating positivism and realism. A considerable emphasis on scientific method is typical of all scientific activity. But it is only as part of a positivist conception of science that the methods of inquiry can come to be of greater importance than the contents and systematic scope of theories for the assessment of a field as scientific. On a realist conception of science, the empirical and logical methods of science are justified instrumentally, by virtue of being the most powerful tools available for the study of nature. On a positivist conception, the empirical and logical methods are (if the phrase be permitted) of the essence of science, and science itself is justified only on broadly instrumental grounds.

The positivist emphasis on the methodological constitution of science is displayed to varying degrees in what can be identified as older positivist thought. In the early days of Copernican astronomy, for instance, the purely mathematical character of the heliocentric astronomical formulations was taken to provide a guarantee that the theory itself was purely scientfic or 'mathematical' rather than metaphysical. The permissible function of the heliocentric hypothesis, like that of the detailed Ptolemaic hypothesis which it superseded, was to 'save the appearances', to enable prediction of the observed motions of the stars and planets without regard to their hypothetical actual behaviour. So long as the heliocentric hypothesis was used and interpreted in such a way, it would be assessed purely on mathematical and empirical grounds; the distinction between mathematical and metaphysical truth served to ensure that the validity of the heliocentric hypothesis was of such a sort that it could not conflict with the physical-cum-metaphysical truth of the loose geocentrism that had strong theological backing at the time. Any defence of the heliocentric hypothesis that claimed it to have physical validity thereby transferred the hypothesis outside of what were taken to be the bounds of science; once outside, it would then be, and was, subject to assessment on explicitly non-scientific grounds.

A stronger and more explicit emphasis on the methodological

38

constitution of science is typical of modern positivism. To a considerable extent, this emphasis marks a reaction against the dogmatic realism typical of much physical science during the last century. Adherence to Newtonian mechanics was so strong in scientific circles around the middle of the nineteenth century that it was possible to define scientific explanation in purely substantive terms, as consisting precisely in the reduction of complex observed phenomena to the principles of Newtonian mechanics. For example, in 1847 Helmholtz, in his classic paper 'On the conservation of force', the paper in which he promulgated the conservation principle, stated:[24]

> The task of physical science is finally to reduce all phenomena to forces of attraction and repulsion the intensity of which is dependent only upon the mutual distance of material bodies. Only if this problem is solved are we sure that nature is conceivable.

Similarly, du Bois-Reymond, a founding member with Helmholtz of the heavily materialistic Berlin Physical Society, observed in 1872 in his (at the time) equally famous paper, 'On the limitations of natural science':[25]

> The cognition of nature is the reduction of changes in the material world to the motions of atoms, acted upon by central forces, independent of time . . . It is a psychological fact of experience that wherever such a reduction is successfully carried through our need for causality feels satisfied for the time being.

The logical positivist Phillip Frank, who strongly disapproves of any such enshrining of scientific theories, underlines the significance of these two passages:[26]

> Is this not an amazing fact in the history of the human mind? As Newton set up his theory the introduction of the central forces of attraction was regarded as a particularly weak point of this theory. It was accused of requiring the introduction of an element that is philosophically absurd. But what happened about a hundred years later? It was claimed as a 'psychologic fact' that just the same thing – the reduction of a group of phenomena to the action of central forces – satisfies our need for causal understanding. And the derivation of physical theorems from the action of these forces, which were formerly

condemned as unconceivable, was now the guarantee that nature is conceivable.

The dogmatically realist tendency which Frank deplores was both a product of and an ongoing stimulant to the overextension of Newtonian principles, the same overextension that came eventually to hinder the progress of physics until the principles were recast in a more limited and hence empirically meaningful form – after which they came to be seen as approximations to limiting cases of the more general principles of relativity theory and quantum mechanics. The recasting of Newtonian principles and the development of new ones required closer attention than had been given previously to the operational specification of any concepts used. The manipulation of these new and revised concepts required, partly on account of their (then) counter-intuitiveness, a rigorous commitment to their logical implications. It was only by such rigorous commitment to the logical apparatus of research that the non-metaphysical (i.e., empirically warranted) components of Newtonian mechanics could be identified and retained, the metaphysical parts discarded, and more generally adequate principles developed. This necessity for a methodological emphasis in the successful practice of physics at the time made apparent the general logical appropriateness of such an emphasis. The detailed construction and development of an unambiguous logical and methodological framework for science which resulted comprises the main contribution of logical positivism to the tradition of positivist thought. For a tradition which has always valued formalisms, this contribution is a significant one.

The consequences of choosing a positivist or a realist orientation within a science vary with the circumstances of that science, and will be treated below. The arguments for or against each are more timeless however, and may be summarized in the form of the objections which can be advanced against each orientation by proponents of the other.

The objection that positivists can bring against realism is that the factual or empirical content of a scientific theory is in no way increased by tacking on to the theory a belief that it is 'true', in any sense apart from or additional to its empirical validity. On the contrary, the theory's factual content is in practice more likely thereby to be reduced. The consequence of seriously treating scientific theories as 'really true' seems to be the extension of the domain of their applicability beyond that point to which their observational warrant properly extends. This practice can lead and has led to gross errors, as discussed above. It was just such errors that led to a crisis in nineteenth-century physics, stifling physical research until the conceptual excesses of Newtonian mechanics were rectified. This argument against realism and in favour of positivism is sufficiently familiar that it need not be elaborated; its validity is almost unquestioned.

The objection that realists can bring against positivism is twofold. First is the claim, illustrated by the quotation from Planck on p. 33, that belief in the reality of a conceptual schema is necessary in order for scientists to undergo the toil and strain of constructing new theories, defending them against opposition, and extending them in the discovery and interpretation of new phenomena. Planck's defence of realism as, in effect, a heuristic principle, thus constitutes a claim about the psychology of creativity. Consequently, it could in principle be investigated experimentally, although the attempt to do so would undoubtedly encounter incalculable difficulties. If one attempts to test Planck's claim with examples taken from the history of science, it receives at best partial confirmation. Some scientists have been positivists and others, perhaps greater in number, have been realists; some are impossible to classify; many seem to alternate between the two orientations; both positivists and realists can be found among the greatest scientists in history.

The second objection is a conceptual rather than a broadly empirical one. Positivism erects a stipulative ceiling on the capacity of science to explain the world; even if scientists respect this ceiling, it is likely that others will not. The ceiling is imposed by the stricture against making scientific explanations refer to physical reality as such, separate and apart from specific controlled observations of it. This ceiling on scientific explanation is much the same as was imposed by medieval scholastic philosophy, both Thomistic and Averroist; it is the same limitation that Osiander insinuated into Copernicanism[27] and that the church forced on Galileo. That it is recognized as the implication of modern positivism is attested to by the ready acceptance of logical positivism by metaphysically sophisticated transcendentalist philosophers such as Jacques Maritain and Ernst Cassirer.

The metaphysician can in effect say to the positivist scientist: 'I will not try to tell you anything about the behaviour of electrons if you will not try to tell me anything about the nature of reality. Discovering the nature of reality is my job; performing experiments and constructing empirically limited theories on the basis of them is yours. I may make reference to your empirical findings as illustrating a principle about the construction of the real world, and in doing so I will explain the significance of your results. I will not be encroaching on your domain, however, because I will not attempt to predict your specific empirical findings.'

The positivist scientist must, whether willingly (as in the case of Duhem) or unwillingly (as in the case of Frank), accept this division of labour. The most he can say is that the metaphysical principles which the philosopher erects will be empirically meaningless. However, the metaphysician has accepted this proviso at the outset, and is not disturbed by it, since any empiricist criterion of meaningfulness is purely stipulative. The metaphysician merely restricts himself to a richer kind of meaning and truth that is not empirical. Furthermore, while the metaphysician cannot derive strictly empirical implications from his philosophical principles, there is nothing to stop him from drawing pragmatic ones, that is, implications concerning the way we can best assume the world to be in charting our daily actions. Thus, with both the most general and the most specific interpretations of scientific theories, as well as reality itself, all marked as his province, the metaphysician is barred only from the experimental laboratory. The positivist scientist is barred from everywhere else.

The realist scientist feels that this arrangement and division of labour is both overly restrictive and excessively cosy. He may feel that the behaviour of electrons has something to do with the nature of reality if anything does (and that he should be involved in deciding whether it does or not), and that he is therefore better qualified to say something about that reality than anyone whose sole qualifications are metaphysical ones. Positivism thus seems to the realist to be abrogating the power and the responsibility of science to discover the truth about nature and surrendering that power and responsibility to those who, even if eager, are unqualified to exercise it.

Both sets of objections, against positivism and realism alike, seem to have some force. The positivist objections against realism clearly have greater logical significance, while the realist objections against positivism have, perhaps, greater pragmatic and systematic

42

significance. However, the positivists do better in such a controversy, for only their objections seem incontrovertible. A logical purist could shrug off the realist objections as being irrelevant to the constitution of science, while few scientists of any persuasion would deny the claims of logic. Thus, if one had to choose unequivocally between the two orientations, one would have to choose between maximizing systematic richness and maximizing logical rigour; between emphasizing intuitive and emphasizing strictly empirical significance; between the danger of developing overextended and empirically degenerating conceptualizations and the complementary danger of 'crippling the flight of the imagination' of many of the 'leading spirits' of science. It would not be a particularly happy choice, but most scientists would probably feel that they had to opt for positivism and logical rigour.

However, there is no need for the choice to be made in so uncompromising a manner, and it has not regularly been made in such a manner in the history of science. The key to the resolution of the conflicting claims of positivism and realism is the recognition that the strengths and weaknesses of each position are complementary, and have complementary degrees of relevance during different stages of scientific inquiry. The weaknesses of realism are particularly disruptive of scientific progress at the same time, or under the same conditions, as the strengths of positivism are most conducive to such progress, and vice versa. In examining the potentialities for an interplay and alternation between positivism and realism in the conduct of scientific inquiry, we will be able to see these strengths and weaknesses in a broader perspective.

2 THE RECONCILIATION OF POSITIVISM AND REALISM

Two Types of Assessment of Scientific Theories

Scientific theories and systems frequently begin and end in periods of intense controversy concerning the appropriateness or meaningfulness of the concepts fundamental to the theory. In between these terminal periods, this kind of controversy is likely to diminish, and controversy and research both centre more typically on the application and extension of the theory in accounting for the range of events in its domain. At the beginning and the end, that is, it is customary to ask, in various ways, whether the explanatory and descriptive concepts used in the theory make sense. In between (if the theory survives the initial examination) it is more customary to ask, in various ways, how great a range of events the theory can be made to account for.

The classic example of this shift of focus is, of course, Newtonian or classical mechanics. When Newton published the *Principia Mathematica* in 1687, there was no question that his account provided an excellent mathematical fit to the observed events which it sought to account for, nor that exact predictions of these events could be rigorously derived from an impressively small set of postulates. Controversy did not turn on these features of his theory. Instead, and in advance of any systematic attempt to try out Newton's theory in the solution of other difficult problems in physics, controversy centred on the admissibility into science of the basic concepts involved in his theory. His conceptualizations of attractive and repulsive forces, action-at-a-distance, absolute space and time, and others, all received widespread criticism. Use of these concepts in physical theory was quite widely regarded as tantamount to a reintroduction of medieval occultisms into natural science.[28] Newton was able to ride out the storm, partly by agreeing with his opponents that many of these concepts would indeed qualify as occultisms if they were taken to have literal meaning, if 'gravity', for instance, was taken to refer to a specific but unknowable quality; but on the contrary, Newton insisted that no such hypostatization was any part of his intention, that his principles were merely 'mathematical' rather than 'physical'.[29]

The provisional and hence unobjectionable character of Newton's physical concepts having thus been established (to the satisfaction of some critics at least),[30] they could then be further assessed and evaluated on the basis of their systematic application, with the need for separate analytic justification for their use gradually diminishing. Evaluating them on the basis of their systematic application involved extending them to cover and account for more and more diverse phenomena. As the Newtonian system was gradually extended to cover observational and predictive astronomy, electricity, pneumatics, hydraulics, heat and heat transfer, physical chemistry, and other previously separate or nonexistent fields of inquiry, the meaningfulness and validity of the fundamental concepts involved came to be taken more and more for granted. Questioning of the status of concepts such as attraction and repulsion came to seem little more than a narrowly academic exercise when the theories based on such concepts were having such unprecedented success in explaining the physical world. Eventually, the fundamental concepts of attraction and repulsion came to seem not only acceptable within science, but absolutely essential to its successful enterprise.

Finally, of course – the story is well known – latter-day Newtonian theories began to encounter more and more serious difficulties. Anomalous findings, such as unexplained perturbations in the orbit of Mercury, and the failure of the Michelson-Morley experiment to locate evidence of an ether drift combined with incomprehensible theoretical predictions, such as those concerning black body radiation, to produce a situation in which the extended Newtonian theory no longer provided a trustworthy guide in the investigation of nature. Having provided the basis for physical science for two hundred years, and an almost unquestioned basis for over a hundred, it had finally begun to show its limitations. That it had any such limitations was a great shock to many scientists, and provoked a reassessment of the status of scientific theories that is still going on. Attempts to preserve what was still valid or valuable in Newtonian theory led some physicists particularly to reanalyse some of the central concepts in the theory and to conclude that in their customary universal form they were misleading – sufficiently misleading that reliance on them was in large part responsible for the crisis in physics. Reformulation of these concepts (especially those relating to space and time) in more limited and empirically warranted forms helped in the development of the theories (relativity theory and quantum mechanics) that accounted for many of the anomalies and eventually replaced Newtonian mechanics altogether.

The reception and career of Wundt's introspectionist structural psychology displayed a similar pattern on a much smaller scale. The scale was smaller both because Wundt's innovations were not so great as Newton's and because his theory did not have such wide application. When Wundt first proposed his system of structural psychology in 1874,[31] he faced opposition from the Comtean positivists (who repudiated *all* introspection on much the same grounds as the behaviourists did later), from the German phenomenologists (who repudiated *analytic* introspection on much the same grounds as the Gestalt psychologists did later) and indeed from the vast majority of German philosophers (who followed Kant or Hering, both of whom denied the possibility of *experimental* introspection). Wundt was able to proceed and gather support and supporters for his system in spite of the opposition, due to three features of his system and of the way he presented it. First, as the experimental background to his psychological system he appealed to physiology rather than to the already extant introspectionist tradition which was dominated by phenomenologists and Cartesians (it was the latter to whom Comte's criticisms were directed). Second, consonant with the character of German philosophy at the time, Wundt's overall classification of the contents of consciousness was respectably *a priori* and speculative; the detailed introspective experiments provided the details concerning the structure of consciousness but not, initially at any rate, the basic structure itself. Third, the elements into which Wundt decomposed conscious experience were, while not widely adopted in German philosophy at the time, familiar and fairly acceptable due to their source in the well-established tradition of British empiricism. The first of these features removed Wundt's system from the ambit of its harshest potential critics, while the second and third reduced its innovative character. Together, they enabled Wundt to by-pass conceptual objections to his enterprise by staking out a small and previously unclaimed area of scientific investigation as his own. The specific means whereby the respectability of his enterprise was established were different from those employed by (and for) Newton, but the general procedure was the same: to gain time for the system to be developed and extended by minimizing its revolutionary or otherwise unacceptable implications.

As Wundt's system became more extended and ramified through his own publications and those of his students and colleagues, the need for defensiveness concerning its propriety diminished and the detailed structure of the system became of primary concern. As a result, the area which it encompassed came to be seen as identical with experimental psychology altogether. Eventually, when other investigators became interested in matters which Wundt's structural approach could not handle – imageless thought, perceptual wholes (Gestalten), animal behaviour, etc. – and which structural psychology, because of its predominance, was hindering the investigation of, the debate over the worth of Wundt's general approach began again in intensified form. In the ensuing controversy Wundtian structural psychology withered away almost entirely, and in America at least, introspective psychology in general lost much of its credibility.

In behaviourist psychology, too, the same kind of alternation is visible, although, because of the particular features of behaviourist research described in the first chapter, the shifting of focus was not so strong or so clear as in the other two examples cited. Conceptual analyses and polemics advocating the focusing of attention on strictly observable behaviour began with Cattell[32] and Meyer[33] and continued through Watson,[34] Weiss,[35] Hunter,[36] and many others. On the other side, blanket refutations of the behaviourist approach were attempted by Lovejoy,[37] Roback,[38] Broad,[39] and, again, many others. By the late 1920s such external and general criticisms were becoming less frequent, partly because of their total lack of effect. Throughout the 1930s and 1940s conceptual analyses and methodological polemics were clustered more within behaviourism, serving principally as ammunition in the rivalry between various behaviourist schools. Also in this period, however, a great deal of detailed and precise experimentation was carried out in support of the positions of the various schools. Such experimentation was relatively free from concern with the conceptual basis of any particular form of behaviourism and was addressed to specific theoretical problems, in much the same way as characterized the middle periods of the careers of the other two scientific systems cited. The second and terminal period of detailed conceptual critiques of behaviourism may be said to have got well under way with publication of the co-operative volume *Modern Learning Theory* in 1954;[40] this book was devoted to rigorous (and devastating) although sympathetic analyses of the logic and structure of the major behaviourist theories of the time. The second period has continued since then, and has witnessed the gradual attrition of behaviourism as any kind of systematic stance.

This alternation of critical focus from theoretical concepts to theoretical application and back again is not particularly surprising, and can be accounted for, in a loose sense at least, fairly easily. If a new theory requires new ways for looking at or interrelating observed events, if it asserts the relevance to an already specified problem area of hitherto ignored or unrecognized phenomena, if in general it requires a reconceptualization of that part of the world to which it is addressed, then its sheer novelty will ensure that it initially receives attention *qua* novelty rather than strictly *qua* theory. It will be considered as a novelty first, and to the degree that the fundamental concepts involved in it are strange ones, to that degree they will require exposure and familiarization as concepts before they are utilized within the theoretical structure. In advance of further elaboration of the theory however, it may seem entirely questionable whether it is worth the effort required to assimilate the new concepts, whether their strangeness is due simply to their newness or rather to their general inappropriateness for dealing with familiar problems. Thus, to the degree that the concepts central to a proposed new theory are unfamiliar ones, critical analysis leading to some acceptance of the concepts is a necessary precursor to their experimental and theoretical elaboration.

If, by whatever means, a theory passes its first conceptual test, then for those who have accepted it on this basis further conceptual justification for it will be relatively unnecessary; *relatively* unnecessary only, for such justification may continue to be necessary in presenting the theory to critics. But for those working within the theory – those for whom questions of the meaningfulness or appropriateness of the theoretical concepts have been resolved, dismissed, or set aside – such justification need play no part in their application and testing of the theory. Such application and testing consists in using the theory to interpret and account for the world, to answer the kinds of questions which it was designed to answer. Thus, the success of the Newtonian physical theory did not consist in postulating the existence of rigid bodies, Euclidean space, rectilinear motion, or principles of attraction and repulsion; rather, once their existence, and hence the meaningfulness of the theory, was allowed, the success of the theory consisted in showing how the principles of attraction and repulsion could account for the rectilinear motion of rigid bodies in Euclidean space. Such achievements are the goal of theory, the goal of scientific inquiry as such, and can be pursued autonomously once the admissibility of the concepts used in the theory has been established.

The renewed interest in conceptual analysis toward the end of the career of a theory can be accounted for in a similar manner. First, the end of one theory frequently overlaps with the beginning of another which replaces it, and if the new theory requires another reconceptualization it will provoke conceptual analysis and examination in the way described above. Second, if a useful theory begins to encounter serious anomalies, to the extent that it cannot consistently be upheld, it might signal an unacceptable loss of economy to reject it outright. There may be nothing of comparable power to replace it with, for the time being at least. Thus, it is necessary to determine the bounds within which the old theory can continue to function and beyond which it is invalid. Determination of these bounds within the limits of the old theory involves recasting it so that it does not extend to the types of situation in which it is inapplicable; it involves, therefore, a reformulation of the theoretical concepts in such a way as to limit their scope. Third, a reanalysis of the foundations of an old theory may be undertaken as part of an effort to repudiate it, to show that its eventual failures were inherent in it from the beginning, and that, as Watson said of structuralist psychology, it 'was founded upon the wrong hypotheses'. All three of these reasons for analysis of a declining theory overlap and can be considered together; when a scientific theory is doing its job, leading to successful investigations of nature, it is relatively unnecessary to question its foundations; when it stops or fails to do its job, or before it is allowed to begin, questioning its basis becomes essential.

The amount of justification required for the fundamental concepts of a new theory depends on the extent to which these concepts are unfamiliar or incompatible with accepted ones. Thus, a new theory which does not require any reconceptualization of the part of nature which it addresses can be assessed at once on the basis of its empirical support. Alternative theories within one theoretical framework are often of this sort. Thus, Hullians could assess Mowrer's two-factor theory[41] on a strictly empirical basis from the beginning; they understood what Mowrer was talking about, and accepted his theoretical terms as meaningful, without any detailed justification of them. At the other extreme, a theory might require so great a reconceptualization of its subject matter that almost all scientists reject it as outlandish, while preserving any bits of it that can be fitted in with current conceptions. This was the fate of Fechner's psychophysical theory;[42] the psychophysical methods which he developed were assimilated into early experimental psychology, while the theory itself was universally dismissed as unscientific and mystical. Unfortunately, it does not seem possible to specify in advance how much 'outlandishness' a new theory will be allowed to have before it is rejected out of hand. Newton's and Fechner's theories were objectionable to their respective contemporaries on much the same basis, i.e., that the fundamental concepts involved in them were mystical, empirically meaningless, and in general not up to current scientific standards.

The Context of Construction and the Context of Reconstruction

Let us label the contexts in which the two different kinds of questions just described are asked of a theory as the 'context of construction' and the 'context of reconstruction'. The context of construction is that in which theories are elaborated and tested in terms of how well they make contact with nature, how well they fulfil their predictive and explanatory tasks. The context of reconstruction is that in which the terms, concepts, and variables out of which the theory is built up are subjected to searching critical examination, in order to establish or disestablish them as appropriate or meaningful.

This terminological convention need not be taken too seriously, but it is at least convenient in the present discussion. Furthermore, the terms have been chosen with some care. 'Construction' signifies a building-up and progressive development of a theory, a house, or whatever; and 'reconstruction' signifies an at least partial tearing down and replacement or strengthening of the foundations, as a preliminary to further building. Scientific work undertaken within these two contexts is often loosely separated in time, for the reasons given. The context of construction is primary while a theory is being extended and elaborated, and the context of reconstruction is primary while a theory is being initially examined and finally abandoned. Work done within the two contexts certainly interpenetrates in time, however, and may well be co-extensive with only variations in relative emphasis throughout the life of a theory.

The criteria for judgment of a theory are not rigidly distinct within the two proposed contexts. They are clearly separable, however, because different questions are asked in the different contexts. If one is pursuing a particular elaboration of an already well-attested theory it is relevant, but usually only tangentially relevant, to be given information concerning the logical and empirical status of the concepts fundamental to the theory. Similarly, if one is examining the elements of a theory to see if they have unambiguous empirical referents, then it is relevant, but usually only tangentially relevant, to be told that the theory accounts for a given phenomenon with such-and-such a degree of success. The two contexts are related hierarchically, in that the context of reconstruction is or should be subordinate to the context of construction, because it is in the latter context that the development of science as such takes place. The context of reconstruction comes into its own most forcefully during the decline of a scientific theory, when the conceptual analysis of the theory is undertaken in order to determine why it is that questions asked in the context of construction are no longer receiving satisfactory answers.

The Differential Relevance of Realism and Positivism to the Contexts of Construction and Reconstruction

The distinction between the context of construction and the context of reconstruction, and an appreciation of the different tasks appropriate to the two contexts, makes possible a resolution of the conflicting claims of positivism and realism in the conduct of science. In brief, the position advanced here is that a realist orientation toward scientific theories and what they account for is most conducive to scientific progress within the context of construction. Conversely, a positivist orientation is most conducive to scientific progress within the context of reconstruction.

The rationale for this position can be stated briefly. In the context of construction, attention is focused on (what is taken to be) the world; there is greatest conceptual economy in assuming that the world autonomously possesses those characteristics attributed to it by the theory and progressively elaborated in the course of scientific discovery. Furthermore, in the context of construction, there is no reason to assume otherwise about the status of such theoretically attributed characteristics; to do so would only distract attention from the task at hand, that of further determining the character of the world through elaboration, testing, and revision of the theory. In the context of reconstruction, on the other hand, attention is focused on the variables and concepts of the theory, primarily as components of the theory and only secondarily as attributes of the world. There is greatest conceptual economy in examining these as they occur, without assuming that they either have or do not have an external reference independent of their specified observational content. Furthermore, within the context of reconstruction, any assumption about the 'objective' (i.e., 'real') reference or lack thereof of such variables and concepts would, as in the previous parallel case, distract attention from the task at hand, which in this case involves analysing their logical implications and observational content.

To put it another way, relating to the pragmatics of science rather than to its semantics, a realist orientation towards a scientific theory can be expected to encourage tenacity in maintaining that theory in the face of potentially disconfirming evidence, and to promote commitment to the general validity of the theory in its future application to specific problems. In the elaboration of a theory which has already received some development, such tenacity and commitment will often be rewarded. A positivist orientation, conversely, can be expected to encourage flexibility and lack of full commitment in the assessment of and choice between theories, a flexibility that is sorely needed when theories are being broken down and examined piece by piece. Such flexibility, however, may reduce to vacillation, and withholding of commitment to nit-picking, as a science incorporating one or more major theories proceeds from strength to strength in the successful investigation of nature. Equally, commitment to the value and validity of a theory may be arbitrary and capricious when a new point of view incorporating it is first expressed; even worse, tenacity may degenerate to dogmatism as the breakdown of a scientific system indicates to an uncommitted observer that something is basically, i.e., conceptually, wrong with the theoretical position.

The differential relevance of the two orientations, in short, establishes the need for an alternation between them, corresponding to the alternation between the contexts of construction and reconstruction. Something resembling such an alternation, indeed, as a function of different problems faced at different times, is apparent in the careers of the scientific systems – Newton's and Wundt's – cited above.

A fuller justification of this position will require a further examination of modern positivism. It will hinge largely on showing that, regardless of our preferences in the matter, a consistently positivist approach is almost impossible to maintain in the context of construction. The analysis will centre on the fine structure and detailed implementation of a positivist orientation in science, for the specific features that limit the applicability of positivism are not such as show up in summary or programmatic statements. The analysis will therefore be directed to the characteristics of modern logical positivism and related movements, for it is only through these that positivism has become sufficiently sophisticated and detailed that it can be examined with anything approaching the necessary precision. This circumstance is also fortunate, in that it was the modern and sophisticated forms of positivism that came to be associated with behaviourism, and so it is with these that we are in any case concerned.

The description and analysis of positivism has already progressed far enough, however, that it can begin to be applied to the development of behaviourism, especially to behaviourism in its initial versions before it became associated with the formal movement of logical positivism. Making some use of the descriptive vocabulary that has been built up in this chapter, therefore, the next will describe the background to, and the initial emergence of, behaviourism; it will show how right from the beginning, within the context of reconstruction, the incorporation of positivism in behaviourism was significantly variant from the usual and appropriate pattern as described here.

III

BEHAVIOURISM'S BACKGROUND: THE INSTIGATION TO BEHAVIOURISM IN STUDIES OF ANIMAL BEHAVIOUR

Two features of behaviourism were cited as central to the movement in Chapter I. The first was the repudiation of unobservable entities and processes – particularly the mind and consciousness, but by extension others as well; it was this repudiation that more than anything else marked the emergence of behaviourism. The second was the adherence to explicit decision procedures as the basis for evaluating scientific statements, concepts, and theories, and as sufficiently establishing thereby the scientific and progressive character of behaviourist theorizing. In Chapter II it was pointed out that these two features also typify different ways of implementing a positivist orientation toward the practice of science. In behaviourism as – at least in modern times – in the physical sciences, the repudiation of unobservables was the initial means for the implementation of positivism, and the adherence to explicit decision procedures was the later, more sophisticated means. We can say roughly that the repudiation of unobservables characterized the positivist orientation of behaviourism from the beginnings of the movement until the development of 'neobehaviourism' in the late 1920s and early 1930s, and that the adherence to explicit decision procedures characterized it thereafter. Chapter IV, correspondingly, will deal in some detail with the use of decision procedures in neobehaviourism and generally in science. The present chapter is concerned with the circumstances which led to the emergence and the initial positivist cast of behaviourism in the early part of this century.

To consider the birth of behaviourism we must look to the early history of comparative psychology. The circumstances which led to the establishment of behaviourism arose around the turn of the present century, particularly in American psychological laboratories, in the context of problems in the study of animal behaviour. What happened in brief was that in such studies, sophisticated methods of experimentation and experimental control v. ere developing in a different direction from the functionalist and evolutionary conceptual framework on which the studies were based. As a result, the attempted evolutionary analyses came to seem outmoded and irrelevant. The experimental results themselves seemed the only valuable outcome of the research programme, and quite independent of their dubious interpretation. Thus, the suggestion that attention might better be confined to mere data, with the theoretical interpretations repudiated on principle, was an obvious and welcome one. The widening gap between data and theoretical interpretation which justified their separation was not, however, an inevitable consequence of animal behaviour research of the time. To understand how this gap developed, and what alternatives to it existed, it is necessary to go back a further step and look in some detail at the development of this behavioural research from which behaviourism sprung.

1 THE CONCEPTUAL DEVELOPMENT
OF COMPARATIVE
PSYCHOLOGY: 1882-1901

Animal behaviour became of interest to psychology as a result of evolutionary theory. The occasional earlier studies on the topic had been carried out mainly by natural historians and breeders. Such studies, while occasionally acute, lacked any systematic theoretical basis for the selection and interpretation of phenomena to be studied. Comparative psychology, explicitly based on evolutionary theory, provided just such a theoretical basis. The goal of comparative psychology, from the time it was first expressed by Romanes,[1] remained that of demonstrating the continuity of adaptive capacities and psychic processes throughout the animal kingdom, and to trace their evolutionary development to their culmination, frequently in man.

The method used to implement this programme combined observations of behaviour, the inference of adaptive capacities on the basis of the behaviour, and the detailed interpretation of the inferred capacities and the behaviour together by means of an analogy drawn between human and animal minds. Observations of selected behaviour which could not be accounted for on the basis of instinct or reflex action – because of the behaviour's novelty in the history of the organism and its adaptive specificity to the requirements of an unfamiliar situation – served as the basis for inference of various adaptive capacities. These capacities were then interpreted as resulting from the action of a mind exhibiting characteristics and undergoing experiences analogous to those typical of a human mind. The description of the animal's mental processes resulting from this procedure was expected to be the same sort of description as would result from introspection of the contents and structure of human consciousness; roughly the same, that is, as resulted from the experiments in analytical introspection typical of human experimental psychology of the time. The method was succinctly described by Romanes:[2]

> For if I contemplate my own mind, I have an immediate
> cognizance of a certain flow of thoughts and feelings,
> which are the most ultimate things – and, indeed, the only
> things – of which I am cognizant. But if I contemplate
> Mind in other persons or organisms, I can have no such
> immediate cognizance of their thoughts and feelings; I can
> only *infer* the existence of such thoughts and feelings from the
> activities of the persons or organisms which appear to manifest
> them. Thus it is that by Mind we may mean either that which
> is subjective or that which is objective. Now throughout the
> present work we shall have to consider Mind as an object; and
> therefore it is well to remember that our only instrument of
> analysis is the observation of activities which we infer to be
> prompted by, or associated with, mental antecedents or
> accompaniments analogous to those of which we are directly
> conscious in our own subjective experience. That is to say,
> starting from what I know subjectively of the operations of my
> own individual mind, and of the activities which in my own
> organism these operations seem to prompt, I proceed by analogy
> to infer from the observable activities displayed by other

organisms, the fact that certain mental operations underlie or accompany these activities.

This general approach to the study of animal psychology has, of course, been entirely discredited, and with fairly good reason. However, it can be, and for some years probably has been, dismissed too easily, on the grounds that it is impossible for us to gain access to the alleged subjective experience of other organisms (which Romanes and those who followed him never denied) and that comparative psychology based on Romanes' method of inference never made any significant progress (which is not strictly true). Indeed, Romanes' inferential method has almost never been critically examined outside of a previously established context of blanket acceptance or rejection. Just such an examination is necessary, however, in order both to show in what respects the method, despite appearances, was viable, and more importantly, to show in what respects, and with what consequences, it was not.

The central feature of Romanes' approach is his use of analogy; that is, it is his reconstruction of the minds of animals on the basis of analogy with the operations, capacities, and subjective experiences typical of his own mind. This 'argument from analogy' depends on two major assumptions. The first is that the operations and the quality of subjective experience typical of human minds are already known, or at least can be readily determined through introspection or objective experimentation.[3] The second is that the minds of animals are similar (or analogous) to the minds of humans, both with regard to their subjective experiences and with regard to their mental functions or operations. To pass judgment on these in a nutshell, the first assumption is incorrect, the second so far as it relates to subjective experiences is strictly speaking untestable but universally agreed (e.g., by Romanes, see below) to be highly dubious; and the second so far as it related to capacities and functions should not be introduced as an assumption at all, as it is the same continuity hypothesis that comparative psychology was designed, and was competent, to investigate. Let us consider each of these in turn.

That the first assumption is incorrect is fairly apparent. We do not have a sufficiently detailed understanding of how our own minds work to use these workings as the basis for constructing the analogy. Even if our own mental operations and private experiences could in principle serve as the basis for the analogy, the construction would have to wait on the development of a human psychology rich enough to systematize and account for them. The notion that the workings of the human mind can easily be understood through casual introspection may be termed the Cartesian fallacy;[4] it was this fallacy that bore the main brunt of the nineteenth-century attacks on introspection, and it was as clearly a fallacy in Romanes' time as it is in ours.[5] The detailed knowledge of human psychology necessary to eliminate dependence on the fallacy was not available to Romanes; nor, indeed, is it available to us. In the absence of such knowledge, not even the first term in the analogy – our own minds – can be built upon with any confidence.

Most of the criticism, however, must fall on the second term in the analogy, relating to the subjective experiences and to the mental capacities (for cognitive functions, etc.) of non-human organisms. Here there are several points that must be made. To begin with, it was generally recognized that the analogy cannot be proven or justified. The analogy constitutes an assumption that certain observable behaviours are accompanied by certain subjective experiences or mental operations, such experiences and operations being somewhat the same as what we humans would have (or perform) in a similar situation or when behaving similarly. However, since we have no access to these elements of inner mental life – it is a truism that the subjective experience or personal consciousness of others is closed to us – we can provide no evidence whatever for the validity of the analogy. This much was freely admitted by Romanes and by all later writers, and accepting this was almost a precondition of the analogy's use. The position of these writers was that the analogy could be justified by its heuristic use in interpreting the minds of animals, and that it was sanctioned by custom, as it was continually used by each of us in attributing consciousness to other persons.

Let us therefore first consider the sanction by custom. It is highly doubtful that the custom exists, that is, that we ever *attribute* consciousness to each other (i.e., make a judgment affirming its existence) at all. It is more likely that, except when we are acting as philosophers, we do not infer consciousness in other persons, but come to *assume* it in the course of socialization – although it is certainly something less than the consciousness of the philosophers that we assume in this way. However, even if the custom may nonetheless be said to exist, the sanction clearly does not. Other people are at least human, and we are not begging any *evolutionary* or *phylogenetic* questions by attributing consciousness to them, and interpreting it, on the basis of our own. But those are just the questions we are begging when we apply the analogy to the minds of animals. Whether animals are conscious (one popular view at the time held that they are not), and what their consciousness consists in, and how it resembles and differs from human consciousness, are all appropriate questions for a comparative psychology of Romanes' sort to investigate. It is hardly appropriate to assume particular answers to them before the investigation starts. In fact it is utterly inappropriate, since the answers implied by accepting the validity of the analogy amount to a pretty full statement of the hypothesis of psychic continuity, which it was supposed to be comparative psychology's task to investigate.

Next, let us consider the heuristic justification. The analogy requires not only that animals be conscious, but also that they be conscious of the same things that we are; it is only to the extent that their consciousness is similar to ours that the analogy can be used. By use of the analogy therefore we can attribute to animals only the same feelings as we would have in a given situation, or the same mental operations as we would perform. As a result, we are unable to deal in any constructive way with all the differences in consciousness that must, on the evolutionary view, characterize different parts of the animal kingdom; we cannot deal either with the diversity of evolved types or with the process of evolutionary development itself.

To consider the matter of diversity: if we use the analogy, we must assume that every creature that can respond to stimulus energy to which we also are sensitive has approximately the same experience when affected by that energy as we do; the alternative, as Romanes stated (see below), is to say nothing at all. But given how generous nature is in evolving a variety of adaptive mechanisms for performing similar tasks, sensory receptors for responding to given energy forms, etc., it would seem unlikely that these would be coupled with no variety at all with respect to subjective experience. This is an *a priori* argument, of course, but it is an *a priori* position that it is being brought against. The point is, once it is accepted that some animals might have a different kind of experience than we do in a given situation, then the presumed universal applicability of the analogy breaks down. But although we may grant on these grounds that the analogy will sometimes fail, we do not know just when it will fail; hence we do not know when it can successfully be applied and when it cannot.

It would not help to make structure the key to application of the analogy, so that, for instance, only sensory receptors morphologically similar to ours would be assumed to yield sensory experience similar to ours. First, this limitation on the use of the analogy is as incapable of any empirical justification as is the analogy itself. Second, it would rule out any possibility of convergent evolution of forms of experience. Third, it would exclude a large and indeterminate portion of the animal kingdom from any place in comparative psychology. That is, it would preclude study of any animals which were structurally dissimilar to man on the dimensions being investigated, and since all animals are structurally dissimilar to man on all dimensions to some degree, we would have to stipulate a somewhat arbitrary cut-off point beyond which we would agree not to employ the analogy.

Finally, the analogy does not allow us to say anything at all about the experiences which some animals have with forms of energy to which we are not sensitive. Bees can sense the direction of polarization of light, and eels can orient themselves by means of faint electrical currents in water; but to interpret these animals' experiences after the model of human experience in the same situation would be, again, to say nothing at all.

These difficulties are thrown into sharper perspective in the explicit context of evolutionary development. It was assumed by most writers who employed the analogy that its adequacy would decrease as a function of the phylogenetic distance separating man from any other given species. The shape of this 'function' is, of course, indeterminable, so that we cannot say how *much* less valid the analogy will be when applied to a cat than a monkey, a pigeon than a cat, etc. But even apart from the question of the shape of the function, this limitation on the application of the analogy renders it of no specifically comparative use. If someone steps on my toe I will experience a certain sensation of pain. If now I step on the toe or other extremity of a dog, a chicken, a frog, a fish, a crab, a flatworm, and a paramecium (the series is not incontrovertible), all I can say about the sensations which these creatures have is that I am progressively less certain as we go through the list that what each experiences is what *I* experienced. I may stretch the point slightly and infer that what each of these animals feels is progressively less like what I felt, but what it is that they did feel, with mounting dissimilarity to what I felt, is completely indeterminable. Thus, the analogy cannot be used in comparing what animals at different evolutionary distances from man will feel in a given situation, nor, *mutatis mutandis,* in comparing what they think (or otherwise do in their minds). On the other hand, if the assumption were not made that the adequacy of the analogy deteriorates with phylogenetic distance, then we would have to assume that each of these creatures felt just what I felt, with no variation due to evolutionary divergence – an assumption which no writers would make, as it would flatly contradict the fundamental evolutionary principle of development. But the alternatives in the comparative use of the analogy are restricted to either denying evolutionary differences or being mystified by them; in either case, the analogy cannot throw any light on such differences as do occur.

The analogy may well be valid sometimes; we have simply to grant this point if we are to discuss the analogy, because it cannot be established in any other way. When the analogy is valid, we shall make more valid interpretations of an animal's private mental life if we use the analogy than if we do not; the surface appeal of the analogy is based on this consideration. Thus, if we step on the tail of a sleeping dog, it will jump up and 'give every sign' of being startled, distressed, etc., and it might seem the narrowest of scientific scruples not to agree that the dog really feels the way it seems to. However, even if we stipulate that the analogy is sometimes valid it is clear that it will not always hold, and that it will hold for some species, and for some components of mental life in a given species, better than for others. Furthermore – and this is the crux of the matter – we can never gain any insight into how well the analogy holds in any particular case. We can assume that the analogy deteriorates as a gross and indeterminate function of phylogenetic distance and morphological dissimilarity, but this assumption, which can only be introduced as such, does not itself provide any insights into the subjectivity of animals as revealed by use of the analogy. The validity of the analogy is thus not only variable but indeterminably variable. Since it is variable, we must know the sources and dimensions of the variability in order to make any informed use of the analogy; but since the variability is indeterminable, we cannot do so. If we ever use the analogy, then we can never find out whether our inferences based on it are valid, and if so to what extent, and in what respects.

Some of the problems in the use of the analogy were recognized by Romanes and by succeeding writers who made use of it. They did not explore its limitations in detail, but felt that its validity was rather dubious, especially when applied to animals far removed from man. Inferences to the mental lives of ants and bees, they agreed, could not be so well founded as inferences to the mental lives of apes and dogs. Nevertheless, they maintained, while we may often distrust such inferences, especially of the former set, we must still continue to use them, even if with great caution, simply because they comprise the only interpretative method available to us:[6]

> That is to say, if we observe an ant or a bee apparently exhibiting sympathy or rage, we must either conclude that some psychological state resembling sympathy or rage is present, or else refuse to think about the subject at all; from the observable facts there is no other inference open. Therefore, having full regard to the progressive weakening of the analogy from human to brute psychology as we recede through the animal kingdom downwards from man, still, as it is the only analogy available, I shall follow it throughout the animal series.

The criticism of the analogy has referred equally so far to inferences concerning what the animal feels (sensations, etc.) and to inferences concerning what it does or can do with its mind (thinking, etc.). This distinction may seem a trifle forced, but was implicit in the writings of the time and, as we shall see, eventually became of considerable importance. We can now narrow the focus specifically to what the animal does or can do - to its thoughts, mental operations, capacities for cognitive restructuring, etc. - in order to show that indeed there was some 'other inference open' than the one based on the analogy from human to animal minds.

All that was said regarding the indeterminable applicability of the analogy applies equally, of course, to everything that supposedly goes on inside an animal's head, to its thoughts and to its feelings. In the case of mental operations such as 'thoughts', however, the analogy is not only more or less useless, it is also irrelevant. Questions about an animal's mental operations, or more properly about its capacities for such operations, are questions about what the animal can do; and such questions can be answered on the basis of objective experimentation. In fact, Romanes himself attempted to answer them objectively. Although for the most part Romanes held true to his subjective method of interpreting the animal mind by explicit analogy from what he knew of the contents of his own mind, he was also very concerned to introduce objective (i.e., publicly applicable) criteria by which the inference from behaviour to mind could initially be justified. As a result, the basis for a minimization of subjectivity was present in his own writings, and was confounded with his subjective methods.

The criterion chosen by Romanes, and retained by most later writers, was essentially the ability to learn, or to modify behaviour selectively in response to the demands of a novel situation. The selectivity of the behaviour differentiated learned responses from reflex ones which, while also adaptive, are fixed and invariable:[7]

> It is, then, adaptive action by a living organism in cases where the inherited machinery of the nervous system does not furnish data for our prevision of what the adaptive action must necessarily be – it is only here that we recognise the objective evidence of mind. . . . Does the organism learn to make new adjustments, or to modify old ones, in accordance with the results of its own individual experience? If it does so, the fact cannot be due merely to reflex action in the sense above described, for it is impossible that heredity can have provided in advance for innovations upon, or alterations of, its machinery during the lifetime of a particular individual.

There was a tension in Romanes' analysis resulting from the fact that two more or less separate lines of reasoning (*objective* inferences based on observations of behaviour and *subjective* inferences based on application of the analogy) were directed toward the same goal, the description of the animal mind. Generally, although not with perfect consistency, Romanes tacitly resolved the tension in the same way as did succeeding writers, by using the objective inferences to detail the operations and capacities of the animal mind, and subjective inferences to describe the animal's subjective experiences. In practice, therefore, and for what will be seen to be very good reasons, the analogy from human to animal mind played much less part in the reconstruction of what the animal could do than in the attempts at describing what it felt.

The differences between the two forms of inference should be made clear. If a particular capacity (for recognizing size relationships, say, or for abstracting the spatial positions of objects from a single perspectival view of them)[8] is necessary for the performance of an action, and if the animal performs the action, then the capacity can be inferred. The procedure is not all that simple, of course; it is not always an easy matter to judge whether the capacity is required for the performance of a given action, or is only consistent with it; and the methodological development of comparative psychology after Romanes consisted largely in refining the bases on which it could be concluded that the capacity was in each case actually required.

Such objective inferences do not make contact with the inner mental life of an animal any more than subjective inferences do. They do, however, make it possible to judge that either a given set of mental operations, or a functionally equivalent set, has taken place. The degree of precision in the specification of what mental operations, if any, may be said to have taken place is dependent only on the degree of precision with which an experimental task is established (cf. the account of Thorndike's analysis, below).

Thus, the operations and functional capacities of mind can be measured and assessed in terms of their behavioural consequences. The same cannot be said of subjective experience, at least so long as experience is considered, in the empiricist tradition, as something separate from action, and especially so long as the experiences being inferred are required to have the same degree of specificity as those considered in introspective psychology. Experience as such has no 'functional equivalents'. Neither has anything else considered *as such*, of course, but mental operations and abilities can be considered primarily in terms of their functional significance, because it is the results to which they lead that establish their presence, while subjective experience, because of its specifically existential significance, cannot. For Romanes and those who followed him, determination of the specific quality of experience was precisely what was of interest. Thus, subjective experience could only be considered in its own right, in the way in which it actually occurred: that is to say, failing any better method, by application of the analogy. The objective criterion could, if used carefully, be used to justify the inference that an animal possessed certain capacities for action, or that it could comprehend relationships (and manifest its comprehension in action), or even that it was conscious, so long as consciousness was considered as a capacity for the sensitization and direction of attention, rather than as the 'quales' which presumably comprised its content; but the objective criterion could not, as we have seen, justify any inference relating to the subjective experience of the organism as something distinguished from its capacities and propensities for action.

In short, subjective experiences are one thing and capacities or dispositions for adaptive behaviour are another, and the bases on which each can be inferred are separate. The inference of cognitive or other capacities can be made on the basis of behavioural evidence, that is, on the basis of behaviour which seemingly cannot be accounted for without postulating the capacity. The inference of subjective experiences analogous to those of humans requires, in addition to behavioural observations, the prior and inescapably *a priori* assumption that such subjective experiences occur and are, in fact, analogous to ours. Inferences concerning an animal's subjective experiences are thus not only separate from but also irrelevant to inferences concerning its mental operations and capabilities; for the latter are sufficiently manifest in observable behaviour and the former are not. It follows that the psychic or mental continuity throughout the animal kingdom can be demonstrated (if present), and the stages in evolutionary development traced, without reference to subjective experience; the task requires reference only to capacities, 'faculties', mental operations, etc., which, while not themselves observable, can be inferred and subjected to critical examination strictly on the basis of their observable effects. What would be left out of such an account is any description of the subjective experiences themselves, and however great that loss might be it could not legitimately be avoided, for given the inadequacy of the analogy and the absence of any alternative, subjective experiences could in any case be introduced into the interpretative account only by what amounted to a fiat.

Thus, the way to overcome Romanes' problem of there being 'no other inference open' than one requiring the attribution of sympathy or rage to bees is to recognize, first, that there are other inferences open, inferences relating to what the bee is capable of doing (including, from the construction given, what it is capable of 'thinking', if anything); and second, that the inference of sympathy or rage is on Romanes' own analysis unjustifiable. Applying this insight requires close specification of the objective criterion which is to justify the inference, of course; more important, it requires specification also, in a form independent of the experimenter's subjective experience, of the mental characteristics which are to be inferred. That these characteristics might still be based initially on ones abstracted from subjective experience is of comparatively little moment; the important requirement is that they be specified independently of such experience so that they can in turn be examined and assessed independently.

The proper subject matter for comparative psychology is thus mind in its external manifestations, rather than mind in its internal constitution and relations. This may seem to be halfway on the road to behaviourism already, but it is not really. In the first place, this formulation of the domain of comparative psychology does not eliminate or even reduce the reference to mind; it merely clarifies the reference. In the second place, and as we shall see, behaviourism was a product of antithesis rather than one of steady development.

Within comparative psychology, the lesson about subjectivity and its limits was gradually and steadily assimilated. That it was not accepted all at once was due to the conviction, shared by most comparative psychologists, that the description of the subjective experience of non-human organisms was a major part of their research activity. The descriptions sought were not required to conform to the conventions of any particular school of introspective psychology, but were expected to be of the same general sort as were characteristic of introspective psychology at the time. Nevertheless, the equivocality of subjective inferences served to reduce their role in the reconstruction of the animal mind and left them to be added at the end; in this way, the subjective inferences were prevented from interfering with the sifting of evidence. Somewhat paradoxically, it was largely because the subjective descriptions of the contents of the animal mind were the goal or end-point of research that they could become, at least, harmless in the course of that research; since they came last, there were few additional conclusions dependent on them.

The reduction of the role of subjective inference in comparative psychology is exemplified in the work of Lloyd Morgan. Morgan's *Introduction to Comparative Psychology*[9] contained much of the same mixture of subjective and objective methods as did Romanes' *Animal Intelligence,*[10] but the relative importance of the two methods was reversed. Morgan insisted at length on the need for subjective inference to round out the picture provided by objective inference,[11] but then made methodological assumptions which served to minimise any role of subjective inferences.[12] First he assumed, with Romanes, that the analogy from human to animal mind deteriorates as a function of the phylogenetic distance from the animal to man. Second, he assumed that the deterioration is not a smooth function of any other objectively ascertainable evolutionary process. Third, and most important, he assumed that the analogy would extend to different capacities or faculties differentially, so that the deterioration of the analogy was not necessarily even monotonic. That is, he assumed that mental evolution is not a unitary process; one species may possess one faculty to a greater extent and another faculty to a lesser extent than another species, and thus some animal species may possess certain psychic faculties to a greater extent than does man (as is obviously the case with perceptual-motor abilities). None of these assumptions was held dogmatically; rather, they were introduced expressly in order to limit severely any systematic but unchecked use of subjective inference. In effect, one was required to assume that the analogy does not hold in a given way in a given case unless objective inferences provided an independent account of the animal's mind such that the questioned application of the analogy could most readily seem to follow. In short, objective inferences were to lead in the characterization of the animal mind, subjective inferences to follow. Thus, while Morgan was not prepared to abandon the dualism of subjective and objective inferences, he was sufficiently sensitive to the demands of his research that in practice he effectively curtailed the claims which could be made on the basis of the former. His method, as he put it, 'is the least anthropomorphic, and therefore the most difficult'.[13]

Morgan posited these methodological assumptions in the context of developing his famous canon of parsimony. Their intent is summed up (and has often been lost) in the canon: 'In no case may we interpret an action as the outcome of the exercise of a higher psychical faculty, if it can be interpreted as the outcome of the exercise of one which stands lower in the psychological scale.'[14] The canon and the reasoning which leads to it thus encourage parsimony in general while, in particular, they subordinate subjective inference to objective reconstruction.[15] The canon also signals the beginning of an attempt to specify the mental characteristics which are to be inferred as faculties or capacities without reference to subjective experience of their operation. It is a bare beginning, but the reference to a 'psychological scale' on which the abilities of man and beast alike are to be placed takes them one step away from their founding in subjective experience and reflection. It is not a step which Morgan took with confidence, however, or at least not one which he followed up, so that while he carefully based each of his inferences to psychic faculties or capacities on detailed and systematic observations of animal behaviour, he just as carefully translated each inference into descriptions of the contents of the animal's conscious experience.

In 1896, Morgan gave a course of lectures at Harvard, where Thorndike was a graduate student, and it has been suggested that he influenced Thorndike to take up the problem of experimental research on animal behaviour.[16] The main publication that resulted from Thorndike's researches, his 'Animal intelligence',[17] is considered a classic for its introduction of a rigorous experimental procedure, its concentration on typical rather than on extraordinary performance, etc. On the issue which we have been emphasizing here, that of the relationship between subjective and objective inferences in the description of the animal mind, Thorndike was not entirely consistent. In parts of his experimental analysis, however, he took the practice of reconstruction of the animal mind on the basis of objective criteria much farther than it had been taken before. He asked the question, for instance, what has been going on in an animal's mind while it has been learning to escape from a puzzle-box and acquire food?[18]

> The commonly accepted view of the mental fact then present is that the sight of the inside of the box reminds the animal of his *previous pleasant experience after escape* and *of the movements* which he made which were immediately followed by and so associated with that escape. It has been taken for granted that *if the animal remembered the pleasant experience and remembered the movement, he would make the movement.* It has been assumed that the association was *an association of ideas*; that when one of the ideas was of a movement the animal was capable of making the movement.

In other words, the animal is held capable of abstracting from its experience in the puzzle-box a representation of those experiences, which it is able to use to guide its subsequent actions. Thorndike claimed instead that the animal is capable of no such abstraction, or at least that no such abstraction guides its behaviour; his reason was that the animal could not initiate the behavioural sequence leading to escape and food by means of a new response.

If a cat is given training trials in a puzzle-box, so that it is made to enter the front door of the box and left to learn the response which will open the door and give it access to food, it will over a series of trials acquire the escape response more and more perfectly. If the cat is then set outside the box on a test trial, with the door open, it will enter the box of its own accord. If, however, the cat is dropped into the box from the top, and learns the escape response to the same criterion, on a test trial it will not enter the box through the front door of its own accord. Thorndike concluded on this basis that the action of walking into the box is indispensable to learning the sequence: enter the box – escape from the box – eat. Ideas cannot be considered to function in any way independent of such specific behaviour, at least in cats, because the cats which were dropped into the puzzle-box from the top[19]

> had exactly the same opportunity of connecting the idea of being in the box with the subsequent pleasure. Either a cat cannot connect ideas, representations, at all, or she has not the power of progressing from the thought of being in to the act of going in.

Thus, whatever cognitions may be said to function in the cat's behaviour are inseparable from the particular responses which the cat has acquired in a given situation.

The evidence in favour of Thorndike's claim is not conclusive. In particular, it depends upon the assumption[20] that the associations involved in learning to enter and escape from the puzzle-box are representative of the associations which the animal is required to make in its day-to-day life. With this important qualification the most significant feature of Thorndike's analysis is that he was able to characterize the mental operations of his cats in unprecedented detail by analysing the different actions which different classes of mental operations would be capable of initiating. He thus carried the process of objective inference of mental operations and capacities to a new level of precision. The 'either-or' form of Thorndike's inference as quoted exemplifies the kind of reconstruction of mental operations that is possible. Either one set of mental operations, or a functionally equivalent set, has taken place; either the cat cannot abstract the reinforcement contingencies from its exposure to the experimental situation, or it cannot utilize this abstraction in the determination of its subsequent behaviour.

On the other hand, Thorndike was quite determined that experimental investigations of the skills and capacities of animals should not only 'give the much-needed information *how they do it*, but also inform us *what they feel* while they act'.[21] Thus, after analysing the mental operations of his cats in the way just described, he went on to consider the quality of a cat's consciousness while it was acting:[22]

> It is most like what we feel when consciousness contains little thought about anything, when we feel the sense-impressions in their first intention, so to speak, when we feel our own body, and the impulses we give to it. Sometimes one gets this animal consciousness while in swimming, for example. One feels the water, the sky, the birds above, but with no thoughts *about* them or memories of how they looked at other times, or aesthetic judgments about their beauty; one feels no *ideas* about what movements he will make, but feels himself make them, feels his body throughout. Self-consciousness dies away. Social consciousness dies away. The meanings, and values, and connections of things die away. One feels sense-impressions, has impulses, feels the movements he makes; that is all.

Thus, for Thorndike, as for Morgan, detailed analysis of an animal's mental operations on the basis of objective inference was followed by descriptions of the animal's private experience on the basis of subjective inference. At the risk of labouring the point, the difference between the two sets of inferences is, again, not one of 'inner' and 'outer'; the operations of mind are at least as 'inner' and unobservable as are the impressions received by that mind. The difference is rather that the objective inferences make contact with observable behaviour through specification of the actions which the mental operations (or equivalent ones) lead to, while the subjective ones do not. The difference may be highlighted by the consideration that the objective inferences can be made as confidently if the subjects are ants or Martians as they can if the subjects are cats or dogs – subject to the qualification mentioned above, which applies to all four species equally – while the subjective ones quite clearly cannot. For those, we must already have some knowledge or conviction concerning the quality of the experiences of the subject organism, a conviction which for Thorndike as for Morgan and Romanes amounted to a predisposition to accept the analogy from human minds to others.

Nevertheless, Thorndike carried further than Morgan the practice of isolating the subjective inferences from the objective ones. Morgan placed limitations on the use of subjective inferences which, in effect, prevented them from interfering with objective inferences. Thorndike in addition treated the two kinds of inference as separate and almost unrelated problems, by virtue of his conclusion that subjective experiences were not much involved in the determination of action.

Finally we may mention the work of Leonard Hobhouse. Hobhouse's *Mind in Evolution*[23] carried the conceptual and methodological development of comparative psychology as traced here to its highest level to that time. Hobhouse formulated his own version of the canon of parsimony, one that was closer to Occam's original razor: 'In comparative psychology the legal maxim must hold, that the thing which does not at some point or other appear in action must be treated as non-existent.'[24] Following on this formulation, he made the clearest distinction to that date between the 'mind' and the 'consciousness' of animals, and with some regrets took the final step in eliminating the experimenter's subjectivity as an analytical tool, and hence in eliminating references to the subjective experience of the animals being tested, from comparative psychology:[25]

> I am not here concerned so much with the kind of consciousness that animals may enjoy, as with the bearings of their experiences on their actions and achievements. In describing the behaviour of an animal, to use terms derived from the human consciousness is often the only way of avoiding intolerable prolixity. Properly guarded and corrected by attention to points of difference as well as resemblance, such usage can lead to so little error that, even if we were ultimately to decide that all animals were automata, no change but that of names would be needed in our account. By 'feeling' in an animal, then, we shall mean a state essentially similar in causation and function to that which we know as feeling in ourselves. Whether it is similar in other respects, is a question which we do not decide by merely using the term. And so with similar terms.

In addition to such conceptual refinements, Hobhouse effectively criticized and corrected the artificiality of Thorndike's puzzle-box studies and conducted his own experiments in situations much closer to the animal's day-to-day life situations. He prefigured in great detail Köhler's studies of insightful behaviour in apes, made sophisticated studies of what was later to be called 'perceptual learning' in cats, dogs, and monkeys, and incorporated his findings into an evolutionary theoretical structure that was in equal parts parsimonious and comprehensive. His work cannot, however, be afforded more detailed treatment in considering the development of comparative psychology because, rightly or wrongly, it was almost totally neglected and had practically no lasting influence.[26] It is at least possible that comparative psychology might have fared better if it had.

In summary, comparative psychology in the first two decades of its existence made numerous advances in investigative methodology and in the scope and precision of its findings. Perhaps even more important, it worked also at achieving a gradually refined, even if usually only implicit, conception of its subject matter, as consisting in the adaptive character and capacities of mind as revealed through its effects in promoting or potentiating the efficient behavioural adjustments of organisms to their environments. Through all of this its goal remained, with remarkable constancy, that of reconstructing the pattern of evolutionary development of mind or of capacities for increasingly complex adaptive behaviour. In Romanes' terms, the goal was 'that of tracing, in as scientific a manner as possible, the probable history of Mental Evolution, and therefore, of course, of enquiring into the causes which have determined it'.[27] For Morgan, it was 'to ascertain the limits of animal psychology',[28] 'to discuss the relation of the psychology of man to that of the higher animals',[29] and 'to indicate the relation of mental evolution to evolution in general'.[30] For Thorndike, 'The main purpose of the study of the animal mind is to learn the development of mental life down through the phylum, to trace in particular the origin of human faculty.'[31] Finally, for Hobhouse, the purpose was 'to trace the main stages of orthogenic evolution, which we have provisionally identified with the evolution of Mind'.[32] The outline of the conceptual development of the science will take on added significance in the context of the two following sections, where it will be seen to indicate a direction that comparative psychology, after becoming embroiled in further difficulties, could possibly have taken but did not; and will serve as a source of contrast by which to highlight these difficulties.

2 COMPARATIVE PSYCHOLOGY AND FUNCTIONALISM

In the attempts at reconstruction of the animal mind as detailed so far there is a possible pitfall. From behaviour we can infer the operations and general functionings of mind. From the analogy between human and animal minds we can infer, it was believed, the subjective experiences or conscious contents that accompanied such operations. What could seem more natural than to explain the observed behaviour as a function of these conscious contents, and thus to show how the mental processes of the animal directed its behaviour? Such a procedure would be in line with common-sense beliefs about the relationship of thought and experience to action, and given that the analogy was to be used at all, there would seem to be little reason not to use it in this way.

The reason for not using the analogy in this way, of course, is that its use is not warranted at all; and the only saving grace attached to its use was that it was coming to be used less and less centrally as comparative psychology developed. Refraining from using the analogy would not constitute a denial of the subjective experience of other organisms, but merely the recognition that its use could not in any case illuminate such subjective experience. That is, the subjective experiences of an animal were not really being *inferred* on the basis of the analogy, but merely *posited,* since the analogy amounts to a statement that subjective experiences of a certain sort (similar to those of man) occur. Attempts based on use of the analogy to show how an animal's subjective experience directs its behaviour would therefore involve the use of an incorrigibly artificial construct in a central role.

None of this, however, was fully appreciated at the time. The only writer among those mentioned who did not rely on the analogy was Hobhouse, and his lead was not followed subsequently. None of the other three writers discussed above entirely avoided the pitfall of explaining behaviour with reference to subjective experience, but for different reasons they did not become altogether ensnared in it. For Romanes and Morgan, as mentioned, the description of probable subjective experience was an end-point in the reconstruction of the animal mind; as a result, such descriptions did not have a major function in any further chain of reasoning. Morgan, in addition, placed such stringent limitations on the use of subjective inference that it was effectively, even if not theoretically, subordinated to objective inference. Thorndike treated the two kinds of inference as separate and only minimally related tasks, being convinced that subjective experiences did not in fact function separate from behaviour in guiding subsequent behaviour. For these writers, subjective inferences were more or less isolated from the rest of the task of reconstruction. Being isolated, such inferences were, if of little use (from our standpoint), at least relatively harmless. By contrast, in most of the behaviour research associated with the American functionalist movement in psychology, there were no such factors operating to minimize the role of subjective inferences and mitigate the consequences of their use.

Functionalism

The difference between British and American post-Darwinian psychology is sometimes summarized by saying that in British psychology the dominant focus of interest was in explicating how we all – men and animals – arrived at our present positions, with the emphasis both in comparative and in differential psychology on these positions as already established; while in the diffuse American movement known as functionalist psychology the focus of interest was more on understanding and harnessing the principles of development and change, with the emphasis on the process of change itself. This interpretation of the difference in the two psychological traditions, as reflecting general differences in national preoccupation, is admittedly facile. It can also be seriously misleading; the most virulent forms of 'social Darwinism' arose also in the United States, as justification for the current distribution of wealth and power. However, whatever was the case in other currents of American culture, it is quite true that a liberal and optimistic version of evolutionary dynamics and their implications underlay much of the functionalist movement in psychology. As a result, the central concern in functionalist psychology was with the processes of adaptation, growth, and development: in the individual, the species, the phylum, and the animal kingdom as a whole, in roughly that order of descending emphasis.

The way in which this concern was expressed marks a more

specific difference between American and British psychology. At first, scientific psychology in the United States was derived largely from German influences, particularly from the introspective experimental psychology of Wundt. This 'new psychology' was a psychology of the fundamental processes or contents of consciousness. The way in which the American interest in developmental processes, individual differences, and the implications of evolutionary theory gradually transformed this abstract conception into the more concrete functionalist one is described in detail by Woodworth.[33] The transformation was remarkably straightforward; what is largely of interest in it is that it was gradual, non-revolutionary, and quite fully recognized at the time. That it was gradual and non-revolutionary is attested to by the piecemeal way in which it occurred and by its relative lack of opposition; its main opponent was Titchener, who did not repudiate it but merely suggested that it was occurring too soon. That it was quite fully recognized by those involved in it is indicated by the early statement of James[34] and the later one of Titchener,[35] both contrasting psychologies of structure with psychologies of function, or as Titchener put it, the 'is' with the 'is for'.

Functionalist psychology was thus an adaptation of the Wundtian, introspectionist, structural psychology to the demands of the American situation. British psychology, by contrast, was from the beginning less inclined toward analytic introspection and experiment than were either the German or the American sort. British psychology was introspectionist, but was not systematically so, and never had such a strong concern with the detailed introspective analysis of the contents of consciousness. Thus, the hold of analytic introspection, and hence of consciousness – the specific and perhaps somewhat artificial kind of consciousness which could be discovered through analytic introspection – as the basic subject matter of psychology, was much stronger in Germany and the United States than in Britain; it was strong enough in the United States that in the course of the passage from Wundtian to functionalist psychology both introspection as a collection of methods and the related kind of consciousness as the subject matter of psychology were willingly retained.

The consciousness that was retained was, nevertheless, regarded in a different way than Wundt (or Titchener) regarded it. The emphasis in functionalist psychology was on the *uses* of consciousness, that is, on how it facilitated the adaptations of organisms to their environments. James[36] wrote at length on consciousness as a regulator of the complex and unstable neural mechanisms of the highly evolved human brain. Angell based his psychology on the principle that 'consciousness is an organic function whose intrinsic occupation consists in furthering the adaptive responses of the organism to its life conditions'.[37] Functionalism, he stated, is the 'psychology of the fundamental utilities of consciousness'.[38]

Neither James nor Angell nor anybody else made the distinction between consciousness as differential sensitivity to different aspects of the environment, and consciousness as a state of awareness consisting of specific experiences, fundamental to their psychological theorizing in the way required by comparative psychology. Nor, for their purpose, was there at first any particular reason to do so, although the distinction is, as we have seen (p. 64), essential if we are to talk about the consciousness of animals, which can be charaterized effectively in terms of attention but not in terms of experience. The distinction was certainly recognized, but what was distinguished was regarded as no more than different points of view in the consideration of consciousness. That is, the distinction was made between what consciousness is and what it does, between its form and its functions, its contents and its operations, its 'is' and its 'is for'. It was, therefore, in light of the gradual way in which the functionalist orientation developed, a distinction that could support a difference in emphasis, but not a difference in basic theoretical and methodological position. While it was the functions or operations of consciousness that were of principal interest to the functionalists, the consciousness thereby studied for its utility was clearly understood to be the same consciousness that could otherwise be studied for its specific content. That is, the functionalists were concerned with the adaptive significance of that same consciousness of which Wundt and Titchener were investigating the content and structure.[39] The distinction between the functions and the contents of consciousness in no way corresponded to a distinction between a consciousness that could be studied and a consciousness that (at least in animals) could not, between consciousness as publicly inferable and consciousness as inescapably private. Indeed, it would have seemed bizarre to any psychologists of the day to suggest that the two distinctions should correspond; consciousness, after all, is what it is, whatever it is, and while it must be studied in different ways in different organisms, it is surely the same consciousness that is being studied.

Functionalist Comparative Psychology

Thus, functionalism was concerned with the adaptive significance or utility of that consciousness which exists as a state of awareness independent of its functions, that is, with the adaptive significance of specific subjective experiences and mental operations. So far as the enterprise was applied to human beings, who are often capable of accurate introspection, it met with a reasonable amount of success. But for comparative psychology, where conscious processes and behaviour could not be observed independently, the consequences of the functionalist position were immediate and disastrous. The general programme of functionalism led comparative psychology quickly into the pitfall of using inferred subjective experiences to account for behaviour, and did so in a particularly debilitating manner. Let us reconstruct the process.

The subject matter of functionalist psychology, human and animal alike, was consciousness as such, considered in terms of its functions and adaptive significance. That is, it was the adaptive significance of the specific subjective experiences or mental operations which an individual was having or performing in an experimental situation; and in the case of animal subjects, of course, these various conscious contents had to be inferred rather than reported. It was therefore of central importance to the programme of functionalist comparative psychology to develop techniques to describe the particular content of an animal's consciousness, just as the functionalists and the structuralists alike described the particular content of human consciousness, so that the specific functioning of this consciousness in directing the animal's behaviour could be demonstrated.

Boring summed up the interpretative method typical of functionalist comparative psychology from the late 1890s to about 1915, in a bald statement of the relationship between observation, subjective inference, and reconstruction of the animal mind based on such inference:[40]

> The rule of functional animal psychology of that date was that, when you have finished your observations of behavior, you use the results to infer the nature of the animal's consciousness and then show how those processes function in the animal's behavior.

Where this rule departed from the method of Romanes was in the addition of the systematic requirement that the inferred conscious 'processes' must be shown, in detail, to 'function in the animal's behavior'. The functionalists, however, possessed no new ways of gaining access to these conscious processes in non-human organisms, and so had to rely more than ever on the analogy from human to animal minds. This necessity for ever more reliance on the analogy, in conjunction with the developing methodological sophistication of experimentation, prevented functionalist comparative psychology from making those compromises with the exigencies of research that established the British programme of work (to which we have effectively assimilated Thorndike)[41] as viable, despite its use of the analogy. Instead, these two features led the movement to an interpretation of the mental life of animals by means of a sensationalistic, 'passive organism' model of unprecedented severity. In the process, the field of comparative psychology inevitably took on the shallow mentalism and estrangement of data from theory against which behaviourism was to be advanced as an explicit reaction.

There were a number of intellectual influences favouring the development of a passive organism model in functionalist psychology (as well as a few opposing it; cf. note 39), and it is necessary to distinguish them in order to be clear about how the functionalist development was unique. First, there was the continuing influence of the British empiricist tradition, in which a kind of passive or narrowly reactive organism account had been developed from Hobbes through the Mills. The continuing influence of this tradition was invoked many years later by Hull[42] as providing the thematic background to the psychology of his own day. However, while this tradition clearly formed part of functionalism's background, it was not sufficient in itself to determine the kind of model chosen; the British comparative psychologists discussed above were equally subject to the influences of British empiricism, but they managed at least in part to go beyond a passive organism conception in considering what animals were capable of doing. Second, there was the direct influence of the kind of theoretical account (as distinguished from the conception of the subject matter) favoured in introspective experimental psychology. Wundt's and Titchener's psychological systems were, by the late 1890s, becoming increasingly sensationalistic (especially Titchener's), and had always been elementaristic. Descriptions of animal consciousness based on the theoretical principles advanced by the introspectionists to account for human consciousness had a high initial credibility in functionalist comparative psychology. Furthermore, the major introspective psychologists themselves made influential statements about comparative psychology. Wundt (cf. note 48) wrote an ambitious work on the interpretation of animal consciousness by means of the analogy.[43] Titchener never undertook any comparative research, but explicitly gave it his blessing as an extension of human psychology, so long as it was based on the analogy.[44] Titchener's student, Washburn, vigorously promoted an introspective type of comparative psychology based on use of the analogy as late as 1936.[45] All of these writers made more or less detailed extensions of their elementaristic psychological theories about man, to cover their less privileged animal subjects. Again, however, this influence does not fully account for the character of functionalist comparative psychology; the comparative psychological writings of Wundt and Washburn never displayed a sensationalistic and reactive orientation to anything like the extent which, as we will see, was typical of many of the functionalist writings.

The additional factor which established functionalism as unique in its employment of a passive organism model consisted, unexceptionably enough, in the methodological constraints involved in making increasingly rigorous studies of the content of animal consciousness. To clarify these constraints, we must look again at the relation between objective inferences (inferences to a functionally equivalent set of mental operations or capacities, based on behavioural evidence) and subjective inferences (inferences to specific mental events, based on behavioural evidence plus application of the analogy). Again, from the observations of behaviour in conjunction with an appropriate criterion we can infer the kinds of adaptive capacities which an animal manifests in its behaviour, and from the application of the analogy to such observations we can supposedly infer the actual mental operations and experiences which are present to the animal's consciousness. The implicit tension resulting from the use of two kinds of inferences for the description of one mind was referred to previously. The tension was reduced for the writers previously discussed by their considering the two forms of inference as relating to more or less separate questions, so that subjective inferences were used mainly to describe what an animal felt, and objective inferences were used mainly to describe what it could do. It was further reduced for Morgan, by his making subjective inferences effectively subordinate to objective ones, and still further for Thorndike, by his conclusion that subjective experiences and 'ideas' play little or no part in the determination of animal behaviour. For the writers associated with functionalist comparative psychology, however, the tension could not be resolved in this way. Subjective inferences could not be subordinated to objective inferences because it was the relationship of specific conscious processes – which because of their specificity could be described only by subjective inferences – to ongoing behaviour that was the focus of interest. At the same time, objective inferences could not be subordinated to subjective inferences because of the increasingly general acceptance that all inferences had in some way to be uniquely determined by observations of behaviour if they were to amount to anything more than rank speculation. What was required, therefore, was some way to assimilate the two kinds of inferences, that is, to combine the particularized content of subjective inferences with the public observational basis of objective inferences: some way, in other words, to place subjective inferences – inferences to particular conscious processes, predicated on the analogy from human to animal minds – under the strict control of objective criteria.

It was of the greatest significance for all later psychology that there was no apparent difficulty in restricting the latitude of subjective inferences in just this way. Such restrictions were constantly increasing as part of the methodological development of comparative psychology. The functionalists were heir to all the constraints on the drawing of subjective inferences which Morgan summarized in his canon, as well as to the methodological strictures in favour of rigorous experimental procedures advanced by Thorndike. Morgan's canon required that all inferences be the minimal ones available. The methodological strictures associated with the development of experimental methods required that the factors relevant to the performance of a task required of an animal be all, as far as possible, explicitly specified and hence controlled in the experimental situation. The subjective inferences were thus to relate as uniquely and precisely as possible to the animal's experience of and reactions to the specifiable parameters of the stimulus situation.

When they were originally introduced, these restrictions did not have quite the same effect as they came to have in functionalist comparative psychology. Morgan and Thorndike employed both subjective and objective inferences, and the function of the restrictions on the drawing of inferences was in large part that of regulating the relationships between the two kinds. The restrictions served to emphasize objective inferences based on observable behaviour, to minimize the latitude of subjective inferences, and consequently to subordinate subjective inferences to objective ones. In functionalist comparative psychology, by contrast, the restrictions could serve only to reduce the latitude of subjective inferences. They could not regulate the relationship between subjective and objective inferences since, due to the emphasis on specific conscious processes, objective inferences were rarely made. It is clear, of course, that subjective inferences could only be *restricted* by these means; they could not be *refined,* in the sense of making increasingly accurate contact with the animal's consciousness, because of the inadequacy and incorrigibility of the analogy, as already discussed. In the British work in the field, the subjective inferences were not becoming refined or more accurate either, but they were being kept out of the way by virtue of following after the account of the animal mind already established on the basis of objective inferences. In functionalist comparative psychology, where practically no objective inferences were drawn, the subjective ones could be held in check only by being restricted by the methodological constraints.

Since such methodological constraints on their use comprised the only check on the drawing of subjective inferences in American research, the increasingly sophisticated employment of these constraints became customary as a means – the only means – for making the inferential accounts precise and unambiguous. But again, while such constraints could make the inferences progressively more 'objective', in the sense of being based on publicly observable events and publicly applicable criteria (i.e., so that different observers could make the same inference), they could not make them any more accurate. Objectivity and accuracy, in this instance, were quite separate and unrelated considerations, even if they were, naturally, not recognized as such.

Thus, the interpretation of experiments carried out within the programme of functionalist comparative psychology came to display a curious pattern. On the one hand the methodological strictures constantly minimized the choice and extent of available subjective inferences; as a result, the inferred conscious contents gradually became correspondingly restricted and impoverished. On the other hand, because of the priorities of functionalist psychology these impoverished inferred conscious contents were accorded enormous functional significance. To put it another way, the strictures on the drawing of subjective inferences (the canon of parsimony, the increase in experimental control) refined these inferences in the only way in which they could be refined and rendered uniquely determined by the experimental situation; they refined the inferences, that is, by rendering them little more than a reflection, or a translation into the sensationalistic language of introspective psychology that was held appropriate for the description of subjective experience, of the animal's behaviour and of the parameters of the experimental situation as they were judged to impinge on the animal's sensory apparatus. But such almost trivially inferred states were supposed to comprise the animal's conscious contents, which were supposed to have functional utility; they were what was held to guide behaviour, and explicating how they did so was taken to be the most significant part of any comparative psychological experiment. In short, at the same time that subjective inferences were becoming so restricted and hemmed in that their artificiality could hardly fail to become evident, their importance in revealing the determinants of behaviour was being magnified as never before.

An extreme version of a sensationalistic, passive organism model of mental functioning was the inevitable result. The alternative to a passive organism model of mental activity is one in which the organism performs internal operations of a sort which do not simply mirror its surroundings and its internal biological conditions. Such an 'active organism' model is certainly compatible with an evolutionary emphasis on the development and functioning of adaptive processes, and was indeed the theoretical goal of much of functionalist psychology. However, the elaboration of such an active organism model would require some attempt at description of the internal activity. The only effective way to make contact with such activity is through objective inferences from the organism's behavioural capacity, because only such inferences relate to internal capacities and operations that can be specified in terms of their functional significance. Functionalist psychology had little place for inferences to such functionally equivalent sets of internal operations, however, because of its concern with individual consciousness. It was thus limited for the most part to subjective inferences. Subjective inferences, in turn, might conceivably have been used for the description of the particular mental operations that an animal was performing in a specific situation. Such inferences could not have been very effective, since subjective inferences, based on the analogy, never are. But they might at least have stimulated the development of objective methods – methods, that is, based on the use of objective inference – for the description and analysis of such mental operations, if the operations themselves had been agreed to be of principal interest. This suggestion is purely conjectural, but it is strengthened by the fact that the replacement of subjective methods with objective ones for making the kinds of descriptions generally desired, those in which the actions of the experimental animal are regarded as reflections of its surroundings and its internal physical states, was much the course that psychology followed in giving birth to behaviourism.

But this is getting ahead of the story. Within the programme of functionalist comparative psychology, subjective inferences – inferences to the private mental lives of individual organisms – could not legitimately be directed to the description of mental operations, regardless of how heuristically valuable such inferences might have been. In the absence of any account based on objective inferences (which could serve to subordinate the subjective ones), subjective inferences could be prevented from lapsing into uncontrolled speculation only by being kept rigorously related to the specifiable parameters of the experimental situation. Mental operations of the sort which would characterize an active organism model could not, almost by definition, be so restricted; such operations were hence outside the range of control which could be exercised over subjective inferences, and such inferences were, accordingly, restricted to the minimal sensationalistic ones.

The passive organism model of mental life which became typical in functionalist comparative psychology was thus a kind of methodological artifact, resulting from the constraints imposed on subjective inferences in an attempt to make them objective. However, the attempt by the functionalists to make objective descriptions of subjective states could never be fully successful; it resulted only in the organism's growing ever more passive. The 'organism' studied in terms of its subjective experiences thus became more and more a mere sensationalistic translation of the stimuli which it received and of the responses which it emitted. Between stimulus and response there figured little more than a mental representation of the stimulus and mental representation of (or instinctive impulse to) the response.

A Representative Experiment

It is only to a limited degree that the emergence and trivialization of the passive organism model was a gradual development, for the artificial quality of the theoretical accounts advanced within functionalist comparative psychology was characteristic of the field from the start, and increased only slightly throughout the short life of the movement. The relationship between observations of behaviour and inferences to subjective experience is shown clearly in as early a study as Small's experiments on learning in rats, in which he introduced the maze as a tool in the study of animal learning. In the experiment quoted here (in which the discussion is unusually concise), a rat was trained to gain access to a portable goal box containing food by tearing off a paper seal which obstructed the door to the box. On the test trial, the door to the box was further secured so that it required a firm push to open it after the seal had been removed. At the beginning of the quotation Small discussed the quality and contents of the rat's consciousness before it encountered the new obstruction:[46]

The train already formed may be figured somewhat as follows: feeling of hunger, sight of box, smell of food (these two probably simultaneous), curiosity, location of food in box by smell (and sight), tearing off paper, getting food, pleasurable state. In some instances, as has been noted in considering the preceding groups, the first term of this hypothetical series drops out, and the mere sight of the box is sufficient to start off the train. (It is quite possible that the instinctive acquisitiveness furnishes the organic basis for the series in such cases. It is highly unlikely that any excitation of a purely sensational character would furnish the motive force.) The connection of these links becomes so intimate that when the rat is normally hungry the appropriate movements are gone through with immediately upon seeing the box introduced into the cage. Now, when this associative process is broken up at the biting-off-paper point, as in this experiment, what happens in the rat's mind? The manifest purpose of the animal is to get inside the box, and this desire to get inside is coupled with the idea of getting in through the door. The modified form of the association train may now be: hunger, a mixed image, motor and visual, of entering the box through the door, getting the food, pleasure. That is, one of the terms of the chain is variable – the association is not determinate. When this term is expunged, another one, perhaps a suppressed one, rises to take its place. Of course it is not necessary to postulate such a process as the following in the rat's mind: 'Biting off paper fails of its usual result, therefore I'll try another method.' The only necessary elements are: the persistence of the feeling of hunger, the location of the food inside the box, either as a present smell-sensation or as a memory of getting the food inside the box, or both, and the memory of getting in at that place. This last accounts for the constant return to, and the poking of, the door, but, as she is not hurt by it, her boldness increases; and this being further stimulated by the smell of food, finally impels her to force open the door.

The pausing of the rat when the door unexpectedly failed to open might seem to imply reflection; but this is not so in any strict usage of the term reflection. Surprise and disappointment would be quite sufficient to restrain activity for the time; and these affections would preclude the possibility of reflection unless reflection is used merely in a descriptive sense to designate the transition from this passive state to an active state under the resurging impulse of hunger. That the rat *feels* 'why' or 'what' is certain, that she thinks 'why' or 'what' is both doubtful and unnecessary. . . .

It is also clear, I think, that what properly may be called ideas, find slight place in the associative process. Crass images – visual, olfactory, motor – organic conditions, and instinctive activities are assuredly the main elements. That these elements may bleach out and attenuate into ideas is not impossible. Analogy with human experience would indeed point to that conclusion.

Small's interpretations of his experimental results were typical of many made during this period, by Kinneman, Kline, Watson, and others.[47] Theoretical debates centred on questions such as the relative importance of sensations versus instincts in the mental life of animals, or the relative role of stimulus-produced sensations versus organic ones in directing behaviour. The inferred train of associations was typically similar to that in Small's discussion, containing sensational, impulsive, and motoric (response) elements indifferently; it was almost classic associationism, of a sort that would have been quite acceptable to the Mills or Hartley, or to Wundt.[48] The animal's mental activity was conceived almost entirely in terms of what it *has*, rather than in terms of what it *does*. In Small's paper there were almost no inferences to capacities or mental operations, such as characterized Thorndike's report a year earlier. Both writers agreed in concluding that 'ideas' play little part in the determination of the animal's behaviour. But for Thorndike this conclusion was reached by considering what responses could be potentiated by the presence and functioning of ideas, responses which his experimental animals did not perform; for Small the conclusion was dependent only on the possibility of postulating a sufficient number of 'impulses' (drives or instincts) that could interact with the animal's experience to stimulate whatever behaviour was observed to occur.

The chain of inferences in Small's discussion started with the rat's behaviour and the characteristics of the experimental situation; progressed to the rat's sensations (of the characteristics of the experimental situation) and feelings (of hunger, which was controlled by deprivation schedules, and curiosity, which was an inborn instinct); and from these in conjunction with behavioural instincts moved back to behaviour again. The inferential chain, in brief, proceeded from stimuli, to the organism, to responses; but the 'organism' component of the chain was entirely passive, consisting of sensations, instincts, feelings, and impulsions. The inferred mentation was a passive process; what the rat did was a function solely of what it subjectively experienced and of the (not explicitly specified) laws of association. In every instance where the possibility arose that the rat was initiating a train of mental operations (reflection, analysis of relationship between action of tearing off seal and expected consequence), Small concluded solely on the basis of parsimony that it was not doing so. His conclusion was spuriously facilitated by his representing the possible mental operations as propositional in each case; but what is more important is that he was able to give no indication of what behaviour the rat could perform that he *would* take as indicative of self-initiated internal operations. Lacking any behavioural criterion by which he could judge whether or not ideas or any other mental operations functioned in behaviour, Small was constrained by the canon of parsimony to assume that they did not. As a result, the evidence of the rat's behaviour could not be implicated in the general direction of the interpretation of its mind or consciousness. This general direction was established in advance by the methodological constraints on the making of subjective inferences.

The irrelevance of behavioural observations to the general direction of interpretation of the animal mind on the one hand, and the polarity of impoverished inferred conscious contents versus the great functional significance attributed to them on the other, together were responsible for an estrangement of data from the theoretical interpretations which were supposed to make sense of them. Thorndike[49] criticized Small's experiments partly on the grounds of the equivocality of any conclusions which could be drawn from them about the constitution of the animal mind; but Thorndike's own ideas about how to proceed in interpreting the animal mind were not sufficiently clear that they could have very much effect – even assuming, as is dubious, that they could have had much effect otherwise.

However, it was not long before a widespread reaction took place against this kind of theoretical interpretation. Small's experiments were the first detailed working out of the functionalist programme in comparative psychology. In the eight years between 1899, when Small's report was published, and 1907, when Watson stopped making use of subjective inferences, there was only a slight intensification of the trends which Small's paper displayed. In the five years between 1907 and 1912, when Watson repudiated subjective inferences altogether, there was only a little more.[50] The behaviourist revolution that Watson inaugurated was a direct and largely explicit reaction against the kind of psychological interpretation exemplified by the quotation from Small. Furthermore, in light of the imbalances of functionalist comparative psychology the reaction was a justifiable one, although the direction which the reaction took in being extended beyond the bounds of comparative psychology was such that these imbalances were never rectified.

3   THE BIRTH OF BEHAVIOURISM

Contrast between American and British Comparative Psychology

In brief, the function of functionalist comparative psychology was twofold. On the one hand, it served to assimilate all considerations of mentality and of psychological organization in animals to the private consciousness of individual animals. Everything about the animal which is presumed to determine or have some effect upon behaviour – in other words, everything related to the animal's mind – has an autonomous status such that it cannot receive any investigation based merely upon a study of its effects upon behaviour but requires, in addition, an interpretative key (use of the analogy) that has no evidential justification and no direct relationship to behaviour. On the other hand, when the analogy was applied to the interpretation of mind, the requirement that the inferences be minimal rendered the mind thus revealed of such a sort that its special status hardly seemed to have any point. The private consciousness to which all mentality was assimilated, and which was therefore so important in guiding behaviour, turned out to contain little more than a copy of observable external factors. Behaviour could not by itself yield evidence about the factors which potentiated it, but these factors, apart from their location in an inaccessible consciousness, turned out to be almost identical to the experimental factors which were in fact the ones systematically manipulated in order to vary behaviour.

In the British research in comparative psychology, by contrast, mind was not so thoroughly separated from behaviour, and so could be characterized in part on the basis of that behaviour. It was largely an accident that this was so, since initially it was the mind of the introspectionists – the mind composed of conscious contents – that the British psychologists were trying to discover in their animal subjects, just as it was for the Americans. For the British, as a result, those aspects of mind which did become assimilated to private consciousness fared no better than in America. They likewise required interpretation by means of the analogy, and were, consequently, incorrigibly artificial; but they were not required to comprise all of the mind. Because of this, the inability of the British comparative psychologists to discover the mind of the introspectionists did not lead them into a dead end. Instead, it led them step by step to a mind that they could discover, the mind that is manifest in the organism's adaptations to complex and ever-changing environmental conditions.

What gave the British comparative psychologists this relative freedom of manoeuvre, so that they did not have to assimilate all of mind to private consciousness, was that they were not primarily concerned with the relationship between conscious contents and behaviour. Consciousness, for them, was of interest for its own sake even more than for its relation to ongoing behaviour. The demands of objectivity in reconstructing the mind on the basis of observations of behaviour therefore led them, not to trivialize their subjective inferences (which would have contradicted their aims), but to supplement them with objective ones which could provide an apparently sounder footing from which the subjective inferences could then proceed. Such a method was not fully suitable for uncovering the relations between consciousness and behaviour, because the variability in the inferred conscious contents and the variability in observed behaviour did not always correspond; but for the British comparative psychologists that was an acceptable limitation. What such a method could do was to make the description of consciousness both detailed and apparently definite (which was initially its main purpose), and also, almost incidentally – although less and less so as the science developed – to allow sophisticated and exact determination from an external viewpoint of the capacities and mental operations involved in an animal's behavioural adaptations.

For the functionalists, however, there could be no compromise with their goal of showing how specific conscious processes guided the behaviour of animals, for explicating that relationship was central to their conception of the task of psychology. They were thus constrained to attack the problem of that relationship head on, by using the analogy without any additional tool which could support and hence vindicate it. In consequence, they could not begin to develop any fundamentally different ways to account for behavioural adaptations until they were prepared to replace the introspectionist model of mind with one that was more appropriate to their purposes – which they could not do for a number of reasons, the main one being that for some time the introspectionist model was the only widely available one that did not carry an unacceptably heavy gloss of Hegelian idealism or theology or both[51] – or, of course, until they were willing to drop the reference to mind altogether.

It is one of the small ironies of history that the functionalists were unable to deal with the adaptive capacities of mind, precisely because they were trying so hard to do just that; while the British comparative psychologists were able to make some progress in the task, precisely because it was not initially their major concern. The irony is resolved by the fact that the two groups of comparative psychologists shared a conception of the mind that is totally inappropriate as a basis for investigating the adaptive capacities of animals; but the British psychologists, because they were not so tied to using it for that purpose, could at least begin to transcend it.[52]

The Behaviourist Reaction

The foundation of behaviourism as a self-consciously new start for psychology was discussed briefly in Chapter I. Let us now examine it in more detail specifically as a reaction to introspective psychology and to functionalist comparative psychology, as expressed in Watson's announcement of the movement's birth.[53]

Given the conceptual difficulties associated with functionalist comparative psychology, one could sympathize with Watson's complaint:[54]

> On this view, after having determined our animal's ability to learn, the simplicity or complexity of its methods of learning, the effect of past habit upon present response, the range of stimuli to which it ordinarily responds, the widened range to which it can respond under experimental conditions – in more general terms, its various problems and its various ways of solving them – we should still feel that the task is unfinished and that the results are worthless, until we can interpret them by analogy in the light of consciousness. Although we have solved our problem we feel uneasy and unrestful because of our definition of psychology: we feel forced to say something about the possible mental processes of our animal.

Watson's initial recommendation with regard to this unsatisfactory situation was an eminently reasonable one. He suggested that since the relation of animal consciousness to animal behaviour is essentially stipulative, experimentally indeterminable, and irrelevant to problems that can be investigated experimentally, it is fruitless to continue trying to solve all those problems which pertain to the relationship:[55]

> Such problems as these can no longer satisfy behavior men. It would be better to give up the province altogether and admit frankly that the study of the behavior of animals has no justification, than to admit that our search is of such a 'will o' the wisp' character. One can assume either the presence or the

absence of consciousness anywhere in the phylogenetic scale without affecting the problems of behavior by one jot or one tittle; and without influencing in any way the mode of experimental attack upon them.

Therefore, he went on, we would be better off to drop all concern with consciousness in comparative psychology, and study only that which can be experimentally investigated, that is, behaviour itself.[56]

> It seems reasonably clear that some kind of compromise must be effected: either psychology must change its viewpoint so as to take in the facts of behavior, whether or not they have bearings on the problems of 'consciousness'; or else behavior must stand alone as a wholly separate and independent science.

How promising such a programme would be would depend on the characteristics of the 'behaviour' which was henceforth to be studied, and on what was eventually going to replace the introspective conception of consciousness. The two considerations are closely related, as the introspective conception of consciousness and the functionalist conception of behaviour (which Watson was starting from) were complementary. As it turned out, however, nothing was to replace the introspective conception of consciousness, and the complementary conception of behaviour was to be left on its own. This became clear as Watson continued his polemic. In the first instance, his analysis supported no more than a demand for the autonomy of comparative psychology. In this restricted field, focusing attention on behaviour could be justified by the sterility of the theoretical models available to comparative psychology. Watson went further, however, and his analysis became a bid for assimilation of the rest of psychology when he carried the argument out of comparative psychology and into general psychology. After arguing for the value of behavioural observations in comparative psychology, Watson detailed the conceptual and methodological problems which he considered would beset any kind of psychology, not just comparative psychology, that depended on introspection. Introspection was an inadequate method and 'consciousness' was an inappropriate subject matter, not only for comparative psychology, but for all scientific psychology:[57]

> I do not wish unduly to criticize psychology. It has failed signally, I believe, during the fifty-odd years of its existence as

an experimental discipline to make its place in the world as an undisputed natural science.... The time seems to have come when psychology must discard all reference to consciousness; when it need no longer delude itself into thinking that it is making mental states the object of observation.... I firmly believe that two hundred years from now, unless the introspective method is discarded, psychology will still be divided on the question as to whether auditory sensations have the quality of 'extension', whether intensity is an attribute which can be applied to color, whether there is a difference in 'texture' between image and sensation, and upon many hundreds of others of like character.

The existing division of labour between introspective and behavioural methods in psychology was not to be reworked, but repudiated. Watson was standing out as the champion of the behaviour which he had been studying all his professional life - the behaviour studied in functionalist comparative psychology – over against the consciousness in terms of which that behaviour had until then been explained: the consciousness studied in functionalist and introspective (structural) psychology alike. Since consciousness could have no observational status as a theoretical construct, and no independently determinable role in the production of behaviour, the natural response to Watson seemed to be simply that of abandoning it. Thus, Watson emphasized one pole of the functionalist duality of consciousness and behaviour to the exclusion of the other, and declared that all genuine problems which previously had pertained to consciousness could be better expressed in the language of behaviour:[58]

> Psychology as behavior will, after all, have to neglect but few of the really essential problems with which psychology as an introspective science now concerns itself. In all probability even this residue of problems may be phrased in such a way that refined methods in behavior (which certainly must come) will lead to their solution.

In contrasting behaviour as it was then conceived, with consciousness as it was then conceived, and affirming that only the former should have scientific status, Watson was, again, attempting to resolve the functionalist duality of consciousness and behaviour by denying it and expressing everything of psychological interest in terms of behaviour alone. The problem with any such attempt is that 'behaviour' is not a pristine concept. In the functionalist model, the characteristics of consciousness and behaviour alike are derived partly from their contrast with each other. Behaviour is thus not given as uninterpreted data, but in part as a fairly simple expression of the conceptual framework in terms of which it has been seen and interpreted. If there is something wrong with the conception of consciousness which was associated with functionalism, there is likewise something wrong with the complementary conception of behaviour, and any programme of research based solely upon that conception of behaviour could be expected to inherit many of functionalism's limitations.

What is wrong with the functionalist conception of behaviour is that it is an impoverished concept. Everything that gives meaning to behaviour, everything that establishes behaviour *as* adaptation to the environment, *as* subserving the economy of the organism, *as* performing broadly biological functions, is separated utterly from the observable aspects of the behaviour of animals, and is assimilated to the contents of a private consciousness that cannot be described in terms of the adaptive functions themselves. What is left as observable behaviour is the movements of a physical body in space. Without the shadowy consciousness that guides and directs behaviour, the behaviour of organisms differs little from the behaviour of stones.

This does not mean that a psychology based on the repudiation of consciousness would be unable to deal with any of the factors responsible for behaviour, or would be unable to distinguish organisms from stones. 'Consciousness' as the guide for animal behaviour was a trivial construct, little more than the means by which external stimulation was transformed into internal agency. Furthermore, the way in which the transformation actually took place, that is, the way in which the private consciousness of the animal actually directed the process of adaptation to environmental conditions, was never made clear; and it could not be made clear so long as the subjective inferences were restricted to the minimal sensationalistic ones. With the repudiation of consciousness, therefore, what was left to determine behaviour was the same experimental and other environmental conditions which had been determining behaviour all along, but through the mediation of consciousness. These external conditions could now be varied explicitly to show their effects on behaviour, and could thus be shown to determine behaviour by themselves without the action of any intermediary, unobservable causal agents. Behaviourism was thus, at the very worst, no worse off for explanatory concepts than was functionalist comparative psychology.

However, it was not all that much better off either. The behaviour which behaviourism could account for remained the behaviour that was studied in functionalist comparative psychology. The focus of control has shifted, from the environment-via-consciousness to the environment itself, but the behaviour that is thus controlled is still isolated from its biological adaptive significance. The meaning or functional significance of behaviour is still not part of the constitution of that behaviour, nor is it one of the determinants of behaviour (through the conception of adaptive capacities); it is at best a result of behaviour, an abstraction from the observed series of environmental-behavioural correlations or stimulus-response connections. Since the functional significance which is the meaning of behaviour still forms no part of the constitution or the immediate determinants of behaviour, what is central to the organism's functioning in the world – previously its consciousness, now its behaviour – remains a mere reflection of environmental conditions. Watson put it quite clearly; the 'principal contention' of behaviourism, he said, is that 'there are no centrally initiated processes. The environment in the widest sense forces the formation of habits.'[59] It follows that the goal of a behaviourist psychology – the only possible goal – is that 'given the response the stimuli can be predicted; given the stimuli the response can be predicted.'[60]

Behaviourism as propounded by Watson was an improvement over functionalist comparative psychology in the important respect that it made the factors which the latter had in fact emphasized in the determination of behaviour – experimental and other environmental factors – into the explicit determinants of behaviour. These determinants were thus unchanged as to their content but were reformulated so as to make them explicitly observable and open to experimental study. Behaviour, consequently, could now reveal the factors that determined it, which it could not do in functionalist comparative psychology except with the aid of the analogy. But behaviourism was not an improvement over functionalist comparative psychology in its conception of the composition of behaviour. Behaviour remained composed of isolated, separable responses, each occasioned separately by specific causal factors and the entire series integrated likewise by external causal factors. Control, whether naturally by the environment or systematically by the experimenter, remained central to the conception of behaviour: not extrinsically, as related merely to the goals of research, but intrinsically, following from the composition of behaviour as essentially reactive, as being evoked in each particular by environmental pressures. Again, it is because of this composition of behaviour as reactive that Watson could formulate the goal of behaviourism: given the stimulus, to predict the response, etc.; for given that behaviour is reactive in this sense (as previously, consciousness had been), achieving that predictive goal would amount to making a complete explanation of behaviour.[61] Behaviourism therefore retained the research programme that had developed in functionalist comparative psychology, that of showing precisely how the organism's functioning (behaviour, consciousness) was a reflection of the specific parameters of the experimental situation. Behaviourism replaced the old sensationalism with a new environmentalism, and conscious processes with responses as the unit of analysis, and thereby structured the programme in such a way that it could be carried out more directly and precisely than before. It is in this sense, which is not quite the one he intended, that Watson was correct in his claim that 'behaviorism is the only consistent and logical functionalism'.[62]

Thus, from the viewpoint of behaviourism's relationship to the psychological tradition from which it emerged, as well as from that of its specific proposals for the future conduct of psychology (cf. Chapter I), the revolution that founded behaviourism was a methodological revolution. Behaviourism consisted largely in an objective reconstruction of the programme of functionalist comparative psychology – or, as we can now say, an *objectivist* reconstruction, since what was central to the reconstruction was the replacement of subjective with strictly objective methods as a matter of principle, and the insistence that only these objective ones were admissible in science. The repudiation of consciousness, the adoption of a stimulus-response model, the tendencies toward environmentalism and minute analysis: all of these characterized the foundation of behaviourism, and all stemmed from the simple elimination of subjective inference and the consequent objectivist reconstruction of the programme and conceptual framework of functionalist comparative psychology.

95

The Incorporation of Positivism

The account as presented so far has, however, an element missing, one which gave the newly constituted behaviourism much of its initial momentum and helped to integrate its diverse trends. It has been left until the end so that the behaviourist reaction could first be presented, as far as possible, in terms of problems internal to the practice of psychology. The last element is the source of the 'principle' by which subjective formulations could be generally replaced with objective ones, both in comparative psychology and throughout psychology. It is here that the incorporation of positivism within behaviourism appears and becomes crucial, for with this incorporation, all of the features of behaviourism discussed above were free to become subtly modified.

The incorporation of positivism within behaviourism must be regarded in two ways: as an internal development within comparative psychology, and as an external influence brought in for the purpose of extending the range of that development throughout psychology. The repudiation of consciousness within comparative psychology was a specific response to a specific conceptual dilemma primarily affecting one area of psychology. The repudiation of unobservables – the unobservables that were causing trouble – in comparative psychology was thus a purely internal development. It was unquestionably a positivist reaction, but one of the sort described in Chapter II as a natural and appropriate response to unresolvable conceptual dilemmas which come to paralyse scientific research in a given field. Whether, if the reaction had stopped there, the positivist recasting of comparative psychology would eventually have given rise to a new set of theoretical principles and presuppositions which gradually assumed realistic significance, is impossible to say with any certainty; but there is no indication in the development of psychology to that time which would cause one to assume that it would not. But the positivist reaction did not, of course, stop with comparative psychology but was extended throughout psychology; as a result, the gradual process by which it could be expected to fade away never began.

What was required to constitute the behaviourist reaction as establishing a positivist orientation throughout psychology was the extension of the repudiation of unobservables throughout the discipline – the repudiation of consciousness elsewhere than in

96

comparative psychology and the subsequent repudiation of other unobservables generally. This extension of the reaction was begun in Watson's original polemic. The conceptual basis for the extension was inherent in the emphasis on rigorous experimental control of environmental conditions as the only means for isolating the determinants of behaviour. That is, there was an implicit environmentalism present in the beginnings of behaviourism, entirely comparable to the sensationalism from which it was derived, and environmentalism is entirely compatible with an insistence that all the determinants of behaviour be observable. However, the rejection of unobservables throughout psychology could not be justified, as the rejection of consciousness in comparative psychology could be justified, simply by appeal to the impossibility of getting on with research while restricted to the old introspective formulations. The more widespread rejection required rather an appeal to the physical sciences as providing an external standard of objectivity against which introspective psychology as a whole could be tried, found wanting, and rejected. In Watson's words:[63]

> Psychology, as it is generally thought of, has something esoteric in its methods. If you fail to reproduce my findings, it is not due to some fault in your apparatus or in the control of your stimulus, but it is due to the fact that your introspection is untrained. The attack is made upon the observer and not upon the experimental setting. In physics and chemistry the attack is made upon the experimental conditions. The apparatus was not sensitive enough, impure chemicals were used, etc. In these sciences a better technique will give reproducible results. Psychology is otherwise. If you can't observe 3-9 states of clearness in attention, your introspection is poor. If, on the other hand, a feeling seems reasonably clear to you, your introspection is again faulty. You are seeing too much. Feelings are never clear.

This application of a hypothetical or ideal external standard of objectivity enabled Watson to carry his argument against consciousness out of its limited ambit in comparative psychology and into psychology as a whole, and to maintain thereby that the controversies in introspective psychology (such as that over imageless thought) could never be resolved. Unless one was 'wedded to the system as we now have it', Watson maintained, one could never believe that 'there will ever be greater uniformity than there is now in the answers we have to such questions', even although 'it is admitted that every growing science is full of unanswered questions'.[64]

Thus, to the home-grown rejection of consciousness in comparative psychology was added its rejection throughout psychology on the basis of appeal to the alleged practices of the physical sciences. It was solely on this that behaviourism's claim to encompass the whole of psychology was initially founded. Psychology's traditional reliance on the concepts of the physical sciences was made the basis for an *incorporation* (rather than merely an autonomous growth) of positivism, by providing a standard for the rejection of all unobservables, specifically all mentalistic ones. The adoption of an external standard of objectivity by which all mental entities could be repudiated was, as we have seen, consistent with the conceptual framework which behaviourism acquired in its reaction to and outgrowth from functionalist comparative psychology, in that the emphasis on the environmental control of behaviour stimulated a search for causes that could be seen, rather than merely hypothesized. Since, again, some sort of appeal to the physical sciences had long been customary in psychology, the addition of the external standard of objectivity was not, at the time, a very large step. It was a step that had profound consequences nevertheless, because it based the restriction of attention to observable entities and processes on a rationale that could have far wider applicability than any argument derived from problems in any particular areas of psychology.

The main effect of the systematic appeal to the external standard of objectivity was to intensify behaviourism's methodological cast. Such a rationale for the repudiation of unobservables, by being more general than any derived from specific psychological problems, was also more widely applicable. The problems within comparative psychology which led Watson to repudiate consciousness – the problems of doing research on animal behaviour within a functionalist framework – were at least related to a substantive issue, that is, environmentalism. Environmentalism was certainly sufficient to stimulate a search for observable causes for behaviour, but these causes were necessarily of a particular sort. Use of the external standard of objectivity as the basis for the rejection of internal 'mental' causes made it possible for the causes of behaviour to be of any sort whatever, so long as they were observable or (later) empirically specifiable. Thus, while Watson never abandoned his commitment to environmentalism – on the contrary, he intensified it – he established the methodological base on which others could dispose of it at will.

The full-scale establishment of positivism in behaviourism, through the rejection of other unobservables throughout the discipline, took some time. Unobservables were weeded out piecemeal, and by the time they were almost all gone it was becoming apparent that behaviourism had to find a more sophisticated logical base than it had previously if it was to continue to grow. However, a general repudiation was implicit from the beginning, in the emphasis on the environmental control of specific responses. Furthermore, Watson took pains to eliminate mentalistic terms from his vocabulary as soon as he announced the behaviourist programme.[65]

'Instincts' and other concepts indicating behavioural dispositions were tolerated longer. They were not seriously objected to until the mid-1920s, largely in response to their excessive use by McDougall and other 'instinct theorists'. The toleration for instincts might have been due in part to the difficulties in making a strictly behavioural translation of them. Even so, as early as 1914 Watson proposed a tentative translation, in his book on comparative psychology in which he still, in other contexts, occasionally made use of instincts:[66]

> In thus arguing against a fundamental difference between the
> behavior of man and brute it must not be supposed that we
> are trying to support the continuity theory of the Darwinians.
> . . . It has often been said that where there is similarity in
> structure, as an observed fact we find similarity in function. . . .
> Logically we must apply the principle consistently. If we find
> man doing something which the animal does not do, it is due
> to one of two things: (*a*) the animal does not possess the
> structure, or (*b*) he does not possess it in a highly enough
> developed form.

Differences in behaviour, in other words, should be accounted for by differences in structure and in environmental conditions, rather than by independently existing behavioural predispositions.[67] Again, however, this way of disposing of instincts required a continuing theoretical commitment. The technique that was more generally used was to allow the dispositional properties expressed by the term 'instinct' to survive in a modified form as 'drives'. Drives, like instincts, are behavioural dispositions, but unlike instincts they can be manipulated by the experimenter; they thereby satisfy at least the requirement of empirical specifiability, while requiring little – eventually almost nothing at all – in the way of theoretical commitment.[68]

Thus, in taking an external standard of objectivity and applying it in blanket fashion throughout psychology, behaviourism acquired a generally methodological character; the more pronounced this character became, the less it needed to be tied to any theoretical principles. In acquiring its methodological cast through the adoption of external standards of objectivity behaviourism also, not unimportantly, helped to assure its own success, since it was the only movement in psychology that vigorously promoted these standards; and these standards, for their part, became more and more influential throughout the scientific culture with the increasing tendency toward positivism in the physical sciences and the philosophy of science. In other words, while the environmentalist and methodologically rigorous conceptual framework which behaviourism acquired in its reaction to functionalist comparative psychology provided the thematic background for extending the positivist reaction throughout psychology, the growing influence of positivist formulations generally in science was largely responsible for the success which the extended reaction was to have. Positivism in psychology was at first a small but important addition to an autonomous methodological development in one part of the discipline; it was introduced by appeal to an external standard that could provide support for the generalization of that development, and was maintained and extended as the expression of the dominant and most progressive methodological currents of contemporary scientific thought.

IV

IMPLICATIONS AND EFFECTS OF THE INCORPORATION OF POSITIVISM INTO BEHAVIOURIST PSYCHOLOGY

1 THE INSTITUTIONALIZATION AND REFINEMENT OF PSYCHOLOGY'S POSITIVISM IN THE TRANSITION FROM CLASSICAL BEHAVIOURISM TO NEOBEHAVIOURISM

It is questionable whether American psychology as a whole was engaged in the context of reconstruction before 1913. Throughout American psychology there was, beginning around 1900, a gradual increase in the use of behavioural methods and a decrease in the reliance on introspective ones for at least some classes of problems, particularly in human psychology (as mentioned in Chapter I). However, this development was broad, diffuse, and evolutionary, much as the earlier shift to functionalism had been, rather than abrupt, revolutionary, or stimulated by the general intractability of current research problems. Conceptual and methodological flexibility was the rule. Comparative psychology was certainly engaged in reconstruction, however, and so was the scientific culture as a whole; and human psychology was certainly caught up in the general trend toward change. If we therefore regard the trend as reconstructive throughout, a good early statement of it is that by Cattell, in 1904:[1]

> I am not convinced that psychology should be limited to the study of consciousness as such, in so far as this can be set off from the physical world. . . . It seems to me that most of the research work that has been done by me or in my laboratory is

nearly as independent of introspection as work in physics or in zoology. . . . It is certainly difficult to penetrate by analogy into the consciousness of the lower animals, of savages and children, but the study of their behaviour has already yielded much and promises much more.

If reconstruction can be said to have started with Cattell's paper, then it continued through the progressively less apologetic statements about behaviour's place in psychology by McDougall, Pillsbury, Thorndike, and others, culminating in Watson's polemic in 1913.[2] Thereafter there was no doubt that the reconstruction was going to be a general one, for even if the tendency toward behavioural methods had not involved a dramatic recasting of psychology before Watson's polemic appeared, it certainly did afterwards, as a result of Watson's successful exportation of the problems of comparative psychology, and of the local response to those problems, to the discipline as a whole. From then on, the reconstruction had a more sharply defined direction of progress. It thus continued through Watson's translation of mentalistic terms into behavioural ones,[3] through the adoption of new experimental methods appropriate to the new conception of psychology,[4] through experimental demonstration of the general applicability of the new approach,[5] through extension of the behaviouristic strictures to include instinct and heredity,[6] and finally, once the battle for objectivity had been won to the extent that Watson could truthfully say 'Most of the younger psychologists realize that some such formulation as behaviorism is the only road leading to science',[7] through the beginning of the settling-down period with concentration on detailed psychological research. It is in this period, starting in the middle and late 1920s, that the context of reconstruction could be expected to give way gradually to the context of construction.

As soon as behaviourism began to settle down in this way, however, it began to become apparent that it did not yet have everything it needed to develop as a science, and in particular that it lacked satisfactory means for expanding experimental results into broader explanatory principles. The development of behaviourism during this period has been described in detail by Koch,[8] and the present account will, accordingly, refer to his statements. Koch summarizes the early development of behaviourism as follows:[9]

Classical behaviorism had been an attempt to escape the
stagnation of the subjectivist psychologies then prevailing
by providing psychology with a *decision procedure,* which, it
was hoped, would make forward movement inevitable. But
though the position soon attained hegemony . . . it degenerated
with comparable celerity into polemicism and inflated
program-making. . . . By the late twenties, there was much
'objective' experimentation but few bodies of clearly stated
predictive principles comparable to the crowning achievement
of physics: its theories. Instead, experimentation seemed aimless,
'theoretical' hypotheses but loosely related to data, and debate
idle.

In short, behaviourism needed some way to safeguard its
achievements in making psychology objective and to make these
achievements the basis for more steady and progressive *theoretical*
development. The priorities of the emerging context of construction
were, characteristically, those of building up theories or other
explanatory accounts. These priorities had been temporarily subordinated during the period of reconstruction, while the foundations
of science agreed to be necessary for implementing them were being
recast. That job accomplished, these priorities gradually acquired a
central position and stimulated concern with what had to be done
if behaviourism was to acquire comprehensive theories. Koch continues:[10]

Neobehaviorism may be seen as a second attempt to
provide psychology with a decision procedure – this time
an effective one that would conserve the orienting attitudes
of [early or classical] behaviorism but recast them in such
a way as to give them teeth. . . . The search for a
'decision procedure' thus became a search for a formulary
of the techniques for 'constructing' *rigorous theory.* . . .
Early behaviorism had primarily involved attempts to guarantee
the objectivity of the descriptive (first-order) concepts used for
empirical data. While not giving up this objective (and indeed
trying to place its pursuit on a more secure footing),
neobehaviorism sought to realize and implement objectivism at
the level of theory.

Implications and Effects

As it happened, the search for objective methods of theory construction was not a difficult one. It met with apparent success almost at once, in the analyses of scientific theories being developed within logical positivism and independent, similar movements. Koch continues:[11]

> In pursuit of these ends, psychology did not go directly to physics but turned instead for its directives to middlemen. These were, for the most part, philosophers of science (especially logical positivists) and a number of physical science methodologists who had been codifying a synoptic view of the nature of science and who, by the early thirties, were actively exporting that view from their specialties to the scholarly community at large. The view was based on a 'rational reconstruction' of a few selected formulations in theoretical physics and put forward a detailed model of the scientific enterprise which came to be known as the 'hypothetico-deductive method'.

It was not entirely coincidental that rigorous formulations of the structure of scientific theories were offered by philosophers of science just when behaviourism needed them. Logical positivism was itself part of the general positivist reaction to the scientific ferment stimulated by the collapse of Newtonian theory, just as (to a lesser extent, and at a greater remove) behaviourism was. Furthermore, the early versions of behaviourism had at least some slight influence on the early versions of logical positivism. Bergmann[12] cities classical behaviourism, along with relativity theory, Poincaré's conventionalism, and the *Principia Mathematica,* as among the chief sources of inspiration for the members of the Vienna Circle in the middle and late 1920s.

Koch describes the 'new view' of science which resulted from the labours of the logical positivists and scientific methodologists:[13]

> This 'new' view held forth an ideal of rigorous theory and seemed to define a route toward its achievement. In barest outline, it asserts theory to be a hypothetico-deductive system. Laws or hypotheses believed fundamental are asserted as postulates, and the consequences of these (theorems) are deduced by strict logical and mathematical rules. The theorems are then to be tested by experiment. Positive results increase the

104

probability of the hypotheses; negative results call them into question. Scientific theories differ from logical and mathematical systems only in that their basic terms are given empirical reference (made to describe the world) by operational definitions (Bridgman) which state the observational conditions under which the terms may be applied. A science aims toward explicit and, if possible, quantitative hypothetico-deductive organizations of events in its domain.

And in summary:[14]

In broad aspect, neobehaviorism may be seen as a marriage between the orienting attitudes of classical behaviorism and one or another interpretation of the 'new' model of science. The general orienting attitudes are to be implemented by translation into theory, or theory-like formulations, in accord with the requirements of the model. As a result, the earlier attitudes are reasserted but in altered form. Thus, for instance, re *objectivism*, the metaphysical overtones of classical behaviorism are, at least by frequent asseveration, sloughed off and attempts are made in a variety of directions to find rationales for a consistently *methodological objectivism*.

While the hypothetico-deductive model of theorizing, as developed by the philosophers of science, was in some ways at the heart of the 'new view', it was not all or even most of what there was to it. The 'formulary of techniques' for theory construction included an extensive apparatus of logical tools for refining and testing concepts and theories; although these could be used in conjunction with the hypothetico-deductive model, they could also be used in virtual independence of it. As a result, they gained widespread use even among those theorists – in fact the vast majority of neobehaviourists – who desired the precision, clarity, and scientific aura of hypothetico-deductive theories but found such theories too difficult and cumbersome for day-to-day use. These logical and methodological tools included operational definitions, meaning criteria such as the verifiability criterion, related criteria for assessing the validity of hypotheses (whether formally deduced from a theory or not), and others. All of these techniques, or decision procedures, were taken to provide a sufficient guide (even without strict adherence to the hypothetico-deductive model) to show not only how to evaluate scientific statements and theories, but also how to put ideas into a form suitable for such evaluation.

The most important of the methodological tools used by the neobehaviourists, and the one that was closest to being home-grown, was the *intervening variable*. Intervening variables were formally introduced by Tolman in 1936,[15] but he had already made use of them in his 1932 book, *Purposive Behavior in Animals and Men*. Intervening variables provided a way in which objective statements could be made about unobservable inner states and processes; these states and processes were defined as consisting in the regularity of the connection between independent stimulus variables and dependent response variables. The specification of the independent and dependent variables thus constitutes a kind of operational definition of such states and processes. Tolman, in fact, called his approach 'operational behaviorism' before he introduced the term 'intervening variable'. Intervening variables differ from Bridgman's operational definitions, since Bridgman's involve specifying the operations used to measure the quantity of something, while intervening variables involve specifying the observations used to define its presence. Tolman's usage was sufficiently influential that it came to provide the model for operational definitions generally in psychology; intervening variables became the main vehicle for introducing theoretical constructs, and were much used by Guthrie and Hull and their students, as well as by Tolman and his. Even Skinner, who disapproved of theories on principle, made some use of intervening variables in his first book.

In general, however, the use which behaviourist psychologists made of the logical positivist techniques tended to be piecemeal and pluralistic. There was little unanimity about the precise logical measures to be employed at each stage in theorizing (although there was fairly wide agreement that the hypothetico-deductive model was an ideal form), but only about the need for such measures in general. This pluralism reflected the unstable situation in the philosophy of science. It gave the positivism of the neobehaviourists a methodological, rather than a strictly logical character. That is, the positivist orientation of neobehaviourism was not tied to the intricacies of the hypothetico-deductive method or to any other logical analyses, but to the availability of any techniques or rules which could provide explicit decision procedures.[16] In the reliance on these rules to guarantee both the meaningfulness and the validity of statements, the atheoretical Skinner was as fully positivistic as the hypothetico-deductive Hull.

Nevertheless, the pluralism of the neobehaviourist use of logical positivist techniques was not unconstrained. Throughout, there was considerable continuity with the orienting attitudes of classical behaviourism. In the transition from classical behaviourism to neobehaviourism what was retained was the feature that gave behaviourism its initial positivist orientation, that is, the in-principle repudiation of unobservables, expressed as an insistence on an uncompromisingly public and objective observation base. While not attempting to account for this insistence, Koch indicates the extent to which it was both prior to and more fundamental than any particular meaning criteria associated with the 'new view':[17]

> Though interpretations of technical meaning criteria imported from the philosophy of science were free and various, certain core beliefs concerning the legitimate observation base for psychological statements were common to all of them. It is significant that these commitments were historically prior to the importation of such criteria, and after importation, they remained untouched by the frequent and radical changes in meaning theory which continued in normal course of professional epistemological scholarship.
> Such rock-bottom commitments concerning the observation base may be suggested via the following reconstructions:
> 1. All lawlike statements of psychology containing *dependent variables* not expressible in, or reducible to, publicly verifiable and thus 'objectively', observable *behavior* indices are to be excluded as illegitimate. . . . The prototypical case of an admissible dependent variable is, of course, the notion of *response* or, more specifically, a 'measurable' index of response, in some one of the varied, if often unspecified, meanings of 'response'.
> 2. Similarly, it is demanded that legitimate *independent variables* of psychology designate references which can pass the test of independent, simultaneous observability *and* are definable in either the observation language of physical science or the concepts of physics. The prototypical case of an admissible independent variable is, of course, the notion of the *stimulus*, again in some one of many rather unseparated meanings.

107

Implications and Effects

However, despite the considerable continuity, a subtle change in the character of behaviourism's positivism resulted from the alliance with logical positivism. As we saw in the last chapter, behaviourism was initially constituted as positivistic through appeal to the standards of objectivity supposedly characteristic of the physical sciences. Such standards justified the exclusion of anything mental from consideration in psychology, because mentality and consciousness could not be observed. However, there was a difference between what behaviourism required in order to encompass all of psychology, and what it obtained by appeal to an external standard of objectivity. What it required was a basis for repudiating mind and consciousness. What it got was a basis for repudiating unobservables as such.

The difference between what behaviourism needed and what it got was not significant until the late 1920s, after which time behaviourism's needs were no longer the same in any case. As long as the insistence was on the 'objectivity of the descriptive (first-order) concepts used for empirical data', so that everything that was going to be talked about in psychology had to be the kind of thing that could be pointed to, the repudiation of consciousness and the general repudiation of unobservables went hand in hand, the former being merely a special case of the latter.

However, the transition to neobehaviourism and the making explicit of behaviourism's positivism involved two trends which inevitably liberalized the anti-mentalistic stand. First, things that could not be pointed to (theoretical concepts such as mass or reinforcement) were agreed to be worth talking about after all, as long as the talk was sufficiently careful. Second, the general positivist orientation including the repudiation of unobservables, which had initially been subordinate to behaviourism's anti-mentalism, became explicit, independent of its polemical background, and articulated by a variety of theorists from a diversity of theoretical backgrounds. The repudiation of mind and consciousness thus could no longer be considered justified by the summary judgment that such things were unobservable. It would have to be based instead on a demonstration that any given mentalistic concepts could not satisfy the meaning criteria which were to determine their admissibility in science.

Now, such a demonstration would be impossible to provide; there could be any number of possible mentalistic concepts and no demonstration could establish the inadmissibility of all of them. Furthermore, by the time such formal meaning criteria were

108

becoming accepted for use in behaviourism, there was little apparent need to continue fighting against mentalism. Introspective psychology was disappearing from the American scene and the dominance of some form of behaviourism seemed assured. Further- more still, if some mentalistic concepts were, against all odds, to satisfy the meaning criteria, could they in good faith be rejected nevertheless? Clearly they could not, not at least if the meaning criteria were to be taken seriously as providing the explicit standards of objectivity – as they had to be, if they were to be used as the basis for theory construction. The possibility thus existed that some refined version of the criteria which had been imported into psychology specifically in order to exclude the mental, might even- tually come to ratify mentalistic concepts. But after all, how much harm would really be done if that happened? The goal of behaviourism was to make psychology an objective science; if mind and consciousness could somehow be rendered objective, then surely mind and consciousness in that form had to be fit subjects for science. They could bear little relation to the ghostly mind and consciousness studied in psychology before the advent of behaviourism.

This reassessment of the possible status of mind and consciousness, and of what was to be excluded from psychology and how, had definite advantages. It answered the common-sense objection that behaviourism tried to argue for the nonexistence of something with which everybody was directly acquainted through personal experience. It put the burden of proof on the other side, so that behaviourists no longer had to find ways to keep mentalistic concepts out of psychology; instead, the 'mentalists' were constrained to find proper ways to bring them in.

The in-principle rehabilitation of consciousness – that is, the acceptance that it was no longer absent from psychology in principle but only in fact – was made explicit by Hull in his presidential address to the American Psychological Association:[18]

> What, then, shall we say about consciousness? Is its existence denied? By no means. But to recognize the existence of a phenomenon is not the same thing as insisting on its basic, i.e., logical priority. Instead of furnishing a means for the solution of problems, consciousness appears to be itself a problem needing solution. In the miniature theoretical system, no

mention of consciousness or experience was made for the simple reason that no theorem has been found as yet whose deduction would be facilitated in any way by including such a postulate. . . . There is, however, no reason at all for not using consciousness or experience as a postulate in a scientific theoretical system if it clearly satisfies the deductive criteria already laid down. If such a system should be worked out in a clear and unambiguous manner the incorporation of consciousness into the body of behavior theory should be automatic and immediate. The task of those who would have consciousness a central factor in adaptive behavior and in moral action is accordingly quite clear. They should apply themselves to the long and grinding labor of the logical derivation of a truly scientific system.

Hull's statement marked the emancipation of behaviourism from its explicitly anti-mentalistic background. The first principle of behaviourism, its rejection of the mental, was to be subordinated to the explicit procedures designed to ensure objectivity in general. It is true, of course, that such procedures still seemed sufficient to exclude mentalistic concepts, even if only in fact. Referring to the 'several centuries' of effort on the part of psychologists and philosophers to establish the 'priority of consciousness or experience', Hull concluded:[19]

Considering the practically complete failure of all this effort to yield even a small scientific system of adaptive or moral behavior in which consciousness finds a position of logical priority as a postulate, one may, perhaps, be pardoned for entertaining a certain amount of pessimism regarding such an eventuality.

The 'formulary of techniques for constructing rigorous theory' which Koch referred to thus served to preserve the original commitment to an objective data-base while de-emphasizing the dogmatic anti-mentalism originally associated with it. The incorporation of these techniques into the ongoing course of theorizing was gradual and piecemeal, but apparently inexorable. It involved abstract analyses of theory construction,[20] elucidatory operationist (and similar) analyses of current psychological concepts and theories,[21] and most significantly, an increasing day-to-day use of operational definitions, axiomatized theoretical structures, high-level theoretical variables with only indirect observational reference (intervening variables), etc., in the experiments and theories of the time.[22] Koch states:[23]

> The neobehaviorist period was ushered in by Hull's advocacy of hypothetico-deductive method [in 1930]. . . . Though Bridgman's work had been cited by H. M. Johnson as early as 1930, it was not until the mid-thirties that a spate of articles on 'operational definition' directed the attention of psychologists to empirical definition and produced the widespread impression that objectivism could be finally implemented only by careful 'operational' practice. It was not until the late thirties that the preceding contexts of discussions were supplemented by analyses which explicitly took the logical-positivist model of science as regulative. Though initially recommendations of axiomatic method and discussions about operational strategy had tended to occur in somewhat separated contexts, both of these topics found an integrative framework in the formulations of logical positivism. Discussions and applications of positivistic meaning criteria began to appear in the literature side by side with operationist analyses.

This concludes the summary description of neobehaviourism's positivism in what Koch calls the 'age of theory', an age which the emphasis on theory development justifies assigning to the context of construction. That positivism was autonomous and explicit; it was free of the dogmatic anti-mentalism of classical behaviourism, and was directed by means of various logical techniques wholly toward the progressive development of psychological theory. It seemed, furthermore, to be well on the way toward accomplishing these aims. The assimilation of the positivist techniques for evaluating theories, their gradual diffusion throughout the scientific culture, and their eventual synthesis into a more or less established, if not completely unified, conception of science, were widely regarded as satisfying neobehaviourism's need for a logical apparatus that would ensure its cumulative and progressive scientific character. Koch speaks of the 'hypothetico-deductive prescription' as the prescription that the conception of science which the formulary of techniques embodies

111

constitutes the way in which scientific investigation can most effectively – and in practice therefore *should* – be conducted; and he defines the 'age of theory' as the optimistic period (c. 1935-50) during which this prescription was, in different ways by different theorists, most widely accepted. He describes the general effects of the adherence to this prescription on the 'self-image' of neobehaviourism[24] as follows:[25]

> The acceptance of the hypothetico-deductive *prescription* had important consequences for the prevailing conception of the aims of psychology, the conception of where psychology stood in relation to its aims, and thus the indicated route for further progress. It was, for instance, assumed by many that a backlog of significant empirical knowledge existed adequate to the 'construction' of broad-scope, if not comprehensive, theories conforming to the requirements of the hypothetico-deductive model. It was believed that psychology was at a stage such that theoretical differences would inevitably and almost automatically be resolved by the 'differential test' of 'derivations' from rival 'postulate sets'. Perhaps of most serious import for the character of actual practice was a cluster of beliefs to the effect that adoption of the forms of the hypothetico-deductive method (or the imagery of its forms) guaranteed that the scientific enterprise would be 'self-corrective'. Such beliefs led, for instance, to the strange expectation that the initial plausibility of a 'postulate' is of little moment in that proper adherence to the forms of the hypothetico-deductive method would almost certainly refine its adequacy or lead to its early demise.

The purpose of the rest of this chapter is to assess and comment on the in-principle adequacy of the kinds of logical techniques which the neobehaviourists hoped would ensure the progressive and self-corrective character of their scientific enterprise as described (with a touch of sarcasm)[26] in this last quotation from Koch. Or rather, the purpose is – as promised in the conclusion to Chapter I – to demonstrate the inadequacy of such techniques for attaining these ends, by means of a review of the limitations that have emerged during the last twenty to thirty years on the applicability of these techniques, and to draw some of the implications of their inadequacy.

We are therefore taking up the discussion of positivism as a basis for scientific inquiry at the point where we left it at the end of Chapter II. The discussion was interrupted there so that it could be related to the particular circumstances of behaviourism. We have traced the unusual set of factors which led to behaviourism's being based on a positivist orientation toward psychology, have described the early form of that positivism, have traced the development of behaviourism to the stage where its positivism became explicit and emancipated from its dogmatically anti-mentalistic background, and have mentioned (see note 26) the significance of neobehaviourism as a unique case study in scientific methodology.

As in Chapter II, the alternative with which positivism will be contrasted is scientific realism. We will try to establish in more detail the greater scientific appropriateness of realism in the context of construction – the context in which neobehaviourism operated – and, conversely, the greater appropriateness of positivism in the context of reconstruction. At first sight, however, the contrast of positivism and realism might seem difficult to apply to behaviourism. Behaviourism never involved a repudiation of realism, either as a common-sense conviction or as a philosophical doctrine. On the contrary, the most influential philosopher who promoted behaviourism in its early days was E. B. Holt, a member of the movement known as the 'New Realism'. Nevertheless, although behaviourism was not founded specifically on an antithesis to realism, and although this fact will be shown to be highly important later on, this antithesis is the one which must be emphasized in discussing behaviourism as an implementation of positivism. 'Realism' must be understood here as it was defined in Chapter II. A realist orientation to science involves not only an intuitive belief about the possible truth of scientific theories but also, as a result, the ascription to an accepted theory of greater validity than can ever be warranted on strictly logical and empirical grounds. Neither Holt nor any behaviourist psychologists were realists in this sense; they all insisted on the priority and unequivocality of strict empirical and logical evidence. Scientific realism involves what on positivist grounds would amount to assigning metaphysical status to empirical scientific theories. The repudiation of such a position is implicit in any approach to science which involves adherence to general methodological critera of objectivity, such as behaviourism did from the beginning; it is explicit both in modern positivist philosophical thought and in neobehaviourism.[27]

2 REALISM AND POSITIVISM IN THE CONTEXT OF CONSTRUCTION

What is most fundamental to a positivist orientation toward science, it was said in Chapter II, is a repudiation of metaphysics or, more specifically, of any inferred entities or processes which are in principle unobservable. But while this simple repudiation might be adequate to ensure the empirical status of data statements, it is not sufficient to ensure the empirical status of theoretical concepts, because such concepts (e.g., mass, force, reinforcement) do not refer to observables in any simple or direct way. This problem of the empirical status of theoretical concepts was the main factor that led behaviourism to seek advice from the logical positivists.

With regard to theoretical concepts, therefore: to implement a positivist orientation within the context of construction, where the development of theories is of principal importance, it would be necessary to have means to ensure that all proposed theoretical concepts could be prevented from referring to any entities or forces which were in principle unobservable. This requirement can be expressed in different ways. In the language of ancient or classical positivism, if a theory is designed to 'save the appearances', to provide an economical description with only 'mathematical truth', it is necessary to ensure that independent existence is not attributed to the explanatory fictions brought in to account for the appearances. Such fictions (e.g., epicycles in Ptolemaic astronomy) cannot be considered to refer to anything except, in a complex way, the phenomena (observed planetary and stellar motions) which they are used to classify. The explanatory fictions can be seen to function as real entities or forces in a theory if, in the elaboration of the theory, they take on properties other than those which have been ascribed to them for the explicit purpose of saving the appearances. It is therefore necessary to have a built-in limitation on the applicability of the explanatory fictions used in the theory.[28] In more modern language, we can say that theoretical concepts may have ascribed to them only those properties which can be empirically specified by reference to the class of observable events to which the theory applies. To put it more simply, the constituents of a theory may be permitted to function in the theory only to the extent that they can be shown to have unambiguous empirical content. Mach's main

114

contribution to the reconstruction of physics, it will be recalled, was to reformulate the concepts of space and time in Newtonian theory in such a way as to eliminate their reference to unobservables.

The problem arises, however, of how to be sure that the concepts in a theory have empirical content and no other. The Newtonian concepts of absolute space and time, after all, clearly had empirical content. The eventual problems in their application arose because they were developed in such a way that they referred to empirical and non-empirical, observable and unobservable, entities and processes equally. The conceptual errors in Newtonian theory which permitted this indiscriminate reference were eventually identified and dealt with; but they came to light only after reliance on them had come to block the progress of physics, and dealing with them required overturning the results of much of the preceding two centuries of physical science. How could such conceptual errors or excesses be prevented from the beginning, before they had such drastic effects? This was the problem facing modern positivist thought.

The answer seemed clearly to lie in the development of formal meaning or demarcation criteria which could be used to evaluate the empirical meaningfulness of any proposed concept before it was incorporated into an ongoing theory. It was important that the criteria be formal ones, since informal or intuitive criteria were obviously unreliable. Newton never intended to handicap science with his theoretical concepts, and neither did Helmholtz or du Bois-Reymond when they asserted that reduction of observed phenomena to the interaction of Newtonian variables was constitutive of scientific explanation. Since concepts receive their meaning through use (the Newtonian concepts of space and time were empirically meaningful in some of their applications, meaningless in others), the appropriate meaning criteria were ones which could evaluate concepts in their simplest applications, that is, in statements. The development of formal meaning criteria for evaluating the empirical status of statements, and later of theories, was the main task undertaken within the loose alliance of interests that constituted logical positivism.

There was some contrast from the beginning, therefore, between the factors that led modern positivist philosophers to develop formal meaning criteria, and those which led behaviourists to adopt the criteria in their scientific practice. The philosophers and logicians developed formal criteria to ensure that metaphysical references could not be insinuated into scientific theories. The behaviourists, for their part, had effected their own elimination of metaphysics from psychology already. Their problem was how to develop theories, given their established commitment to an objective observation base. Thus, they adopted the formal positivist measures, not so much to keep their theories free of metaphysics, as to enable them to develop theories at all. This difference in approach accounts in part for the piecemeal and pluralistic use that behaviourists made of the techniques resulting from the logical positivist analyses.

Problems in the Development of Meaning Criteria

The development of formal meaning criteria was originally thought by many logicians to be a relatively simple task. It proved more difficult than expected, however, to develop meaning criteria that would set the boundaries between empirical and non-empirical (or metaphysical) statements in the right places, so that they would allow all statements which were 'obviously' meaningful and disallow all statements which were 'obviously' nonsensical. To begin with, the verifiability criterion – the first meaning criterion proposed in any detail – was obviously empirically meaningless by its own standard, and hence could have only stipulative significance. More important, it also condemned all general scientific laws as meaningless, since there is no way that universal statements (e.g., *'all* swans are white', 'for *every* action there is an equal and opposite reaction') can be verified, short of enumeration of all possible instances, which is usually impossible in principle. This limitation of the verifiability criterion is a consequence of the logical invalidity of induction, in that there can never be any *logical* guarantee that the next instance (of swans or actions) will conform to the law. The problem might in principle be avoided, therefore, by making falsifiability, rather than verifiability, the criterion of meaningfulness. Universal statements cannot be verified, but they can be falsified by a single negative instance; their empirical meaningfulness or their status as scientific statements[29] can thus be established on falsificationist grounds by specifying the conditions which would constitute their falsification.

Falsificationist logic has problems of its own however. The exact falsificationist counterpart to the unverifiability of universal statements is the unfalsifiability of existential statements. Existential

116

statements (e.g., 'some swans are black') are not falsifiable, except (as in the corresponding case) through exhaustive enumeration of all possible particulars. To deal with this difficulty, Popper, the chief modern exponent of falsificationism, argues persuasively that existential statements, as such, are indeed non-scientific and therefore metaphysical.[30] His argument about isolated existential statements has some force (he assimilates them to statements such as 'Somewhere there is a philosopher's stone, a holy grail, a golden isle'); but it does not apply to statements containing both universal and existential quantifiers (e.g., 'For *every* pure solid at a given external pressure there *is* a temperature above which it becomes either gaseous or liquid'). Such statements are often encountered in science, but strictly speaking they are neither verifiable nor falsifiable. It is impossible to examine every pure solid, while if any solid resists a change of state, it is always possible that it needs merely to be heated a little more.

There are, in addition, further problems for formal meaning criteria that affect verificationist and falsificationist approaches equally. A trivial example will show the kinds of difficulty which can arise.

In order to sanction the use of at least some universal statements, logical positivist analyses from about the time of Ayer's *Language, Truth and Logic*[31] began to emphasize 'confirmability' rather than 'verifiability' as the criterion of empirical meaningfulness. A statement is confirmable if an observation statement can be deduced from it or from a set of statements of which it forms an essential part. More precisely, a statement M is confirmable if and only if it can be observationally verified or if in conjunction with some other statement P it implies an observationally verifiable statement O not implied by P alone. This confirmability criterion makes allowance for universal statements and for others which are not immediately verifiable or falsifiable, but requires them to have a kind of specifiable observational content nonetheless. As it stands however, this criterion renders any statement confirmable, in the following way. Let M be any statement at all, O any (true) observation statement, and P the statement 'M implies O'. Then, from the conjunction of M and P, but not from P alone, we can deduce O. O is true by observation, hence M is confirmed. The same example can be used to show that any statement M forms part of a falsifiable set of statements. Let M and P be the same as in the preceding example,

117

and *O* any falsifiable statement (it need not be true, nor be observationally falsifiable). Again, the conjunction of *M* and *P* implies *O*. Thus, specification of the events which would falsify *O* serves also to specify the events which would falsify at least one of *M* and *P* and hence their conjunction. Such universal confirmability or falsifiability is, furthermore, not easy to avoid. Church[32] has shown that with somewhat more complicated logical manipulation, any *M* can still be confirmed even if limitations are placed on *P* so that it must be either analytic, observationally verifiable, or independently confirmable.

Of course these examples are, as mentioned, trivial ones, but it does not in the least follow that they are irrelevant or unimportant – in fact, quite the opposite. If we need formal criteria of meaningfulness because informal or intuitive ones are unreliable, then it is pointless to have to resort to informal criteria for deciding when the formal ones are to be applied. Hence, trivial 'mistakes' made by applying a proposed criterion are relevant precisely because they are trivial. Trivial mistakes are easily recognized, while non-trivial ones often are not. There is, however, no formal criterion of triviality, and no guarantee that naturally occurring mistakes will be either trivial or easily detectable. Hence, trivial mistakes serve effectively to invalidate a proposed criterion; if we cannot trust it in a trivial and transparent situation, then we cannot assume that we can trust it in a serious and difficult one.

The attempts to develop formal meaning criteria continued to encounter difficulties such as these, as well as more complicated ones, to such an extent that many logicians abandoned the attempt to construct formal criteria of any sort.[33] Others continued to seek formal criteria but came to concentrate on analysing the empirical meaningfulness of theories rather than of statements.[34] Statements and concepts alike are now widely agreed to take their meaning from the theories in which they occur, from what Feigl calls their 'locus in the nomological net'.[35] This kind of account does greater justice to the complexities of the scientific use of concepts than did the earlier analyses of statements. However, attempts to replace the older meaning criteria have encountered difficulties of their own. Feigl's, for instance, so far contains only a sketch of the characteristics which a completed account will have to have. Carnap's, while more complete, has the same problem as the confirmability criterion, sanctioning absurd and (informally) meaningless constructions such as 'The cosmic mind dislikes cheese' and 'Last night everything doubled in length'.[36]

The main problem with any formal analysis of meaning that applies to an entire theory is its complexity. A theory which is to be analysed must be formulated in such a way as to have the exact logical structure demanded by the analytic criterion. The same holds true for the analysis of statements, of course, but is less of a problem there. Most declarative sentences have the necessary logical form for the application of either a verifiability or a falsifiability criterion. By contrast, the logical form which a theory must have for Carnap's criterion to be applied to the concepts in it is neither simple, nor easily obtained, nor typically present in existing theories. As a result, it is difficult to apply criteria such as Carnap's, and in fact no such criterion has yet been made generally applicable to existing theories. The consequence of complexity, therefore, is that there exists at present no technique which can be applied to determine whether a given statement or concept, or theory in which they appear, is meaningful or meaningless, empirical or metaphysical. No analysis of theories has come any closer than the analyses of statements to providing a usable criterion, and indeed it is now doubtful that such a technique could exist even in principle. That is, it is not certain that it is possible even in principle to give a formal and complete account of the empirical meaningfulness of theories by means of such global analyses.[37] Unless a proposed analysis is both formal and complete, no criterion can follow from it for identifying the non-empirical components of any theory that has at least some empirical content. Making such identification possible for therapeutic ends was, of course, the purpose for which meaning criteria were developed in the first place.

In summary, the development of meaning or demarcation criteria which could be used to prevent conceptual excesses such as those which eventually vitiated Newtonian theory has been frustrated. The formal criteria for assessing the empirical status of statements proved incoherent, and no refinement was able to improve them significantly. The few formal criteria for assessing concepts or statements in theories are equally incoherent, and in addition their complexity and the difficulties in applying them would make them of dubious generality even if their technical problems could be overcome. No proposed criterion has been of much practical value in assessing the meaningfulness of statements or theories.

Problems in the Application of Testing Criteria

We can already see that it is extremely difficult, if not impossible, to formulate concepts, statements, and theories guaranteed to be 'clean', to have empirical content and nothing else, simply because the criteria for assessing the empirical status of concepts, etc., have so far been inadequate and resistant to improvement. Such problems in the development of meaning criteria do not so drastically affect a realist approach to science in the context of construction, for in a realist approach metaphysical baggage (or what positivists might consider such) is not prohibited, and in the context of construction considerations of purity can legitimately be subordinated to considerations of theoretical fruitfulness. Such problems do, however, clearly make it difficult for a rigorously positivist approach even to begin functioning in the context of construction.

Scientific concepts and theories must not only be formulated and judged admissible, whether clean or not; they must also be used. Theories must make contact with nature in the context of construction; they must be tested, developed, accepted or rejected as providing information about the world, however that world is conceived. Criteria for testing the validity of statements and theories have the same logical form as those used to test their meaningfulness. The verifiability criteria, for instance, make the meaning of a statement dependent on specification of the operations which would be involved in its verification. Testing the validity of a statement acknowledged as meaningful simply involves carrying out the operations. Problems arise in interpreting the results of such operations, however, so that in testing the validity of statements and theories, as in testing their meaningfulness, formal criteria are inadequate to the task. Three arguments support this conclusion.

First, every scientific theory has its share of anomalies, experimental results incompatible with the theory. Some of these anomalies are repeatable, some not. If a theory is regarded as a hypothetico-deductive system, it will almost certainly entail predictions which should refute the theory or some part of it. Every theory 'lives in an ocean of anomalies'; each one is 'born refuted'.[38] Hull's behaviour theory,[39] for instance, was 'born refuted' by the results of latent learning experiments[40] and was further refuted in infancy by the demonstration of elation and depression effects on response strength.[41] Newtonian mechanics was born refuted by the failure of the moon to follow the orbit apparently ascribed to it by Newton's equations, Copernican astronomy by the absence of any detectable stellar parallax, etc.

Reaction to such anomalies in science can take many forms, depending on the circumstances of their occurrence and on the inclinations of particular scientists. Given a theory, and an anomalous finding, should the finding be considered peripheral or central? That is, can the anomaly be passed by as belonging to a class of events of only tangential relevance to the theory, or does it call for intensive investigation as the key, for good or ill, to the theory's claims to validity? If the latter, should the theory be considered wrong or merely incomplete? That is, does the theory need to be replaced or merely extended? Such questions are fundamental and unavoidable in dealing with anomalies. They call for judgments which cannot be made on the basis of any strict criteria of confirmation or refutation, because such judgments have to go beyond the available evidence to assess the relevance of the anomaly in the context of knowledge which has not yet been acquired. They involve an estimation of the consequences of treating the anomaly in one way or another, an estimation which therefore has the character of a prediction of future knowledge.

Thus, anomalies, like other unsolved problems in science, may provoke intense efforts at assimilation, or force *ad hoc* revisions of theory, or be shelved pending further development of science, or simply be ignored. Only rarely do they serve to refute a well-attested and ongoing theory. Given how widespread anomalies are, this reluctance to accept them as refutations is entirely appropriate. Many anomalies are eventually assimilated within further extensions or more precise applications of current theory. Hasty acceptance of them as refutations of theories would thus lead to the rejection of theories which in some cases would later prove perfectly competent to account for the anomaly, or which in other cases might in the same interim period lead to other new achievements which could render them worth retaining despite the presence of the anomaly. Such a suspicious attitude towards anomalies is consistent with a realist orientation to science (if nature is assumed 'really' to be the way the theory says it is, then an experimental result which blatantly contradicts the theory will naturally be looked on with some suspicion), but is clearly not consistent with any rigorous commitment to formal testing procedures.

Second, if in some respects formal testing procedures are too harsh on a theory, in other respects they are too easy. Any anomaly can be accommodated within a theory by making an *ad hoc* addition to the theory or by referring the anomaly to some other theory which must be assumed valid for the theory under examination to be tested. As Feigl puts it, 'from a purely formal point of view it must be admitted that adjustments in any part of the theoretical network may result in a better empirical "fit".'[42] Thus, Newtonian theory could have been 'saved' from the moon's anomalous orbit by postulating that the moon was of variable density, so that its centre of gravity was not at its middle. The moon's density distribution could have been chosen so as to yield just that correction in its predicted orbit that would make it conform with the observed one. Indeed, Newtonian theory was later saved in such a way from the results of the Michelson-Morley experiment. Fitzgerald's equations predicted that a body would contract in the direction of travel to an extent which would precisely counterbalance the effect of the ether drift; the failure to find an ether drift thus no longer formally told against the theory. This formal rehabilitation of Newtonian theory did not, of course, prevent the Fitzgerald equations from being used by Einstein for quite a different purpose, in the establishment of special relativity theory.

In short, a strict insistence on compatibility of theory and observation would require that every anomalous result be dealt with when it occurred, but would allow the dealing-with to be *ad hoc* and trivial. Indeed, the insistence would *force* the dealing-with to be *ad hoc*, since it would rule out any delay in considering the anomaly if the theory was to be maintained.

Third, and closely related to the availability of *ad hoc* modifications to a theory, is the fact that a theory can never be compared with all the alternatives. There is always more than one possible theory that will predict a set of experimental results and account for a set of events. Alternatives to a given theory which are thus empirically equivalent may be trivial, as contrived examples usually are. For instance, as an alternative to theory T we could propose theory $T + M$, where M is a meaningless statement sanctioned by the inadequate meaning criteria described above. On the other hand, each alternative may be a highly developed theory in its own right. For instance, the relevant parts of Newtonian mechanics were empirically equivalent to special relativity theory, or could easily have been made so, when special relativity theory was first proposed. Again, Copernicus' and Tycho Brahe's astronomical theories were empirically equivalent with respect to events within the solar system – in this case for the rather special reason that they were also geometrically equivalent.

Choosing between empirically equivalent theories cannot, by definition, be done on the basis of the evidence in favour of each. Such theories can, nevertheless, often be forced apart by elaborating them to the point where they make different predictions. Such a procedure can be effective, however, only if strict limits are imposed on the amount of *post hoc* accommodation that will be permitted to the theories. Such limits, furthermore, cannot be formally specified any more easily than meaning criteria can be specified, and for much the same reasons. Imposing such limits on *post hoc* accommodation in the absence of formal criteria therefore amounts to placing limits on what will be accepted as attributable to the world. Doing so is thus consistent with a position of scientific realism, but is not consistent with a position which forbids any systematic deviation from rigorous and explicit criteria for the assessment of theories.

On the other hand, choosing between two well-developed empirically equivalent theories, in the absence of what is accepted beforehand as deciding evidence, is not made any easier by adopting a realist approach than by adopting a positivist one. Nor is there any reason why it should be easier. The systematic function of realism in the context of construction (as contrasted with its psychological function as emphasized by Planck) is not to provide a basis for making judgments in the absence of evidence, but to provide a basis for making judgments on the basis of evidence which is not logically compelling. When the choice must be made, therefore, between Copernican and Tychonic astronomy, between Newtonian mechanics and special relativity, scientists who make the choice on realist grounds may disagree fundamentally and irreconcilably in their choices. As we shall see, the circumstances in which such choices are made often mitigate the arbitrariness and 'all or nothing' character of the choice.

Some of the considerations which have been mentioned here in support of a realist position – the impossibility of making unequivocal tests or crucial experiments to decide between competing theories – led Poincaré[43] and Duhem[44] to adopt an opposite position. They maintained that since scientific theories cannot be unequivocally tested or compared, we cannot assume that they make definite contact with the real world. The truth that is sought by scientific theories is presumably univocal, even if the theories can never be. Therefore, they maintained, the multiplicity of possible theories dictates that theories cannot be considered 'true' in anything like an absolute sense, but should rather be considered as conventions, to be adopted and discarded alike on the basis of convenience.

This is the position, of course, of the positivist movement known as conventionalism (see the discussion in Chapter II). It is a consistent and ingenious position, and it offers one means for resolving the difficulties generated by reliance on formal testing procedures; a means that was, as we shall see, appropriate at the time the position was advanced. There is no reason to accept the conventionalist position as either generally appropriate or logically compelling, however. It amounts merely to the demonstration that one cannot be committed both to formal testing procedures, with the practically limitless *ad hoc* adjustments to theory which such procedures allow, and to a realist account of science. Specifically, conventionalism combines commitment to formal testing procedures with a keen appreciation of their fallibility, and uses the conjunction to justify withholding commitment from the theories which the procedures sanction. Conventionalism does not, however, provide grounds for being committed to the use of such fallible testing procedures. Thus, it does not tell against the realist position advanced here, which addresses the same problems as conventionalism did (resolving them by de-emphasizing the testing criteria rather than by de-emphasizing theories), but which is also vindicated initially by the incoherence of formal criteria even in advance of their application to theory testing. Furthermore, the choice between competing theories is not really simplified by designating the theories as conventions.[45] That designation does little to solve the problems that conventionalism was developed to deal with, problems associated with choosing between competing theories, except in the special case where an out-of-date but familiar theory is maintained on the basis of its everlasting truth. Such cases belong, as a rule, to the context of reconstruction, and will be considered there.

Problems Arising from the Resort to Methodological rather than Logical Criteria

Strict and consistent logical analyses so far seem inapplicable for assessing either the empirical meaningfulness or the validity of scientific statements and theories. A positivist orientation toward science thus cannot, on the available evidence, be coherently implemented as a formal programme. Nothing has yet been said, however, to suggest that positivism cannot be consistently maintained as an *attitude* toward scientific practice, even in the absence of adequate formalizations. Thus, some philosophers of science have claimed that the value of the formal criteria of meaningfulness and validity is not altogether nullified by the logical weaknesses they display. These philosophers maintain that the purpose of constructing such criteria - that of ensuring the unequivocally empirical character of science - can best be served by applying the best available criteria to the best of our ability. At the very least, they maintain, such a procedure, while not proof against errors, is better than none at all. This orientation toward meaning and validation criteria is a *methodological*, rather than a *logical* one. It is interested in the formal techniques in so far as they can lead to a desired end, that of ensuring the empirical character of science; the techniques are to be judged on the basis of how well they can achieve that end rather than on the basis of their logical properties as such. Maxwell summarizes this orientation as follows, in discussing the confirmability criterion:[46]

> It is true that the criterion will not do as it stands; but what is intended is quite clear. Let us modify it to read something like, 'Some observation sentence must be derivable from M and P, and P must function non-trivially and in an uncontrived manner in the derivation. It is true,' this position continues, 'that we may not be able to give formal criteria for triviality and for uncontrivedness - criteria which will meet all of the logician's trick cases. Nevertheless, we know what is meant and will be able to recognize triviality, etc. (in this sense) when we see instances of it.'

This methodological position amounts to treating the available criteria *as if* they were appropriate, and adapting them to meet the special cases in which they are not. The problem with any such pragmatic use of the formal criteria concerns the identification of the special cases where they are inapplicable, and the decision about what to do with them once they have been identified. The 'logician's trick cases' can be recognized easily enough, if for no other reason than that they are put forward by logicians. But as pointed out before, the value of such trick cases is that they show that a proposed criterion can lead to unacceptable conclusions and they show it in such a way that the conclusions can easily be identified as unacceptable. If a proposed criterion leads to problematic conclusions in the analysis of complex theories, there is no way of knowing for sure whether the conclusions are acceptable or unacceptable, right or wrong. It is precisely in these difficult cases where common sense cannot be trusted that the application of the criterion is most relevant; and it is precisely in those situations that the logical fallibility of the criterion will render its applicability most in doubt. In short, a fallible criterion will abdicate its responsibility just when it is most needed, when confronted with the most difficult tasks; it will do so not because it is more likely to lead to absurd conclusions when applied to difficult tasks, but because the informal checks to which it must constantly be subject are themselves most in doubt when the tasks are difficult.

Let us apply these considerations to the two most influential methodological positions put forward to date: falsificationism and operationism. Both were initially developed before the search for formal criteria reached its peak, and both remain influential at present, in the face of the reduced influence of formal criteria.

Falsificationism Falsificationism as a methodological position is associated almost entirely with Popper and his more faithful students. Popper is not and never has been a positivist, in the sense in which that term has been used here. On the contrary, he has always regarded the goal of science as the attainment of absolute truth. He regards this goal as unattainable in principle, however, and has devoted most of his philosophical career to the development of formal decision criteria for the unambiguous logical and empirical assessment of statements and theories. These criteria are different from, but entirely comparable to, the meaning criteria developed by logical positivists. Popper's appreciation of the fallibility of human knowledge, however, has led him to stress the provisional character of any such criteria. Against the hopes, at least, of some logical positivists, he declares that the application of such criteria can never lead to any certainty regarding either the truth or the falsity of any statements: 'If you insist on strict proof (or strict disproof) in the empirical sciences, you will never benefit from experience, and never learn from it how wrong you are.'[47] Since his falsificationist criteria are parts of a general methodological position, Popper can supplement them when alone they are insufficient to guarantee the empirical character of science. For instance, in countering the charge that any theory could be made to resist falsification on his criteria, simply by making *ad* and *post hoc* adjustments to it as necessary, Popper states: 'the *empirical method* shall be characterized as a method that excludes precisely those ways of evading falsification which, as my imaginary critic rightly insists, are logically possible'.[48]

How far do such methodological supplementations render falsificationism workable? Three major problems for logical (rather than methodological) falsificationism have been mentioned so far. They are the admission of meaningless statements of the sort sanctioned by the confirmability criterion, the 'immunization' of theories against refutation by an injection of *ad hoc*-ness, and the unfalsifiability of existential statements. Concerning the first of these, Popper has little to say, trusting presumably that such cases can be recognized when they occur; the dangers inherent in this trust have already been mentioned. Concerning the second, Popper's answer is that an addition to theory is rarely identifiable as simply *ad hoc* or not; there are degrees of *ad hoc*-ness and degrees of empirical significance. For instance, while the Lorentz-Fitzgerald contraction equations and theory are not completely *ad hoc* (cf. above, p. 122) they generate fewer testable consequences than does special relativity theory, which, Popper, claims, is therefore to be preferred on the basis of its greater empirical content. Such an answer is certainly acceptable in principle, but it only pushes the problem back a step: How does one now go about comparing the revised theory (Newtonian mechanics + Lorentz-Fitzgerald equations) with the new one (special relativity) on the basis of the amount of their empirical content? Empirical content can be defined as a function of the number of testable predictions entailed by a theory, and, again in principle, two theories might be compared on this basis. A technique for making such comparisons is difficult to develop, however, because most theories entail either an infinite number of empirical predictions or else none at all. Popper sketches the outlines of such a technique, but his account is no more than schematic; it is more an analysis of the problem than an attempt at a solution. Neither Popper nor anyone else has yet been able to develop such a technique to the point where it could be applied in any concrete instance. In the absence of such a technique, the placing of restrictions on *ad hoc*-ness can only be based on the *content* of the *ad hoc* additions and their patent theory, considered separately from their *number*. Such a practice, therefore, cannot be given a general justification, methodological any more than logical, which is separate in any way from the substantive issues related to the particular case. It constitutes, that is, the placing of limitations on what will be accepted as attributable to nature over and above those which can be justified with reference to any (methodological or logical) decision criteria. Such a practice, when based – as it must be, if it is not to be random – on broadly theoretical considerations, typifies a position of scientific realism.

The third problem is that existential statements are not falsifiable, and hence on strict application of a falsificationist criterion are non-empirical or metaphysical. Many such statements nonetheless appear in important positions in scientific theories. Therefore, Popper maintains a strict falsificationist criterion only in the case of isolated existential statements. For those included in theories he is more lenient:[49]

> . . . an *isolated* existential statement is never falsifiable; but if taken *in a context* with other statements, an existential statement *may in some cases* add to the empirical content of the whole context; it may enrich the theory to which it belongs, and may add to its degree of falsifiability or testability. In this case, the theoretical system including the existential statement in question is to be described as scientific rather than metaphysical.

Again, Popper's answer is entirely acceptable in principle, but cannot easily be put into practice. No matter how pragmatic we wish to be about testing theories, whether a theory entails strictly falsifiable predictions or not is a purely logical question. From the conjunction of an existential and a universal statement, no new universal statements are entailed. New existential statements may be entailed, but existential statements still cannot, for Popper, constitute theoretical predictions, because as such they are not falsifiable. Hence, no existential statement can increase the falsifiability of a theory; none, that is, can increase the theory's empirical content in the strict logical sense of generating additional falsifiable predictions.[50] Since all existential statements are on a par in this respect, Popper's emphasis on *'some cases'* is potentially misleading. The falsifiable predictions made by a theory that includes existential statements are the same whether the existential statements are transcendentally metaphysical or (in some sense) empirically meaningful. On grounds of falsifiability alone, if any existential statements are allowed in a theory, then all of them are. The falsifiability criterion cannot distinguish between good ones and bad ones.

And yet, Popper is surely correct when he says that some existential statements, but only some, enrich a theory and add to its empirical content. The example he gives is the discovery of the element Hafnium, and the inclusion in chemical theory of existential statements about it, after some of its properties had been predicted by Bohr on the basis of strictly universal entailments from theory. The identification of Hafnium as exhibiting these properties enriched chemical theory, may have been instrumental in the discovery of further elements, etc. The existential statements about Hafnium were thus clearly meaningful and possessed of empirical content in some important sense. But that sense is not one that can be defined or measured by any use of the falsifiability criterion, as has just been shown. The empirical content of such statements can be assessed, if at all, only on the basis of criteria other than that of falsifiability. Existential statements must be judged empirical or non-empirical, meaningful or meaningless, quite apart from their inclusion in any theory which receives *its* evaluation strictly on the basis of its falsifiability. Such judgments can certainly be made on theoretical grounds, but not according to Popper's rules, not, that is, by the use of his version of 'empirical method'.

In short, the use of falsifiability as a methodological rather than a logical criterion does not eliminate any of the difficulties concerning existential statements. Strict (logical) falsificationism bars them all; methodological fiat, if it admits any, admits them all and cannot discriminate between them; their evaluation and the choice between them can be made only on substantive grounds independent of the falsificationist methodology. Such grounds, if they are to have any systematic rigour, can only be theoretical grounds, but it follows that they must be occupied in the absence of, or to an extent greater than that warranted by, strict adherence to the falsificationist criteria. The occupation of such grounds, to such an extent, constitutes, again, a position of scientific realism.

In both cases, making falsificationism a methodological rather than a logical position provides a *licence*, for repudiating *ad hoc*-ness and for admitting some existential statements respectively. But it is only someone who has bound himself to the falsificationist rules who needs a licence to deviate from them, and the licence does not carry any guidelines for doing so. Methodological falsificationism cannot tell us *how* to repudiate *ad hoc*-ness and look discerningly at existential statements; it cannot tell us how to do anything more than the strictly logical position can.

Operationism An independent technique for establishing the empirical meaningfulness of concepts was developed by Bridgman,[51] under the name of 'operational analysis', usually shortened (to Bridgman's distaste) to 'operationism'. The basic tenet of operationism is that the meaning of a concept is determined by the operations performed in applying it. As Bridgman summarized it:[52]

> The fundamental idea back of an operational analysis is . . .
> that we do not know the meaning of a concept unless we can
> specify the operations which were used by us or our neighbour
> in applying the concept in any concrete situation.

Operationism, like most of the other decision procedures described, was part of the reaction to the overturning of Newtonian mechanics in the modern scientific revolution, in a spirit of 'How could we have been so wrong?' Bridgman's avowed aim was to 'render unnecessary the services of the unborn Einsteins'[53] in recasting our conception of the universe. His technique has been applied more, however, to rendering unnecessary the services of the unborn Watsons, as it has been much more influential and widely adopted in behaviourist psychology than in physics. Unlike most logical positivist analyses, and like Popper's, operationism was never intended as a formal criterion of meaningfulness but rather as a technique, backed by an attitude, for keeping theoretical constructs in touch with observations. Nevertheless, it has some familiar problems of a logical nature, as well as some new ones stemming from its practical character. These will be considered in turn.

We can operationally define an object's length as the reading taken from a yardstick placed against it, and we can specify the operation as precisely as we wish. Similarly, we can define an object's brittleness as the force of a hammer blow that it takes to shatter it; or we can stipulate a brittle–not brittle dichotomy by assigning an arbitrary cut-off point on the continuum of force. None of this is problematic. Often, however, we need to attribute a property to something without performing the designated operations for defining or measuring that property. It would be inconvenient to measure the length of a body every time we refer to its length. It would be impractical to shatter a body every time we refer to its brittleness, especially if we wish to speak of whole brittle bodies. We therefore have to phrase the operational definition as a conditional statement. The meaning of 'This flask is brittle' is operationally given by the conditional 'If I hit this flask with a hammer at the designated force, the flask will shatter.' The meaning of 'This desk is three feet wide' is given, similarly, by 'If I place a yardstick against the side of this desk, the yardstick will yield a measurement of three feet.' The validity of a conditional statement that is untested in a given case is dependent on generalization from a test case; the desk was measured yesterday, a sample of flasks from the carton each shattered when hit with the hammer. From this reconstruction of operational definitions, there are two problems which arise, the first from the form of conditional statements, the second from the process of generalization.

The first problem is that the conditional 'If X is hit with a hammer, X will shatter' is satisfied by any X that is not hit with a hammer; this is a consequence of the logic of conditional statements, which are falsified only if the antecedent is true and the consequent is false. Thus, in the example given, everything that is not hit with a hammer is operationally defined as brittle, and every desk that is not measured is three feet wide. These consequences are obviously unacceptable, but they follow inevitably from the use of conditional statements, and it is hard to see how such statements can be avoided. Hempel[54] suggests that the problems in the use of conditional statements generally in science can be overcome only by relating the consequent to universal (theoretical) laws which account for it. As applied to operational definitions, such a procedure would involve deducing the property to be defined from a theoretical account, and hence would subsume operational definations under the general class of observation statements entailed by a theory. Making operational definitions thus dependent on theory, however, completely negates the purpose for which they were developed, which was that of defining a concept independent of its place in a theory so as to place limits on its extension within the theory.

This first problem might seem to be one of the logician's trick cases, and hence irrelevant for practical purposes. The second problem, however, leads to much the same conclusion about the relation of operational definitions to theories, and does so on eminently practical grounds. Generalization from a test case – which, as we have seen, is necessary if operational definitions are to be used – involves an inductive risk; it requires the judgment that a given case is similar to the test case with regard to the property considered. We must assume that the desk did not change its width overnight, or that the quality control at the glass-blowing works is sufficient to guarantee that each flask in the carton is equally likely to break. The fact that these assumptions can be made only within certain limits is not a concern in these cases. We can safely make the necessary assumptions in these cases, because we are familiar with the way in which desks and flasks generally behave. That is, we know what variables can be considered irrelevant in attributing the same property to two different flasks or to one desk at two different times. More precisely, we assume that the operationally defined value of a designated variable is invariant with respect to changes in the value of certain other variables, in order for our operational definitions to have even the slightest degree of generality. We assume that desk-width (as operationally defined) is invariant with respect to time, and that flask-brittleness (as operationally defined) is invariant with respect to denumeration.

Thus, from the necessity of inductive risk we are led to assuming the invariance of certain variables with respect to others.[55] These assumed invariances establish the limits within which operational definitions can be considered valid. They are not specified in reports of experimental procedure because they are, in fact, infinite in number, comprising all of the unique circumstances under which any operational definition was made. The only variables with respect to which invariance is not assumed are those specified in the operational definition itself. Thus, the operational definition of 'intelligence' as 'the score achieved on an intelligence test' assumes invariance with respect, among other things, to choice of test. The operational definition of 'intelligence' as 'the weighted average score achieved on the verbal and performance scales of the Weschler Adult Intelligence Scale, current edition, administered by a trained tester and in conformance with the test instructions printed in the test handbook' assumes invariance with respect, among other things, to sex, age, and social status of the tester.

Thus, operational definitions are always definitions with respect to certain variables and without respect to all others, which are presumed irrelevant. An operationally defined concept is presumed variable with respect to the specified variables and invariant with respect to the rest. The assumption of invariance can be justified on, at best, two bases. First is informal familiarity with the objects and properties involved; there is no reason to expect that desk-width varies with time because it has never happened before and besides, desks don't do that sort of thing. Second is a theoretical account that specifies that behaviour appropriate to the objects involved; the definition of a solid in conjunction with the heat expansion coefficients of steel and wood, for instance, may enable us to predict, or may be taken to guarantee, that the desk will not change its width overnight. The assumption of invariance (or irrelevance) is not rigid, of course; it can be tested with respect to any variables chosen for consideration and available for measurement. The choice of variables to test in this way may be made on almost any basis whatever – common sense, hunches, random selection, theoretical expectations – but is not implied in any way by the procedures of operational definition itself, and can never be exhaustive.

In short, operational definitions can limit the application of a concept only along those dimensions where its propriety is already suspect.[56] Use of the technique to limit concepts in any other way would rest on a choice of variables or dimensions random with respect to the theory in which the concepts appear; such use would be, in the context of the development of the theory, gratuitous at best and disruptive at worst. In between, it may be merely trivializing. The choice of variables to control for – that is, the selection of suspect dimensions – cannot be made on the basis of the rules of operational definitions themselves; such variables or dimensions are not specifiable independent of the theory and the problems with which they are connected. If the choice of such variables is to be systematic, it must rest on broadly theoretical considerations, but in the absence of a finished theory that entails the relevance of specified variables – that is, in the construction and development of a theory – the choice must proceed on grounds other than entailment. Such grounds, again, involve the implicit attribution to the theory of greater validity than can be strictly warranted; and again, the holding of such an assumption constitutes a position of scientific realism. So, operational analysis, like methodological falsificationism, requires for its systematic utilization in the context of a developing theory a position of, or equivalent to, scientific realism.

3 POSITIVISM AND REALISM IN THE CONTEXT OF RECONSTRUCTION

It was stated above that the systematic function of realism in the context of construction is that it provides a basis for making judgments on the strength of evidence which is not logically compelling. Therein lies the strength of realism, and also its weakness: it enables decisions to be made, but by the same token may encourage them to be made wrongly. Drawing conclusions on the basis of non-compelling or, strictly speaking, insufficient evidence necessitates a relaxation of critical standards. Such standards are in part replaced by reliance on the power of a theory, or of the fundamental insights which the theory exemplifies, to serve as a guide in the continuing investigation of nature. The theory's power must be relied upon sufficiently that it can be held to warrant neglect of the flood of anomalies that besets any theory, as well as of the innumerable alternative theories that are always possible. A theory that is relied upon in such a way need not be monolithic; the realist commitment will not be to the theory in all its details but to what are taken to be its fundamental insights. Thus, the theory can be revised and improved by applying these insights to the solution of further problems. The fact of commitment, however, places certain stringent limitations on the direction and extent of theoretical development. In particular, it makes it very difficult for the theory, or for the scientists who maintain it, to accept any explanation of observed events which contradicts the fundamental insights of the theory and which is therefore incompatible with (what the theory claims to be, hence what is accepted as) the real world. If the investigation of nature by means of an accepted theory leads to a situation in which such 'unreal' interpretations are called for, then the realist approach to science runs into very serious trouble.

Such a situation can arise when experimental results or theoretical analyses incompatible with the fundamental insights of the accepted theory become prominent. They may become prominent and thus emerge from the perennial flood of anomalies in a variety of ways. They may be refutations of theoretical predictions which stem directly from the theory's most fundamental insights; recognizing the anomalies as particularly important thus proceeds, in this case, from the very fact of the realist interpretation of the theory. They may become prominent as a result of external cultural factors, such as the demand for better calendars or intelligence tests; such demands can sometimes stimulate more intense interest in unresolved problems than they would receive on autonomously scientific grounds. They may be unexpected achievements which exemplify the different fundamental insights of a competing theory.

Although such anomalous findings and interpretations may come from many sources, and be judged important for as many reasons, it is the commitment to a realist interpretation of the accepted theory that renders them of crucial significance. Once it has been agreed that they must be dealt with, that is, that they can be neither ignored nor explained away, then a continuing failure in fact to deal with them within the accepted theory places a realist interpretation of that theory in a double-bind. The realist commitment to the truth of the theory simultaneously assures them major systematic status and precludes the use of any easy stratagems (such as *ad hoc* modifications to the theory) for dealing with them.

Thus, however such problems arise, they constitute a challenge that cannot be ignored but that also, within the constraints of a realist interpretation of the accepted theory, cannot be met. Such unresolvable problems that cannot be by-passed or ignored have a devastating effect upon the tenets of scientific realism. In the presence of enough of them, the realist conviction that science can disclose the truth about the real world may begin to crumble; or it may be upheld but be divorced from its formally inadequate (and now also practically inadequate) empirical foundations. Either reaction involves re-examining the relationship of the theory *qua* theory to its empirical base, in order to see how the two came to diverge. That is, either reaction (and they are not that much different) requires a consideration of the theory and its component parts primarily as abstract constructions rather than as representations of the world. Either, therefore, makes the context of reconstruction central in the scientific enterprise.

In short, the context of reconstruction becomes primary when scientific focus is shifted from that part of the world which the theory addresses, to the theory itself. There are three tasks for scientific inquiry in the context of reconstruction. First is the determination of why the accepted (or formerly accepted) theory is no longer proving adequate to the demands made of it. This task involves identifying the factors within the accepted theory which have come to vitiate it. Such factors may include the fundamental assumptions involved in formulating or applying the theory, the choice of variables in terms of which theoretical explanation is given, etc.; some or all of these may be identified as empirically unwarranted, overextended, or simply meaningless. Second is the correction or elimination of these vitiating factors, either by recasting them in an empirically more warranted form or by replacing them with altogether new ones; in the former case the appearance, at least, of the theory may be preserved. Third is the resolution of the intractable problems that led to the crisis in the first place. These three tasks impose demands, both of a technical and of an attitudinal kind, which can be met much more easily within a positivist orientation to science than within a realist one.

Essentially, what makes a realist approach unsuitable for these tasks is its relative inflexibility in dealing with substantive issues. A realist approach facilitates a close focus on what is known or taken to be important; it is well suited to highly directed activities such as adding new findings on to old frameworks, expanding a theory built on an established base, or rejecting one of an indifferent pair of incompatible theories. This close focus has a price, however; it produces a comparative blindness outside the area of focus. A realist approach is incapable of supporting a critical analysis of all components of an accepted theory equally, since some fundamental components will be treated as almost unquestionable, or at least less questionable than others depending on how fundamental they are. If some of these fundamental components are the ones responsible for the theory's difficulties, a realist interpretation of the theory will actually hinder its critical analysis. It is here that tenacity in the defence of a theory may degenerate to dogmatism: the attitude does not change but its appropriateness does.

A positivist orientation, on the other hand, involves no commitment to the truth of the fundamental insights of a theory, but only to the theory's empirical foundations. Such an orientation helps in the performance of the tasks which arise in the context of reconstruction, both in general and in specific ways.

The general way in which a positivist orientation helps is a simple consequence of its lack of commitment, its refusal to agree that a theory must be either true or false; it reduces the stakes in the evaluation of theories. Positivist analyses of scientific theories as classifications of data or freely chosen conventions reduce the tenacity with which an old theory can be maintained, because they reduce the status of all theories; or at least, they do so for those who accept the analyses. Such analyses may be attractive, furthermore, to those who are intellectually and even emotionally tied to the old theory but who understand the depth of its problems. By divorcing the absolute truth of a theory from its empirical support, positivist analyses enable a discredited but well-loved theory to be maintained as true, and any new ones considered merely as aids to calculation. In this way, the insistence on the truth of a well-known but increasingly untenable theory can be rendered harmless in the course of science. Additionally, such positivist analyses can reduce the diffidence that a scientist might feel in proposing a new theory that is grossly counter-intuitive or that contradicts already existing theories. This last benefit of positivism, the encouragement of free flights of creative imagination through analysis of theories as conventions, was the one most emphasized by Poincaré.[57]

In the identification and analysis of the factors that have vitiated a theory, a positivist approach provides, besides an appropriate intellectual climate, the beginning, at least, of a set of analytical techniques. These techniques include all those used to implement the basic positivist requirement that the terms and statements of a theory have unambiguous empirical content. That is, they include all the recent meaning and demarcation criteria (in their application as methodological techniques) that were criticized above in relation to the context of construction. They were not adequate in that context, even as methodological rather than logical criteria, because the development and elaboration of theories required decisions about the admission and interpretation of data which these criteria simply could not be used to make. In the present context, however, with regard to identifying and analysing the disruptive elements of a theory, the relevant questions concern precisely the unambiguous empirical content of *selected* concepts and statements in the theory. The kind of meaningfulness and validity that can be designated as trouble-free is precisely that restricted but unequivocally empirical kind that can be checked through use of the techniques. Any surplus meaning carried by the concepts and statements in the theory is legitimately suspect in the present case. It is typically necessary to extend theoretical concepts beyond the range of their unambiguous empirical warrant, and thus to invest them with surplus meaning; but certain instances in which they are so overextended are the ones that lead to trouble for the theory, and these require identification and analysis. It was, for instance, through analysing the possible observational implications of the current theoretical conceptions of space and time that Mach was led to conclude that the concepts of *absolute* space and time were meaningless. Such an analysis can be carried out at any time, of course, and the positivist techniques are always the appropriate ones for doing so; but since theoretical concepts are quite typically overextended, the analysis is called for only when such overextension has to be identified to account for a breakdown in the theory.

The correction or elimination of the disruptive factors in a theory follows on their identification and analysis. In some cases the concepts or assumptions selected for examination may be concluded to be incorrigible or meaningless, and in need of complete replacement. However, if the selected concepts have any ascertainable empirical content, they can be reformulated so as not to go beyond it, by application of the analytical techniques, e.g., by the operational definitions[58] of the concepts or by the description of their confirming or falsifying instances. Such strict reformulation of the concepts renders them of less power in any proposed new theory, of course, but in a sense prepares them for receiving surplus meaning of a new sort in future theories by stripping them of the particular surplus which they carried in the old theory. Of more immediate importance, the recasting of the offending components of the old theory facilitates the extraction from that theory of those parts or applications of it which are still useful. Such extraction is necessary; the old theory may still be useful in some scientific investigations, and may have many practical applications as well. It cannot be maintained as true on a realist account, because its acknowledged failings are too great, but to reject it altogether as false would, in the absence of an alternative theory of comparable power and scope, involve an unacceptable loss of economy. On a positivist account the theory can be maintained in whatever form can be empirically justified; in such a form the theory may have lost much of its elegance and systematic unity, but some of its utility is preserved while it is prevented from acting as a straitjacket on the development of alternative, possibly incompatible theories and models.

Such alternative theories and models may be directed primarily at resolving the outstanding problems that touched off the reappraisal of the old theory. The solution of such problems is the major substantive achievement made in the context of reconstruction. In the attack on such problems, a positivist approach encourages a conceptual flexibility that permits the tentative pursuit of diverse and even incompatible routes towards their solution; again, this is the feature of positivism emphasized by Poincaré. In addition, a positivist orientation contributes an emphasis on conceptual precision and rigorous data determination that draws attention to the fine structure of the experimental phenomena, and that may thereby aid in focusing attention on previously neglected aspects of the problems. In short, in the solution of outstanding problems a positivist orientation promotes a narrowing and intensification of focus on the phenomena related to the problems and does so without a corresponding systematic commitment. The combination of intensity of focus and conceptual flexibility would, indeed, provide an ideal orientation for the practice of science, if science were not also concerned with the construction of theories possessing maximum scope and generality.

In discussing positivism in the context of reconstruction it may be valuable to distinguish generally between its *critical* and its *mediating* function. The critical function of positivism is exemplified by the analysis of unsound theoretical concepts and by the recasting of such concepts, where possible, in such a way as to give them more solid empirical reference; this function has already been discussed in sufficient detail. The mediating function of positivism is exemplified by its analysis of the status of theories as conventions, classifications of data, etc. By reducing the stakes involved in the assessment and comparison of theories, a positivist orientation mediates between successive dominant theories or sets of theories in a branch of science, easing the transition from one to the next. It does so by being available for use simultaneously as a conservative and as a radical influence. The influence of positivism is a conservative one, in that it permits the retention of old theories, or old views about the nature of reality, in the face of new and – from a realist standpoint – disconfirmatory evidence. At the same time the influence is a radical one, in that it facilitates the development of new ideas and theories with a minimum of opposition predicated on their 'outlandishness' or counter-intuitiveness, and stemming from the inertia attained by the ideas associated with the old system. In modern physics, the conservative influence of positivism may be exemplified by the 'saving' of Newtonian theory by the Lorentz-Fitzgerald equations when they were first proposed; the radical influence may be exemplified by Einstein's use of the equations in the construction of special relativity theory. Thus, different scientists, depending on their preferences, can look upon either the old or the new theories as either absolutely (and hence non-empirically) true, or as mere aids to calculation, or indeed as both, so long as the two kinds of validity are not confused; separating the two kinds of assessment of scientific theories enables the old and the new theories to co-exist as long as proves necessary.

Co-existence is only necessary, however, so long as the old theory retains its vigorous proponents, and until one or more of the new theories has been developed to the point of being able to replace the old theory, either by accounting for most of its successes (as well as some of its failures) or by successfully devaluing them in favour of a new set of achievements. Specifically, it is in the solutions to the outstanding problems that led to the decline and reappraisal of the old theory, and in the extension and systematization of such solutions, that the context of reconstruction merges into and is eventually replaced by the context of construction. Once the critical problems have been solved, or shown to be pseudo-problems and replaced with others that are more amenable to solution, the opportunity arises to maximize the range of applicability of the solutions so as to make them the basis for a theoretical account of as much of the field of inquiry as is possible. And on any account of the nature and function of science – whether science is supposed to be seeking truth or classifying data – it is considered desirable to maximize the range of phenomena for which an account can be given and to eliminate any potential contradictions in explanation. Such systematic considerations may be less powerful in a positivist than in a realist approach, and may be more subordinated to stringently empirical considerations, but they are by no means repudiated. Approaching this goal of systematization is the function of science in the context of construction, and in its pursuit the new theory or theories may be expected gradually to modify or abandon altogether their positivist cast in response to the exigencies associated with their development. The replacement of positivism with realism may be a slow process at best, tied to the entry into the scientific field of younger scientists who are not restricted in their options, as some of their elders may be, either to a positivist renunciation of the search for truth or to an outdated common-sense commitment to the truth of the old theory.[59] With time, nevertheless, if a new theoretical system is to achieve maximum scope and power, it is essential that it come to be accepted as having genuine reference to real things.

The characteristics of realism and of positivism are the same, whether in the context of construction or in that of reconstruction. The primary characteristic of realism is the commitment to the truth of a scientific theory (or the falsity of a competing one) to a greater extent than can be strictly warranted by empirical evidence and the rules of whatever logic has been adopted; realism thus encourages systematization at the expense of rigorous logical and empirical analysis. The primary characteristic of positivism is the refusal to make any such commitment, and the insistence on evaluating theories and statements strictly on the basis of explicit logical and empirical criteria; positivism thus encourages rigorous logical and empirical analysis at the expense – largely for technical reasons – of systematization. In the shift from the context of construction to the context of reconstruction and back, what changes is the relative appropriateness of these two contrasting orientations to science. In the context of construction realism is most appropriate, since what is required is the systematic development and elaboration of theories. In the context of reconstruction, positivism is most appropriate, since what is required is the critical examination, analysis, and dismemberment of theories.

4 A NOTE ON PARADIGMS

The account of the contexts of construction and reconstruction as developed here bears close comparison with Kuhn's account of revolutions and normal science,[60] and the two analyses can be mapped on to each other fairly easily. The 'fundamental insights' of a theory which are the focus of the 'realist commitment' correspond at least roughly to a 'paradigm', the 'context of construction' to periods of 'normal science', the 'context of reconstruction' to periods of 'crisis' and 'revolution', etc. The compatibility of the present account with Kuhn's is, furthermore, quite intentional. What, therefore, is the difference between the two, and if they are fully compatible, what is the point of the present one?

One difference, of course, is that the account given here attempts to be more general than Kuhn's. The present account claims that a pattern similar to that described by Kuhn is the usual and appropriate one in science, but also permits a description of exceptions, such as behaviourism. The main difference, however, is that the present account is based mainly on an analysis of the philosophy of science rather than, as Kuhn's is, of the history of science. The routes taken in the two accounts, even if they lead to similar conclusions, are thus completely different. As a result, the kinds of cogency the two accounts have, even if they should be equally cogent, are also different.

Kuhn's account was originally presented as a description of the pattern of progress in science. His account takes on normative significance for those who accept it and who want their science to be 'mature'. But while Kuhn's account may thus provide prescriptions for how to run a science, it gives, or so some readers have complained, little rational justification for them. If science operates the way Kuhn says it does, goes the complaint, then science may work, but is not rational, it depends on various kinds of coercion and conversion rather than on a rational spirit of inquiry. As a result, critics of Kuhn have charged that his analysis is based on irrationalism,[61] mob psychology,[62] and catastrophism.[63] Kuhn has responded to these charges at length,[64] but has been unable to convince many of his critics of the rationality of the scientific enterprise as he describes it. They cannot see why science should operate in the way Kuhn says it does and, in the absence of any such reasons, tend to reject his analysis.

The present account specifically attempts to provide reasons why science should operate along lines similar to those Kuhn sketches, and at least in this one respect the different route taken in this account may make it an advance on Kuhn's. The reasons are derived, not primarily from the history of science, but from an almost historical analysis of the most general methodological features of scientific inquiry. The factors which make realism (or a paradigm) necessary in the context of construction arise directly from the problems involved in interpreting and selecting data and relating the data to a theory. Without some such realist commitment the cumulative development of science is impossible, because the logical 'rules of inquiry' are inadequate tools for answering the questions that arise. A realist commitment can thus be justified as the best and most rational means for extending and systematizing the results of scientific research, and it can be justified for each individual who makes the commitment. The justification involves reference to the scientific field and to the problems encountered in extending it, but requires only minimal reference to the ethos of the community of practitioners in the science. As a result, both Kuhn's account and the present one imply that the conduct of science will involve personal commitment by scientists, tacit devaluation of some of the claims of logic, and the selective blindness that results. But neither implies irrationalism, unless 'reason' is equated with 'logic'; and it has been apparent from some time that no such equation can be made.

5 BEHAVIOURISM AND ITS POSITIVISM

At the end of Chapter I an explanation was promised as to why neobehaviourists were wrong in their conviction that 'commitment to the procedures of science' and possession of 'a set of decision procedures, appropriate to all sciences indifferently' would guarantee the viability of their scientific enterprise. The explanation has been some time in coming, for it required a look at the historical background of behaviourism as well as an overview of the relation between methodological and substantive factors in science generally.

How Adherence to Explicit Decision Procedures Results in Theoretical Fragmentation

Contrary to the neobehaviourists' expectations, the rigorous use of explicit and formal decision procedures – rules for arriving at any kind of conclusions about hypotheses, theories, and data – can guarantee neither the development of a scientific field as a whole nor theoretical convergence of competing positions within that field. This conclusion holds true whether the rules are ones imported from the technical philosophy of science, ones developed for use in other successful sciences (e.g., operational definitions), or ones developed by psychologists for use in their own discipline (e.g., intervening variables). Instead, if such use is accepted as fundamental to scientific progress, it can *prevent* theoretical development and convergence. The systematic use of the various kinds of decision procedures had this effect on neobehaviourism in two complementary ways, through the relative superordination of methodological issues and through the relative subordination of substantive ones.

The potentially fragmenting effects of the superordination of methodological concerns was treated at length in a general way above. It is entirely consistent with adherence to explicit decision procedures to make an unlimited number of alterations to a preferred theory in order to maintain it in the face of negative findings. In fact, Hull considered this unlimited alterability of methodologically rigorous theories – specifically his own – to be essential to their scientific character; it guaranteed that such theories would gradually approach perfection, since negative results would be as important as positive ones in their development. But, as we have seen, such unlimited alterability merely leaves theories incapable of refutation. The history of neobehaviourism, furthermore, illustrates this conclusion far better than it illustrates Hull's faith. Throughout the neobehaviourist period the theories of, say, Guthrie, Hull, and Tolman were each constantly being criticized on both logical and experimental grounds by the proponents of the others. The criticisms had their effect: they stimulated accommodation in each theory in order to meet the objections, and such continual accommodation was widely regarded as demonstrating the corrigible, hence progressive, character of each. But while the competing theories were thus refined to the point where, in their areas of overlap,[65] it became difficult to derive different predictions from them, this 'empirical convergence' was accompanied by no comparable theoretical convergence. At the level of theory, the Guthrians, Hullians, Tolmanians, etc., remained as far apart as ever. Their shared methodological commitment helped to keep them theoretically disunified by making their disparate positions empirically defensible, rather than to bring them any closer to basic theoretical agreement.

The separate effects of the subordination of substantive principles were more subtle. The brunt of the earlier parts of this chapter was that some kind of logically indefensible ontological reference or unformalizable substantive insight is not merely desirable or appropriate as a basis for theoretical development, but is absolutely *indispensable* to it. They provide the only possible systematic basis on which many crucial theoretical decisions (on how to interpret data, on what variables to implicate in operational definitions, etc.) can be made. It follows that the neobehaviourists must have incorporated some such indefensible ontological references into their theories, since otherwise they could not have developed even their own positions. And indeed, such indefensible references can be found throughout neobehaviourist theories, *if one looks hard enough for them.* And there is the rub: such references are explicitly denied – are methodologically banned – in neobehaviourist theories; being denied, they make their appearance only covertly; being covert, they are idiosyncratic to the particular theory in which they appear (or in which they are hidden); being idiosyncratic and covert, they are out of the public domain, unavailable to other theorists either to adopt or to criticize.

What was covert about the substantive principles in neobehaviourist theories was not their existence as such but rather the fact that they were inevitably indefensible on strict methodological grounds. Their content was not fully specifiable in terms of the methodological rules which purportedly governed the use of theoretical terms, and they were usable within the various theories precisely by virtue of their ambiguity. Almost all the theoretical terms and postulates in neobehaviourist theories had covert substantive implications in this way. They are responsible for most of the unique content that remained in the various theories after theoretical accommodation had gone as far as it could go; it was largely the covert content that was manipulated and elaborated in the different theories. As Scriven observes:[66]

> I remember the glee with which I discovered that nobody actually produces operational definitions, even when they say they do. Hull's work is replete with examples of allegedly operational definitions. Within three lines of many of these he will insert an ontological addendum but still insist that the defined term has no meaning except as an intervening variable.

The two best documented classes of theoretical terms with covert and unjustifiable substantive implications are also the two most widely used classes of theoretical terms in neobehaviourist theories: intervening variables in the theories of Guthrie, Hull, Skinner, Tolman, and their students, and hypothetical constructs (as postulates) in the theories of Hull and his students. Both of these classes of variables are supposed to be completely definable, in different ways, within a theory, and their use is supposed to be restricted to what follows from their explicit definition.[67] In fact, they are practically never thus definable, and their use depends upon the ambiguity of their reference, upon informal extrapolation from their formal definitions, and upon the implicit granting to them of autonomous status to the extent that their properties can be *discovered* in the subsequent elaboration of the theory.

That the contents of the neobehaviourist theories have this character does not need to be demonstrated here. The demonstration was made independently, and in a sympathetic spirit, by the authors of *Modern Learning Theory*,[68] in their extremely detailed logical analyses of the theories of all the major neobehaviourists, and most especially of Hull and Tolman. The covert character of the content of neobehaviourist theories has consequently been widely accepted for many years as showing that the theories are flawed (although the function of the covertness has not been emphasized before). Furthermore, the logically indefensible status of their theoretical constructs was eventually recognized by the neobehaviourist theorists themselves. In his posthumous final book, *A Behavior System*,[69] Hull retracted all the claims to generality in his 1943 systematization of the laws of behaviour, and while continuing to hope that a comprehensive and rigorous behaviour theory might someday prove possible, judged that even his latest attempt 'will serve mainly to call attention to the problem'.[70] Tolman came eventually to repudiate the hope of ever making a complete definition of any intervening variables and declared that, if they were not to be abandoned altogether, then at best all they could be considered was 'an aid to thinking'.[71] Guthrie eventually repudiated the very possibility of making a methodologically secure anchorage of theoretical terms as the basis for their subsequent use, as follows:[72]

> The fact that it had taken Russell and Whitehead some 400 pages to establish the conclusion that one plus one equals two, and that every intervening step could be challenged and would require more proof, and that the steps of these added proofs would require still more, has made me impatient with the notion that there can be any completely rigorous deduction, or ultimate validity in an argument. This scepticism colors my notions of the nature of scientific facts and scientific theory.

146

Guthrie, who was a logician before he became a psychologist, nevertheless attempted to use intervening variables to provide solid anchorage for the terms of his own theory. His statement thus represents a gradual realization, acquired over a period of forty years, that the limitations of pure logic as exemplified in the *Principia Mathematica* apply also to the application of logical principles to the construction of psychological theories. (Skinner, who also made some use of intervening variables and later repudiated them, is, as in many other respects, a special case, and will be considered separately in Chapter V.)

The presence of some logically indefensible surplus meaning functioning as covert content in neobehaviourist theories may thus be taken as generally accepted. The way in which the covert status of the theories' contents helped to maintain theoretical fragmentation was, as indicated, through keeping the theoretical principles from the public domain, or rather, through rendering them subtly and ambiguously different from the explicit principles which were in the public domain. Each theorist tended to construe his own theoretical principles in terms of what he meant by them, what function he intended them to serve, while maintaining and sincerely believing that their operational or postulational specification provided a firm warrant for the use which he was making of them; conversely, he tended to construe the theoretical principles advanced by a competing theorist in as firm and rigid a manner as possible. Each theorist or school of theorists, therefore, tended to expect that the results of 'crucial experiments' cited by them would be impossible to explain by a (rigorously construed) competing theory. But they continually found that the results of 'crucial experiments' advanced by their competitors could readily be explained by their own theories, at least after their own theories were given minor modifications perfectly consistent with their original spirit. Experimental evidence brought against theories by the proponents of competing theories thus had little effect. Each group of theorists tended to see the mutual impenetrability of each other's theories as evidence of the basic worth of their own approach and of the deviousness of that of their opponents. This pattern of off-centre criticisms and rebuttals was especially characteristic of the relationship between the most directly competing groups of theorists, who also had the firmest commitment to elaborate and methodologically rigorous theories, those centred around Hull and around Tolman. The drawn-out controversy between these two groups on the subject of transposition behaviour, for instance, was conducted largely in terms of 'crucial experiments' that were supposed to settle the issue for once and for all – but of course never did.

Hence, even the minimal 'realist commitment', if such it can be called, of neobehaviourist theorists to the principles of their own theories helped to maintain the theoretical fragmentation of the discipline, simply because it was never clear just what the commitment was *to*. The strictly unwarrantable substantive principles which they adopted were kept secret and disguised (for themselves as well as for their opponents) as explicit and methodologically justifiable constructions, and consequently were unavailable for systematic comparison with alternatives. The way out of this dilemma of uncomparability, it should be clear by now, does *not* lie in enforcing ever more rigid rules on the composition of theoretical constructs; it was the inapplicability of such rules that gave rise to the dilemma in the first place. Rather, it lies in the determined effort to specify what of substantive import is being claimed by a theory, whether through rigid entailment or not; if the implications of a theory cannot all be rigorously derived from postulates, they can at least be made public, as far as possible at any given time, by its proponents.

Summary of the Character of Behaviourism's Positivism

The essential role that a positivist orientation can play in scientific inquiry has been sketched out in this chapter and in Chapter II. In behaviourism, however, the role that positivism played was quite a different one. Let us therefore review the systematic differences between positivism in behaviourism and scientific positivism in general. The differentiating factors were all operative in the data-based positivism of classical behaviourism and continued to be operative, without significant change apart from their refinement, in neobehaviourism.

As stated in Chapter III, we can distinguish two versions of positivism present in the founding of behaviourism. The first is exemplified by Watson's statement that:[73]

It seems reasonably clear that some kind of compromise must be effected: either psychology must change its viewpoint so as to take in facts of behavior, whether or not they have bearings upon the problems of 'consciousness'; or else behavior must stand alone as a wholly separate and independent science.

The second is exemplified by his statement a few pages further on, that:[74]

The time seems to have come when psychology must discard all reference to consciousness; when it need no longer delude itself into thinking that it is making mental states the object of observation.

The first statement constitutes a declaration that in Watson's field, that of animal behaviour, the dominant conceptual framework had become so cumbersome that it needed to be escaped from, in order to allow unimpeded concentration on experimental studies. This first version of positivism was thus purely internal to comparative psychology, and was, on the analysis presented here, an appropriate response to the dilemma affecting research in the field. The second version, however, as represented by Watson's second statement, was very different. It constituted a kind of intellectual imperialism, an extension of the indigenous positivism of comparative psychology to the discipline as a whole. The circumstances which led to this step, and those which led to its gradual acceptance throughout psychology, were both unique. Both were discussed in Chapter III, but may be reviewed here from a slightly different perspective.

The circumstances which led to the extension of positivism throughout the discipline stemmed from the same conceptual framework of functionalist comparative psychology that Watson was, from a different direction, rebelling against. That is, the sensationalism of functionalist comparative psychology became, with the removal of consciousness, environmentalism. Environmentalism, in turn, is a general position; it cannot be applied to animals and not to man, unless man is credited with an immaterial mind or soul, completely different in kind from whatever it is that animates animals. Thus, if environmentalism is established by the rejection of consciousness as a subject matter, it is natural that the position be extended to include man. The alternative would be an uncompromising dualism established for man alone, a dualism which would therefore have theological implications.[75] Neither the substantive nor the research-based methodological arguments in favour of environmentalism and the repudiation of consciousness were strong enough to gain general acceptance in human psychology at the time, however, despite what would seem from the standpoint of comparative psychology to be their universal applicability. Thus the more general methodological argument derived from physics, concerning the general requirements of objectivity, was necessary in establishing Watson's position. This argument was one which could be applied universally, without requiring experimental validation at each step (such is the advantage of methodological arguments). Thus, the unique circumstance leading to the extension of the positivist reaction throughout psychology was the unique relevance of a general methodological argument to the establishment of a position that had both methodological and substantive components.

The circumstances which led to the general acceptance of the extension of positivism throughout the discipline were likewise unique. They comprised the growing positivist orientation of the whole scientific culture, a positivist reaction of unprecedented extent in the history of science. This reaction was occasioned by the overturning of Newtonian mechanics, with the immediate effects described in this chapter and in Chapter II, and was maintained by the intuitively incomprehensible findings of quantum mechanics and, to an only slightly lesser degree, relativity theory. While formally positivist philosophy did not have a wide currency in the United States during behaviourism's early years,[76] there was a widespread appreciation of the limits of scientific explanation, as consisting in closely determined empirical generalizations of observed data with relatively little systematic import. This burgeoning and implicit positivism accounted in large part both for the growing popularity of a positivist approach to psychology and for its gradual divorce from any specific systematic issues.

The fact that behaviourism's positivism was neither introduced nor retained purely as a response to internal problems had significant implications for both its critical and its mediating functions, as these functions were described previously in this chapter. The critical function of positivism was not, after the beginning, directed toward specific concepts and variables that had been identified as troublesome. Even at the beginning, when concepts indicative of mind and consciousness were being criticized, the criticisms were directed toward such concepts primarily as they occurred in human psychology, rather than as they occurred, most problematically, in comparative psychology. Thereafter, the critical function was exercised as a kind of a weapon, directed at any concepts that appeared to be gaining a central role in non-behaviourist theories (e.g., the concept of instinct), and eventually came, with the development of neobehaviourism, to be applied in blanket fashion to all theoretical concepts. The critical function of positivism was thus divorced from its specific context of application to problematic concepts. In being required to be universal, the application was inevitably haphazard and unsuccessful. But although the application was unsuccessful in ridding psychology of theoretical terms with empirically unspecifiable references, it forced the references to become covert and separated from their central position in the development of theory, as we saw above.

If the critical function of positivism was thus misdirected, the mediating function was almost entirely absent, both from classical behaviourism and from neobehaviourism. It is significant that hardly any behaviourists ever made a definite repudiation of realism, in either its common-sense or its philosophical varieties, even though they adopted their methodological formalisms from a movement (logical positivism) which was expressly based on this repudiation. While a *pro forma* rejection of realism specifically as a metaphysical position was sometimes made, the general assumption was that use of rigorously objective methods at all levels of investigation would ensure that behaviourist theories were *as true* as any theories can possibly be – without detailed concern about just *how true* that was (such a concern being a philosophical one). Thus, behaviourism rarely adopted or, more to the point, developed and acted upon, any conventionalist analyses of the status of theories as freely chosen 'conventions' – analyses which exemplify the mediating function of positivism – and never acquired the freedom which such analyses can confer, freedom to engage in unrestrained flights of creative imagination. Instead, the scientific enterprise was expected to be self-consciously pedestrian from the outset. Every theoretical development had to be rigorously justifiable, and thus had to proceed in accordance with the rules of rigorous theory construction. As a result, rather than providing a place for unfettered imagination, which could then be brought down to earth by controlled experimentation, the development of theory was to be what Hull described as a 'long and grinding labor'.[77] It was partly due to the limitations thus imposed that behaviourist theories, while highly receptive to ideas that could be made objective, were not particularly marked by radically new ideas of their own. Similarly, the insistence on 'objectivity', as having a firmer and more distinctly regulative character than many philosophical positivists could themselves grant it, militated against an emphasis on creativity or its product – creative ideas – as being most fundamental to the development of theories. At the same time, this insistence promoted the entirely erroneous dependence on the notion of 'crucial experiments', as we saw above, a dependence that might well have been avoided had behaviourism's positivism included more conventionalist insights.

V

CONCLUSION: TOWARD A
GENERAL EVALUATION OF
BEHAVIOURISM

We now come to the question of just what implications these specific analyses of the origins and systematic foundations of behaviourism have for a general evaluation of the movement. It will become clear that while there are some important respects in which the analyses can support a general evaluation, there are other equally important respects in which they cannot. Let us begin by making all of these explicit.

The analyses given here have concentrated on the systematic foundations of behaviourism. Fairly definite conclusions have already been made about those foundations, and they can be extended to cover any theoretical positions which depend on those foundations. The conclusions cannot be applied, however, to specific pieces of behaviourist research, separate from their systematic context. The negative judgment which has been made about that context certainly reflects on the research conducted within it, but does not apply to any of the individual pieces of research themselves, in so far as they can be considered separate from their context. Neither can the conclusions already arrived at be applied, except very conjecturally, to the contemporary positions in psychology which are called 'behaviourist' but which share few, if any, of the systematic characteristics of either classical behaviourism or neobehaviourism. Finally, when we try to describe the main positive contribution which behaviourism has made to psychology, it will be necessary to go beyond the analysis presented so far and to consider some aspects of behaviourist research which were independent of, and almost unaffected by, any systematic considerations.

1 SYSTEMS AND SYSTEMATIC METHODOLOGY IN BEHAVIOURISM

The fundamental *systematic* contribution of behaviourism lies in its practical demonstration of the untenability of the methodological principles on which it was founded. This may seem a harsh and negative judgment, but it should be stressed that the contribution was a major one. As emphasized previously, behaviourism was the only – or at least the most detailed, uncompromising, and sophisticated – serious attempt ever made to develop a science on methodological principles alone. Developing a science in such a way has long been a dream of philosophers and methodologically orientated scientists, but has never before been undertaken in detail. That the attempt failed utterly at two levels (that the attempt to keep ontological references at bay by means of formal techniques was unsuccessful, and that even the attempt was sufficient to stifle the science's substantive development) has or should have profound consequences for our understanding of the complementary roles of method and substance in science.

Philosophers have often maintained that the philosophical, methodological, or logical presuppositions embodied in a scientific investigation should be made explicit, since otherwise they will influence the investigation in ways that escape detection and possible control. Such a claim may be invalid; when such presuppositions are made explicit they may exercise far more control than they can when they are implicit, and if they cannot be successfully organized into a coherent formal system they may, in their explicit form, have very negative effects on scientific inquiry, as we have seen. On the other hand, the substantive features of scientific inquiry – what it is about, and what it puts forward as causal or otherwise explanatory factors – should clearly be made as explicit and open as possible, regardless of their formal or formalizable status. This conclusion would be entirely unexceptionable and even uninteresting, were it not that many of the substantive features of neobehaviourist research were indeed covert, and were thereby prevented from playing a central role in the process of inquiry.

Of course, a commitment to both substantive and methodological principles is needed for the cumulative development of science. But while both substantive and methodological principles are necessary, the substantive ones are more important, both because they are what scientific inquiry is addressed to developing, and because they alone can provide the crucial implicit indications of when and how the inevitable deviations from the methodological principles should occur. Even in the context of reconstruction, when positivist methodological analyses are called for, they need to be directed by independent judgments of which particular substantive principles are responsible for the science's difficulties, since otherwise the analyses may be random and thus haphazardly disruptive. Any tendency of methodological considerations to direct research needs, therefore, to be subordinated to the particular substantive issues present in individual cases in science. There is no methodological substitute for good ideas, at every stage of research, and no guaranteed methodology for acquiring them; and while methodological tools are necessary for comparing and developing these ideas, scientific progress is possible only if the tools, rather than the material to be worked, have the supportive role. The systematic contribution of behaviourism, therefore, lies principally in demonstrating the general applicability of these points, or rather, in demonstrating the in-validity of their contraries.

With regard to the substance of the neobehaviourist attempts to systematize psychology, it can fairly be judged that the ambitious systematizations of Hull, Tolman, Guthrie, and their students have, apart from what was just discussed, little or no enduring significance. To the extent that they constituted the road leading to some contemporary positions in psychology (e.g., Miller's psychobiology, Bolles' cognitive motivational theory), and to the extent that these contemporary positions prove of lasting worth, then the grand systems will have played a worthwhile propaedeutic role; but such a hope can provide only the most tenuous vindication for the enor-mous amount of effort expended on the systematizations. The basic explanatory principles advanced in these systems likewise do little to vindicate them. These principles – reinforcement, drive reduction, cognitive maps, expectancy, contiguity, etc. – were for the most part not original, but consisted in objectivist reformulations of explana-tory principles acquired from physiologists, philosophers, other psychologists, and common sense. The failure of the grand systems did not even demonstrate the invalidity of these principles, since the methodological characteristics of the systems were sufficient on their own to vitiate them, although the extreme use made of these principles in the grand systems may well help make them less popular in future psychological theories.

2 CONTEMPORARY VARIETIES OF 'BEHAVIOURIST' THEORY

Almost all of the comments made here about behaviourist theories, in attempting to develop an explanation for their failure, have been about theories that have already been agreed on other grounds to be inadequate. This diffidence reflects one of the themes that has been implicit throughout this monograph, that the progressive development of scientific theories can occur by means of any number of methodological orientations, so long only as these are not taken sufficiently seriously as to be accorded more weight than the substantive principles which scientific inquiry develops. This consideration makes it impossible to give a general assessment of most contemporary varieties of behaviourism. Most contemporary varieties do not rely on the systematic methodological foundations of neobehaviourism, nor on the narrowly anti-mentalistic positivism of classical behaviourism. Rather, they are behaviourist only minimally, through the decision – based on grounds of personal preference and historical familiarity – to avoid as far as possible the use of introspective and impressionistic methods of investigation. It is only in terms of their historical context that such minimally related positions can be described specifically as 'behaviourist'; in many cases there is nothing more about them related to any of the systematic features of behaviourism than there was in the position of Cattell in 1904, quoted at the beginning of Chapter IV. Any detailed evaluation of the theories associated with contemporary varieties of behaviourism must be based, therefore, on the specific content of the theories and of the experiments which back them up. To the extent that the content of contemporary 'behaviourist' theories is not subordinate to their methodological characteristics, and to the extent that their methodological characteristics are not expected to justify them more or less independent of their content, these theories cannot be evaluated on methodological grounds.

And yet, that much said, one can hardly avoid acquiring some impressions about the way in which even the slight methodological constraints of much contemporary behaviourism have subtly influenced it. Consider the approach of sophisticated contemporary behaviourists such as Hebb, for whom 'CNS' has meant *conceptual* nervous system for twenty-five years, and who has developed elaborate models of the ways in which cognition, self-consciousness, and even moral sentiments can be represented in such an idealized structure; or Eysenck, who has developed a comprehensive personality theory based on the operation and interplay of a small number of inborn traits; or Broadbent, whose research concentrates on discovering the basic structures of cognitive functioning; or Berlyne, who has made pioneering studies of humour and aesthetics. The work of these psychologists comprises much of the best of contemporary psychology. All of these psychologists call themselves behaviourists, or 'methodological behaviourists', and in the sense that they avoid subjective and introspective methods and use observations of behaviour as their sole source of data, they undoubtedly are. And yet it is difficult to escape what is, again, an impression, that 'behaviour' for these theorists is mainly a *metaphor* in terms of which human activity as a whole can be elliptically described, and that they employ it because they find it personally congenial – and that they find it congenial because of the lingering belief that, despite everything, observations of behaviour alone, even though it is often highly complex verbal behaviour that is being observed, have some unique scientific validity. It is hard to explain why theorists investigating concept formation, personality dynamics, and aesthetics avoid any direct involvement with the personal (subjective) experience of their human subjects – who, unlike animals, can tell them about it – except by means of the unjustifiable assumption that behaviour data are the only scientifically valid ones and that introspective and impressionistic data are incorrigibly untrustworthy. To the unknown extent that these psychologists and other contemporary behaviourists restrict themselves to behaviour data on the basis of such assumptions, their methodological behaviourism is no more than the lingering traces of the behaviourist anti-mentalist prejudice. This is not, however, to condemn these psychologists; we all need a point of view from which to view human activity, and theirs, based on the behavioural metaphor, has become broad enough that it does not restrict their vision any more than another point of view might do. But it is to insist that to the extent that this prejudice is the basis for *their* behaviourism, then the reliance of these psychologists on the behavioural metaphor cannot be considered more than a personal preference, without any particular scientific justification, a preference that may be explained, but not scientifically justified, by psychology's history. Thus, while these psychologists are influential figures, it may be too much to expect – and hardly something to hope for – that their personal choice of investigative methods will continue to influence those who follow in their theoretical footsteps.

3 UNSYSTEMATIC POSITIVE CONTRIBUTIONS OF BEHAVIOURISM

Apart from theoretical considerations, the applications of behaviourist techniques in the field of behaviour modification may be cited as behaviourism's chief contribution to psychology in general. Various techniques of behaviour modification have had widespread application in therapeutic, educational, and other contexts; they are sufficiently well known as to make a review unnecessary. However, without questioning either the significance of behaviour modification techniques (but see note 20 to this chapter) or the close association that they have had with behaviourist psychology – but, on the contrary, to clarify that association – one can question the extent to which the introduction and use of behaviour modification techniques have been an *outgrowth* of behaviourism.

Behaviour modification started to become influential, specifically as behaviour *therapy*, with its practical development by psychiatrists disillusioned with psychoanalysis, mainly Salter[1] and Wolpe,[2] and was initially based on a muscular relaxation technique developed by the physiologist Jacobson.[3] Behaviourist psychologists quickly enough became interested in the possibilities of behaviour therapy and refined the techniques, but they were not responsible for introducing it as a method of treatment. Some prominent behaviour therapists such as Wolpe and Eysenck maintain that behaviour therapy is rigorously based on Hullian and Pavlovian theory. However, since the critical review of the theoretical basis of behaviour therapy by Breger and McGaugh,[4] and the resulting controversy, it has become very dubious whether behaviour therapy has any firm relationship of any sort to any behaviourist theories. In fact, the debate on the theoretical basis of behaviour therapy faded somewhat at the beginning of the 1970s, when it became generally recognized that the techniques are far more viable than any of the theories on which they are supposed to be based. London[5] celebrates this trend as marking 'the end of ideology in behavior modification', and observes that dependence on outdated behaviourist theories is something that behaviour therapists may be better off without. Finally, it no longer seems feasible to credit behaviourist psychologists with inventing behaviour therapy. The demonstration by Watson and Rayner[6] of conditioned and deconditioned fear responses in 'Little Albert' is often cited as the first exemplary case of behaviour therapy. However, Freedberg[7] has shown that behaviour therapy of quite an advanced sort was practised in the United States from about 1890 onwards, with Morton Prince and Boris Sidis as its chief innovators. The techniques used came, by 1909, to be held to be based on Pavlovian theory, although the relationship was not much clearer then than it is now. The techniques were comparable both in procedure and in effectiveness with some of the early modern ones, but their application did not involve the modern de-emphasis of conscious processes – a de-emphasis that, as Breger and McGaugh have shown, is in any case strictly *pro forma*.

None of this is to deny, however, that behaviourist psychologists have been more involved than anyone else in developing, extending, applying, and validating the techniques used in behaviour therapy, as well as in other, derivative, types of behaviour modification. Indeed, the characteristics of behaviourism which enabled it to serve as the basis for developing and extending these techniques constitute the principal contribution that behaviourism has made and can continue to make to psychology. The characteristics of behaviourism which enabled it to perform this function are not, however, among the ones emphasized in most accounts of behaviourism. They were features which emerged from the animal laboratories, where behaviourism itself was born. They stemmed from work which was remote from any areas of human concern, but they were remote also from the system-building concerns which were the primary interest of most neobehaviourists. They can best be described in a slightly roundabout way, through a brief discussion of the psychological practice of Skinner, in which, out of all the highly developed versions of neobehaviourism, they figure most prominently.

4 THE PRINCIPAL UNSYSTEMATIC CONTRIBUTION OF BEHAVIOURISM AS EXEMPLIFIED BY CERTAIN FEATURES OF SKINNER'S PSYCHOLOGY

Skinner has never accepted the hypothetico-deductive method, and until recently avoided theorizing of any sort. He clearly figures as a neobehaviourist nevertheless, because of his uncompromisingly methodological orientation to psychology. He was probably the earliest advocate of operational definitions in psychology, although he did not publish on the subject until some time later.[8] Even more than any of the other neobehaviourists, Skinner has insisted that the proper use of rigorous methods, both at the experimental and at the systematic level, was necessary and sufficient for the construction of a scientific psychology. He merely found no profit in going beyond simple generalizations in his reporting of results. His one bow to the fashions of neobehaviourism, the intervening variable concept of 'reflex reserve' in his first book, was later described by him as 'an abortive, though operational, concept which was retracted a year or so after publication. . . . It lived up to my opinion of theories in general by proving utterly worthless in suggesting further experiments.'[9] Consistent with his rejection of formal theories, the covert substantive principles in Skinner's position are not postulates or theoretical concepts with disguised ontological references. Instead, they function at a higher level, as basic metasystematic orienting assumptions. These assumptions are fairly prominent in Skinner's system, and account for all of its general systematic (although atheoretical) character.

The metasystematic orienting assumptions in Skinner's psychology are those of *environmental* and *speciational generality*. These assumptions are to some degree characteristic of all neobehaviourist theorizing, but are present in no other system so forcefully as in Skinner's. The assumption of environmental generality, to put it excessively crudely, asserts that the Skinner box is representative of all environments. The assumption of speciational generality, equally crudely, asserts that the pigeon is representative of all species of organisms. The two assumptions together provide a warrant for extrapolating from the behaviour of pigeons in Skinner boxes to the behaviour of all animals in all environments, and specifically to the behaviour of humans in complex social situations.

This caricature of Skinner's assumptions genuinely conveys their import, but they should in all fairness be stated less crudely. They are actually second-order, rather than first-order, assumptions, serving to indicate the procedures required for extending the range of a descriptive schema. The assumption of environmental generality is more properly that the modifications in descriptive terminology which are necessary in order to generalize a description of behaviour displayed in a Skinner box to cover that displayed in another, dissimilar, experimental environment, such as a runway or a slide, in which the stimulus features to which the animal responds are different, are sufficient to ensure the adequacy of the description (or rather, the descriptive schema of which the description is an instantiation) when applied to behaviour displayed in any environment. The assumption of speciational generality is that the modifications in descriptive terminology which are necessary in order to generalize a description of behaviour displayed by one species to cover that displayed by another, unrelated, species, are sufficient to ensure the adequacy of the description (or descriptive schema) when applied to any species. The upshot of the two assumptions is thus that a descriptive schema which proves adequate to characterize the behaviour of rats and pigeons in two different kinds of Skinner boxes is adequate to characterize the behaviour of all organisms in all environments.[10]

These orienting assumptions are fundamental to the systematic status – or systematic pretensions – of Skinner's psychology. Once identified, they can clearly be seen to be invalid. With regard to the assumption of speciational generality, it is plain that there are major differences in the behaviour displayed by different species even in highly controlled and comparable experimental environments. These differences are sufficiently great that they make descriptive terms applied to the interchange between organism and environment irrespective of species – such as 'reinforcement', applied as a descriptive term – only trivially applicable. That is, the behaviour of organisms in controlled operant environments varies so greatly as a function of species differences that the description of such behaviour by means of general rubrics such as 'reinforcement' and 'response shaping' forces the overlooking of much of the observable and systematic variability of the behaviour. To take a trivial instance, it is relatively easy to condition a rat to make a standard operant response (a bar press) for shock avoidance, but almost impossible to condition a pigeon to make a standard operant response (a key peck) for the same reinforcer. Various forms of the assumption of speciational generality were criticized by Beach,[11] but in a context that made his criticisms difficult to apply to purely descriptive formulations; furthermore, his criticisms did not focus on the behaviour of different species in similar, controlled environments. By contrast, Seligman[12] has surveyed a wide range of experiments that make the criticism incontrovertibly applicable to the description of behaviour emitted in Skinner boxes.

The assumption of environmental generality is, if anything, even more clearly fallacious. That is, it may be possible to restrict the experimental environment sufficiently so that some limited, but specific and useful, descriptive generalizations can apply to a broad range of species within such environments. With the relaxation of rigid restrictions on the composition of the environment, however, the variability of behaviour even within a single species becomes so great that the only descriptive generalizations that can be made applicable throughout the range of environmental conditions are those so broad and diffuse as to be practically meaningless.

For instance, Breland and Breland[13] have reported numerous examples of well-established conditioned behaviour chains which became severely disrupted when the experimental animals were removed from the original conditioning apparatus and placed in a complex situation more closely resembling the animals' natural environment. In the more complex situations the animals consistently interrupted their conditioned response chains with behaviour segments which the Brelands considered 'instinctive', which were never reinforced by them, which prevented the animals from receiving reinforcement, and which were very highly resistant to extinction. In many cases, furthermore, the animals proved very recalcitrant to 'reconditioning' in the more complex situation, but impossible to condition initially *at all* except within the control apparatus. The Brelands concluded that the language of operant levels, reinforcement contingencies, etc., was utterly inadequate to the description of behaviour in complex situations as observed by them; that is, application of this descriptive terminology simply did not permit them to describe what was going on.

Furthermore, the invalidity of the assumption of environmental generality can be demonstrated, again, even within the confines of a Skinner box. Even within a controlled operant environment, the behaviour of a given organism under a given reinforcement contingency with a given (operationally defined) motivational state will vary systematically as a function of the specific response chosen for examination, the specific discriminative stimuli serving as cues for the emission of the response, and the specific reinforcer contingent upon that response. To give a simple example, it is fairly easy to condition a pigeon to key peck with food as a reinforcer, but very difficult to condition it to do so with shock avoidance as a reinforcer. As a more elaborate example, Lawicka[14] has elegantly demonstrated the relationship between choice of discriminative stimuli and choice of response in dogs, with reinforcer held constant. In his experiment, dogs were trained to make a stimulus discrimination, which served as a cue to indicate which of two responses the dog would be reinforced for emitting. In all, the experiment had two sets of discriminative stimuli (location of tone as coming from upper or lower speaker versus pitch of tone as higher or lower) and two sets of responses cued by the discriminative stimuli (choosing the correct alley of a T maze versus running or not running down a runway); different dogs were assigned to each of the four combinations of stimulus discriminations and paired response choices in a 2 × 2 factorial arrangement. Lawicka found that dogs will learn to discriminate differences in pitch much more readily than differences in spatial position (of the speaker) when the discrimination cues a go-stay response choice. Conversely, they will learn to discriminate differences in spatial position much more readily than differences in pitch when the discrimination cues a left-right response choice.[15] Again, the terminology of reinforcement contingencies, operant levels, response shaping, etc., is entirely inadequate for describing the behavioural variability observed in such experiments. Such terminology is thus insufficient for providing descriptive generalizations about behaviour manifested in different environments, even when the environments are varied only in extremely specific and highly controlled ways.

Studies such as this establish the systematic pretensions of Skinner's writings, whereby he extends his descriptive account of the behaviour observed in his own animal studies to cover complex human behaviour,[16] as thoroughly unjustifiable. The metasystematic assumptions on which Skinner's systematic extrapolations are based have been treated at some slight length, so as to contrast them vividly with the other kind of covert principles which he makes use

Conclusion

of, broadly methodological ones in this case, relating to the perceptual specifiability of stimulus and response. Again, these features are, like the assumptions just considered, characteristic of other neo-behaviourist approaches to psychology than Skinner's, but not to the same extent. To treat these covert methodological principles, it will be necessary to reconstruct the way in which Skinner's approach to psychology can be considered to serve as the basis for purely descriptive, rather than explanatory, formulations.

Despite the impression one sometimes receives, Skinner is not an environmentalist, in the sense of assuming that environmental pressures cause all behaviour. His position in this regard is not simply a positivist disavowal of 'causes',[17] but accounts also for his total disinterest in physiology. Whether or not behaviour is *caused* by the environment, it takes place in an environment. Any recognizable piece of behaviour can be observed in its environmental setting. The behaviour may occur randomly with respect to all discernible features of the environment. More typically, a piece of behaviour may occur more frequently under some environmental conditions than under others. The environmental conditions include anything that can be described in the environment, so that the absence of females in mating season, for instance, comprises part of the environmental conditions under which certain birds are more likely to exhibit vacuum courtship activity. Description of the environmental conditions under which a piece of behaviour is most likely to occur comprises the most important part of a description of that behaviour in relation to the environment. Whether the environment forces, compels, elicits, potentiates, or provides an opportunity or a cue for, that behaviour, is irrelevant to the description of the behaviour as occurring in the environment.

When a piece of behaviour occurs, it usually has what we describe as an effect upon the environment. That is, some of the environmental conditions change either concomitant with or subsequent to the behaviour. Opening a door is an example of the first sort; the change in the environment is inseparable from the behaviour. Typing is an example of the second sort; the behaviour of hitting a key is generally followed by the action of a type die hitting the paper. In almost all cases of the second sort (as well as in some of the first, such as turning on a light), the change in environmental conditions is perceptibly separate from the behaviour of which it is considered an effect. For the change in environmental conditions in such cases to be identifiable as an effect of the behaviour (since the environment is constantly changing), it is therefore necessary that it be observed to be subsequent to the behaviour (or concomitant with it) on more than one occasion.

Certain changes in environmental conditions which we thus describe as effects of behaviour, may be among the observable conditions under which the behaviour can be identified as most likely to occur. That is, the conditions under which the behaviour is most likely to occur may include some conditions only in so far as they can be identified as effects of a previous occurrence of the same behaviour (in a sense of 'same' which is yet to be explained). Such conditions, if present other than as effects, are not ones under which the behaviour is most likely to occur. Description of these conditions *as* effects of a previous occurrence of the same piece of behaviour thus comprises an important part of the description of that behaviour in relation to the environment in which it occurs. Many pieces of behaviour may in this way be described as being most likely to occur under conditions which come about as effects of a previous occurrence of that behaviour. It is possible to attempt to discover, through careful observation, whether the effects of behaviour always constitute some of the conditions under which the behaviour is subsequently most likely (or least likely) to occur. To the extent that such relationships between the effects of behaviour and the subsequent occurrence of that behaviour can be discovered, they can be elaborated into systematic statements of the relationship between behaviour, the effects of the behaviour, and the environment, without in any case either addressing or begging the question of the causes of that behaviour.

Now, all of this is a very roundabout way of saying that behaviour may be reinforced by its consequences and that the behavioural repertoire may to some extent be described as a function of previous reinforcement. The roundabout way of expression, however, emphasizes the purely descriptive, rather than explanatory, character of (at least much of) Skinner's psychology. Tracing and manipulating the observable regularities is the sole focus of interest. It is important to establish this point, because it is only in so far as Skinner's psychology – and by extension other varieties of behaviourism and neobehaviourism – can be regarded as purely descriptive in the sense of this reconstruction, that the following comments can apply.

Conclusion

We have seen that the descriptive schema which Skinner developed in line with the foregoing analysis cannot in fact be applied universally, even before we consider human behaviour. But that is not the point. The point is that for the description to be applied at all, it is necessary to be able to identify the referents of the terms of it, the 'pieces of behaviour' and the 'environmental conditions'. This identification cannot be done – or at least it has not been done – in any consistent and formal way. Rather it involves a training of perception, the acquisition of the ability to *see* stimuli and responses, and the subtle effects of one on the other, in the flux of environmental conditions and organismic movements.

This training of perception is a subtle process, requiring considerable exposure to and practice in experimental situations. It has been the subject of almost no systematic investigations (at least within psychology), but constitutes the 'apprenticeship' component of the training of experimental psychologists. The final product of a simple conditioning experiment, such as a bar press by a rat, is usually identifiable by physical criteria such as the depression of the bar to a criterion depth. But the shaping of the bar-pressing response requires close and trained observation of the behaviour of the rat in the Skinner box, to serve as the basis for recognizing and reinforcing the rat's successive approximations to the desired response. Even closer and more sophisticated observation is necessary in order to shape the complex trick behaviours of demonstration animals, such as the playing of ping-pong by chickens, or the guiding of missiles by pigeons.[18]

Out of all the varieties of neobehaviourism, the work of Skinner and his students has exhibited the most highly developed and sophisticated instances of such trained and skilled perception. Skinnerians have excelled other animal psychologists in this respect, because of their emphasis on precise description and on control of the fine grain of the behaviour of individual animals, and conversely, because of their distaste for abstract theoretical structures. To a somewhat lesser extent, however, this acquisition of perceptual skills has been part of the training of experimental psychologists, especially animal psychologists, of every stripe. The acquired ability to *see* stimuli and responses, independent of the physical specification of either, and the skill involved in being able to recognize what groups of motions of an experimental animal have the necessary integrity or 'grouped-togetherness' to serve as the unit of description and control, have been the unacknowledged foundation on which all behaviourist practice has been built. The unique contribution of Skinner and his students has been to establish this foundation more firmly than any other psychologists have done; and it is a major contribution, because the foundation of perceptual skills remains intact when all of the systematic edifices built upon it, including Skinner's own, have crumbled.

This emphasis on the acquisition of perceptual skills helps to resolve one of the many long-standing anomalies in the theory and practice of behaviourist psychology, that concerning the identification of stimuli and responses. The complaint has often been made that although behaviourists insist on a purely objective observation base, they have never been able to define it, and their usage of the terms 'stimulus' and 'response', fundamental to that observation base, has been ambiguous and inconsistent. Much of the problem about use of the terms stemmed from the attempts to make explicit definitions of what was to count as stimulus and response; Koch refers to these problems in the quotations in the first section of Chapter IV. In practice, there was little or no problem in the use of the terms. Stimuli and responses are what one has learned to see as stimuli and responses. They are not initially, but they *become*, directly observable.

Training in ways of seeing, acquiring skill in the recognition of the functional significance and structural integrity that establish some physical movements as responses, learning to recognize the meaning of behaviour as established by these features of it as among the givens in what one is observing: all of this constitutes training in what can only be called applied phenomenology. The training is phenomenological in that it involves a subordination of one's preconceptions to the situation that is being observed, in order to discover the perceptual givens in the situation. The practice – as opposed to the theory – of behaviourism is thus in this sense based on applied phenomenology, and has been, furthermore, from the beginning.

It may seem absurd to suggest that behaviourism is based on phenomenology. The apparent absurdity, however, is due to little more than the fact that the two are not often thought to be related, and more specifically, that phenomenology is often thought to have close affinities with subjectivism and (most curiously) introspection. Nothing can be done about the strangeness of mentioning phenomenology and behaviourism in the same breath, but the supposed relationship of phenomenology with subjectivism and introspection can easily be disposed of.

Phenomenology is a way of looking; it does not specify the direction of looking. Introspection can be, but need not be (and usually is not) phenomenological, just as 'extraspection' or looking at the world can be, but need not be (and usually is not) phenomenological. Phenomenology involves merely the setting aside of our abstract and intellectual interpretative schemas in order to discover what is given in perception and how it is organized, apart from our knowledge of it. The 'givens' can be either those that are given as internal or those that are given as external to the self.

Neither does phenomenology necessarily involve any blurring of the boundaries between the self and the world. To be sure, the expressive power of a painting, say, may be such that we 'read into it' qualities of warmth, spirituality, or whatever; and in a phenomenological description of the painting these qualities will be referred to the painting even though we know that they are 'really' constituted by our reaction to the painting. But this is not a blurring of the boundary between self and world; on the contrary, the *dasein* of the object, or its quality of being-over-there separate from self, turns out to be one of the most general givens in any phenomenological account of objects. The fact that a phenomenological account may ascribe properties to objects that they do not 'really' have, as in the example given, may seem to make such accounts of scant utility in providing a basis for dealing with such objects. But it is precisely this feature of phenomenological accounts that makes them relevant; the fact that stimuli and responses are given in perception is what makes it possible to deal with them, despite the impracticality or even impossibility of making an unambiguous, purely physical specification of them.[19]

It may be objected that the process of learning to see stimuli and responses is the very opposite of a phenomenological process, since it is artificial, as shown by the fact that it requires directed training, and hence amounts to imposing a conceptual schema on the objects of inspection. There are two replies to this objection. The first is that it is not at all certain how widely such imposition occurs; among the Skinnerians in particular, close observation has typically preceded any description. The second is that it doesn't make any difference. Once the conceptual schema stops operating at the conceptual level and is incorporated into perception, then its implementation becomes one of the givens in perception; and the study of the givens in perception, regardless of their alleged source, is a phenomenological study. Consideration of how these givens become givens, or any attempt to restrict them, removes the enterprise from the phenomenological field. It is thus an error to say that phenomenology deals with the givens of perception only in so far as these are independent of learning. The consequence of such a position is that the organization of perception must be referred to something outside of perception (Köhler's neural fields, Husserl's quasi-Platonic pure ideas) in order to distinguish the 'truly givens' from the mere 'apparently givens'; and such a procedure, again, is not phenomenology. By contrast, looking at the physical movements that constitute the activity of a rat or a pigeon, and coming to see in those movements *meanings* – intimations of or approximations to the ultimate response that one wishes to shape – this, however strange it may seem, is phenomenology.

In this sense, therefore, despite the unfamiliarity and counter-intuitiveness of the claim, it is not unfair to judge that the practice of behaviourist psychology has long been based on an unrecognized and covert kind of applied phenomenology. The use of a covert phenomenological approach in determining the units of the subject matter in animal experiments constitutes an outstanding example of a methodological strategy that was both implicit and successful, and that was capable of being successful largely because it was implicit. Descriptive analyses of behaviour of a covertly phenomenological sort have gradually grown sufficiently detailed and acute, particularly but not solely in some of the formulations of Skinner and his students, as to justify being described as a 'phenomenology of behaviour'. This gradual and covert development of a phenomenology of behaviour may well constitute the most important positive contribution of all the varieties of behaviourism to the future development of psychology. In particular, it is the perceptual skills which many behaviourists have acquired in the course of their phenomenological training – skills in the identification of and subtle discrimination between responses as embodied in an ongoing stream of behaviour – that have equipped them to be at the forefront in developing and extending the techniques of behaviour therapy and other forms of behaviour modification.[20]

But while the inadvertent contribution of behaviourism and

neobehaviourism to the development of psychology may thus have been great, and especially notable in the various fields of psychological technology, that contribution is nevertheless, as a phenomenological contribution must almost always be, a propaedeutic one, not science but some of the groundwork on which science is built; and in psychology the science which could be built on that groundwork still lies an indeterminate distance away, in one of psychology's many possible futures. What behaviourism as the most important single influence in the continuing development of modern psychology can be said to have left us, besides the important negative lessons discussed earlier, is some portion of the tools appropriate for building a science – but not the science itself, and very little even in the way of durable preliminary structures which can be taken into the science.

NOTES

I INTRODUCTION

1 E.g., A. Paivio, W. D. Rohwer, Jr, W. W. Reese, and D. S. Palermo, 'Imagery in children's learning: a symposium', *Psychological Bulletin*, 1970, vol. 73, pp. 383-421; R. W. Sperry, 'A modified concept of consciousness', *Psychological Review*, 1969, vol. 76, pp. 532-6.

2 T. S. Kuhn, *The Structure of Scientific Revolutions,* Chicago, University of Chicago Press, 1962. Among the numerous attempts to apply Kuhn's analysis to psychology are D. L. Krantz, 'Research activity in "normal" and "anomalous" areas', *Journal of the History of the Behavioral Sciences,* 1965, vol. 1, pp. 39-42; D. S. Palermo, 'Is a scientific revolution taking place in psychology?', *Science Studies,* 1971, vol. 1, pp. 135-55; E. M. Segal and R. Lachman, 'Complex behavior or higher mental process: is there a paradigm shift?', *American Psychologist,* 1972, vol. 27, pp. 46-55; and W. B. Weimer and D. S. Palermo, 'Paradigms and normal science in psychology', *Science Studies,* 1973, vol. 3, pp. 211-44.

3 T. S. Kuhn, 'Logic of discovery or psychology of research' and 'Reflections on my critics', both in I. Lakatos and A. Musgrave (eds), *Criticism and the Growth of Knowledge,* Cambridge University Press, 1970.

4 M. Masterman ('The nature of a paradigm', in Lakatos and Musgrave, *op. cit.* [note 3; all cross references within square brackets are to notes within the chapter in which the cross reference is made]) has distinguished twenty-one separate senses of the term 'paradigm' in Kuhn's *Structure of Scientific Revolutions.* Some of these are trivial (e.g., number 13, 'an anomalous pack of cards'), but the remainder give evidence of what is at least a considerable breadth of usage.

5 Kuhn, *op. cit.* [note 2], p. x.

6 *Ibid.,* p. 10.

7 *Ibid.,* p. 11.

8 E. Heidbreder, 'Functionalism', in M. Henle, J. Jaynes, and J. J. Sullivan (eds), *Historical Conceptions of Psychology,* New York, Springer, 1973, pp. 280-81.

9 It was, in fact, the problem of understanding some of the differences between psychology and physics, or the social and natural sciences in general, that led Kuhn to the notion of paradigms. Kuhn states (*op. cit.* [note 2] p. x):

171

Notes to pp. 5–9

I was struck by the number and extent of the overt disagreements between social scientists about the nature of legitimate scientific problems and methods. Both history and acquaintance made me doubt that practitioners of the natural sciences possess firmer or more permanent answers to such questions than their colleagues in social science. Yet, somehow, the practice of astronomy, physics, chemistry, or biology normally fails to evoke the controversies over fundamentals that today often seem endemic among, say, psychologists or sociologists. Attempting to discover the source of that difference led me to recognize the role in scientific research of what I have since called 'paradigms', ... Once that piece of my puzzle fell into place, a draft of this essay emerged rapidly.

10 E. L. Thorndike, 'Animal intelligence: an experimental study of the associative processes in animals', *Psychological Review Monograph Supplement,* 1898, vol. 2, no. 8.

11 G. J. Romanes, *Animal Intelligence,* London, Kegan Paul, Trench & Trubner, 1882.

12 C. L. Morgan, *An Introduction to Comparative Psychology,* London, Scott, 1894.

13 See I. P. Pavlov, *Lectures on Conditioned Reflexes* (2 vols), New York, International Publishers Co., 1941.

14 There were, of course, political influences on the development of psychology in Russia, both before and after the Revolution, and the dominance of the Pavlovian position owes something to these. However, these influences would not prevent a Kuhnian analysis of Pavlovian psychology, for two reasons. First, Kuhn's analysis can take account of external pressures on the development of a science (cf. Kuhn, *op. cit.* [note 2], p. xii). Second, and more important, however much Pavlovian psychology may have depended on political factors to establish it as dominant in Soviet psychology, it has proved sufficiently viable there to retain its dominance on scientific grounds. It thus contrasts sharply with, say, Lysenkoist genetics, which became dominant on political grounds in the apparent absence of any scientific merit. For a review emphasizing the systematic character of modern Soviet psychology and its relation to Pavlov, see P. K. Anokhin, 'Ivan P. Pavlov and psychology', in B. B. Wolman (ed), *Historical Roots of Contemporary Psychology,* New York, Harper & Row, 1968.

15 J. B. Watson, 'Psychology as the behaviorist views it', *Psychological Review,* 1913, vol. 20, pp. 158-77.

16 E. G. Boring, *A History of Experimental Psychology* (2nd ed), New York, Appleton-Century-Crofts, 1950, p. 642.

17 J. B. Watson, 'The place of the conditioned reflex in psychology', *Psychological Review,* 1916, vol. 23, pp. 89-116.

18 R. C. Bolles (*Theory of Motivation,* New York, Harper & Row, 1967, p. 317) notes:

There was roughly a decade from about 1916, when Watson first promoted conditioning, to at least 1926, during which conditioning was accepted as a valid explanatory device and sometimes even proposed as the basis for all learning. All this time there was virtually no empirical support for the claims made for conditioning.

19 J. B. Watson, *Behaviorism,* Chicago, University of Chicago Press, 1961, pp. 3-5 (first published, 1924).
20 Boring, *op. cit.* [note 16], p. 642.
21 For detailed discussion and references see G. Humphrey, *Thinking: An Introduction to its Experimental Psychology,* London, Methuen, 1951.
22 R. S. Woodworth, *Contemporary Schools of Psychology,* New York, Ronald Press, 1931, p. 48.
23 Watson, *op. cit.* [note 19], pp. 5, 6, 18-19.
24 A. P. Weiss, *A Theoretical Basis of Human Behavior,* Columbus, Ohio, Adams, 1925.
25 In 1929; see B. F. Skinner, 'The operational analysis of psychological terms', *Psychological Review,* 1945, vol. 52, pp. 270-7.
26 C. L. Hull, 'Mind, mechanism, and adaptive behavior', *Psychological Review,* 1937, vol. 44, pp. 1-32.
27 E. C. Tolman, 'A new formula for behaviorism', *Psychological Review,* 1922, vol. 29, pp. 44-53.
28 E. C. Tolman, *Purposive Behavior in Animals and Men,* New York, Appleton-Century-Crofts, 1932.
29 I. Krechevsky, ' "Hypotheses" in rats', *Psychological Review,* 1932, vol. 39, pp. 516-32.
30 W. B. Cannon, *The Wisdom of the Body,* New York, Norton, 1932.
31 C. L. Hull, *Principles of Behavior,* New York, Appleton-Century-Crofts, 1943.
32 K. W. Spence, 'Theoretical interpretations of learning', in S. S. Stevens (ed), *Handbook of Experimental Psychology,* New York, Wiley, 1951.
33 C. D. Spielberger and L. D. deNike ('Descriptive behaviorism versus cognitive theory in verbal operant conditioning', *Psychological Review,* 1966, vol. 73, pp. 306-26), discussing 'theorists in the Hull-Spence tradition', state:

> The model developed by these theorists was designed to account for the behavior phenomena exhibited by nonarticulate organisms or by humans in simple learning situations in which the operation of higher mental processes was minimal, for example, in eyelid conditioning and rote learning. A major difference between the views of descriptive i.e. Skinnerian behaviorists and those of Hull and Spence is that the latter never claimed that their concepts would hold for complex verbal processes.

34 Hull, *op. cit.* [note 31].
35 The term was coined by E. J. Dijksterhuis (*The Mechanization of the World Picture,* Oxford, Oxford University Press, 1961) to satisfy the need for a noun corresponding to 'mechanistic'.
36 S. Koch, 'Psychology and emerging conceptions of knowledge as unitary', in T. W. Wann (ed), *Behaviorism and Phenomenology: Contrasting Bases for Modern Psychology,* Chicago, University of Chicago Press, 1964.
37 E.g., J. Dollard and N. E. Miller, *Personality and Psychotherapy,* New York, McGraw-Hill, 1950; B. F. Skinner, *Science and Human Behavior,* New York, Macmillan, 1953; B. F. Skinner, *Beyond Freedom and Dignity,* New York, Knopf, 1971.
38 E.g., J. Dollard, L. W. Doob, N. E. Miller, O. H. Mowrer, and R. R. Sears, *Frustration and Aggression,* New Haven, Conn., Yale University Press, 1939.

II POSITIVISM, REALISM, AND BEHAVIOURIST PSYCHOLOGY

1 T. Hobbes, *Concerning Body (de Corpore)*, in W. Molesworth (ed), *The English Works of Thomas Hobbes*, London, John Bohn, 1839 (first published, 1655).

2 P. Gassendi, *Syntagma Philosophicum* (*The Constitution of Philosophy*) (vols I and II of his *Opera Omnia*), Stuttgart, Frommann-Holzboog, 1964 (first published, 1658).

3 J. Locke, *An Essay Concerning Human Understanding*, ed. A. C. Fraser, New York, Dover, 1959, p. 26 (first published, 1690).

4 D. Hume, *A Treatise of Human Nature*, extracts in A. Flew (ed), *Hume on Human Nature and the Understanding*, New York, Collier, 1962, p. 7 (first published, 1739).

5 Wundt is discussed by D. B. Klein, *A History of Scientific Psychology: Its Origins and Philosophical Backgrounds*, New York, Basic Books, 1970, p. 853. The other examples are from W. L. Davidson, 'Professor Bain's Philosophy', *Mind*, 1904, vol. 13 (n.s.), pp. 161-79.

6 K. Pearson, *The Grammar of Science*, London, Scott, 1892.

7 E. Mach, *The Science of Mechanics: A Critical and Historical Exposition of its Principles*, La Salle, Illinois, Open Court, 1893 (first published in German, 1883).

8 Cf. S. S. Stevens, 'Psychology and the science of science', *Psychological Bulletin*, 1939, vol. 36, pp. 221-63.

9 L. Kolakowski, *Positivist Philosophy from Hume to the Vienna Circle*, Harmondsworth, Penguin, 1972.

10 *Ibid.*, p. 11.

11 *Ibid.*, pp. 11-12.

12 *Ibid.*, p. 13.

13 *Ibid.*, p. 15.

14 *Ibid.*, p. 17.

15 *Ibid.*, p. 34.

16 *Ibid.*, p. 35

17 P. G. Frank, *Modern Science and its Philosophy*, New York, Braziller, 1949.

18 The other two proposed rules of positivism – the fact-value distinction and the unity of scientific method – are of less importance here. They have traditionally been held as part of a hard-headed empiricist orientation to science, whether positivist or not. On the unity of science, see the statement of Helmholtz, below, p. 39. There are, it is true, fundamental differences between positivist and non-positivist conceptions of the unity of science, and these will be clarified below.

19 Frank (*op. cit.* [note 17]) points out that Mach's position has often been treated as equivalent to Berkeleyian idealism, to the position that perceptions are the only real existents and hence that reality is ultimately mental. Such an interpretation is evidently unfair to Mach. His claim was that perceptions are, not all of reality, but all that can be available to us; talk of anything existing independent of perceptions is thus empirically meaningless. The motto for Mach's position would not be Berkeley's *esse est percipi*, to be is to be perceived – but rather *cognosceri est percipi*, to be known is to be perceived. The interpretation of Mach's analysis as idealistic seemed to be the main basis for its rejection

as a basis for the implementation of positivism as an explicit programme for
psychology (cf. Stevens, *op. cit.* [note 8]).

20 Quoted by Frank, *ibid.*, p. 63.

21 All other descriptive or declarative statements of fact, that is. Analytic statements
(the validity of which is determined on purely logical grounds), imperative
statements ('Shut the door') and emotive-expressive statements ('I love you') do
not denote supposed facts; hence, the verifiability criterion cannot be applied to
them. They are empirically empty rather than empirically meaningless. There
may be meaningless imperatives ('Eat gloob!') but the verifiability criterion will
not identify them as they stand. Similarly, the same words ('I love you') may
denote a fact or express an emotion, or do both at once; but it is only in so far
as they do the former that they comprise a statement the meaningfulness of
which can be tested with the verifiability criterion.

22 Frank, *op. cit.* [note 17], p. 175.

23 Cf. Einstein's aphorism, 'God is subtle, but He is not malicious.' One of his
biographers (R. Clark, *Einstein: The Life and Times,* New York, Avon, 1972, p.
38) comments, 'With these words he was to crystallize his view that complex
though the laws of nature might be, difficult though they were to understand,
they were yet understandable by human reason.'

24 Quoted by Frank, *op. cit.* [note 17], p. 213.

25 Quoted by Frank, *ibid.*, p. 213

26 *Ibid.*, pp. 213-14.

27 In his unauthorized introduction to Copernicus' treatise on heliocentric
astronomy; see A. Koestler, *The Sleepwalkers: A History of Man's Changing Vision
of the Universe,* London, Hutchinson, 1959, for discussion.

28 See A. Koyré, *From the Closed World to the Infinite Universe,* Baltimore, Johns
Hopkins Press, 1957.

29 Newton's disclaimer (quoted by E. A. Burtt, *The Metaphysical Foundations of
Modern Physical Science,* London, Routledge & Kegan Paul, 1932, p. 219) appears
in his *Opticks*:

> To tell us that every species of thing is endowed with an occult specific
> quality by which it acts and produces manifest effects, is to tell us nothing:
> But to derive two or three general principles of motion from phenomena,
> and afterwards to tell us how the properties and actions of all corporeal
> things follow from those manifest properties, would be a very great step in
> philosophy, though the causes of those principles were not yet discovered:
> and therefore I scruple not, to propose the principles of motion
> above-mentioned, they being of very general extent, and leave their causes
> to be found out.

30 Others, such as Leibniz, remained unconvinced to the end, raising substantive
objections to Newton's fundamental concepts that, in retrospect, seem prophetic
(see Koyré, *op. cit.* [note 28]).

31 W. M. Wundt, *Grundzüge der Physiologischen Psychologie,* Leipzig, Engelmann,
1874.

32 J. McK. Cattell, 'The conceptions and methods of psychology', *Popular Science
Monthly,* 1904, vol. 66, pp. 176-86.

33 M. F. Meyer, *The Fundamental Laws of Human Behavior,* Boston, R. C. Badger, 1911.

34 J. B. Watson, 'Psychology as the behaviorist views it', *Psychological Review,* 1913, vol. 20, pp. 158-77.

35 A. P. Weiss, *A Theoretical Basis of Human Behavior,* Columbus, Ohio, Adams, 1925.

36 W. S. Hunter, *Human Behavior,* Chicago, University of Chicago Press, 1928.

37 A. O. Lovejoy, 'The paradox of the thinking behaviorist', *Philosophical Review,* 1922, vol. 31, pp. 135-47.

38 A. A. Roback, *Behaviorism and Psychology,* Cambridge, Mass., Sci-Art, 1923.

39 C. D. Broad, *The Mind and its Place in Nature,* London, Kegan Paul, 1925.

40 W. K. Estes, S. Koch, K. MacCorquodale, P. E. Meehl, C. G. Mueller, W. N. Schoenfeld, and W. S. Verplanck, *Modern Learning Theory,* New York, Appleton-Century-Crofts, 1954.

41 O. H. Mowrer, 'On the dual nature of learning: a re-interpretation of "conditioning" and "problem-solving"', *Harvard Educational Review,* 1947, vol. 17, pp. 102-48.

42 G. Fechner, *Zend-Avesta,* Leipzig, Voss, 1851; G. Fechner, *Elements of Psychophysics,* New York, Holt, Rinehart & Winston, 1966 (first published in German, 1860).

III BEHAVIOURISM'S BACKGROUND: THE INSTIGATION TO BEHAVIOURISM IN STUDIES OF ANIMAL BEHAVIOUR

1 G. J. Romanes, *Animal Intelligence,* London, Kegan Paul, Trench & Trubner, 1882.

2 G. J. Romanes, *Mental Evolution in Animals,* New York, AMS Press, 1969, pp. 15-16 (first published, 1884).

3 There are at least three different meanings of the 'objective-subjective' dimension, and they should be briefly distinguished. In the first, frankly evaluative sense, 'objective' means 'free from bias' or 'concerned with observable events, without fear or favour'; 'subjective', the antithesis, means 'biased' or 'swayed by personal considerations'. It is in this sense that introspective methods purported to be objective. In the second, more strictly descriptive sense, 'objective' means 'external to the perceiving organism' or 'publicly observable', while 'subjective' means 'dependent on the private or personal experience of the observer'. In this sense, the introspective methods were all subjective. In the third sense, 'objective' has something to do with 'objects', and with the observational methods (supposedly derived from physics) for dealing with them; the assumption in this sense is that objective observations are the only genuine ones, so that 'subjective' means 'concerned with unobservable inner entities or processes'. This last sense is the one that was called 'objectivist' in Chapter I, and was the usual sense used in behaviourist writings. It amounts to a combination of the first, evaluative sense, with the second, descriptive sense. However, in this chapter, unless otherwise stated, 'objective' and 'subjective' will always be used in the second, purely descriptive sense.

4 Even if it was mainly Descartes' followers, rather than Descartes himself, who committed it.

5 It should be clear that the introspective psychologies of, say, Wundt, Külpe, and Titchener were not guilty of this fallacy, at least in their studies of human consciousness. The introspection carried out by these psychologists was anything but casual and, more important, was not assumed to provide any easy, immediate, or incontrovertible information about the mind's contents and operations.

6 Romanes, *op. cit.* [note 1], p. 9.

7 *Ibid.*, pp. 4-5.

8 These examples are not taken from Romanes' writings, but from the later behaviourist controversies over transposition and cognitive maps, respectively.

9 C. L. Morgan, *An Introduction to Comparative Psychology*, London, Scott, 1894.

10 Romanes, *op. cit.* [note 1].

11 Morgan, *op. cit.* [note 9], pp. 36-52.

12 *Ibid.*, pp. 53-9.

13 *Ibid.*, p. 58.

14 *Ibid.*, p. 54.

15 Besides the desire for scientific rigour and the need to counter the prevalent tendency to anthropomorphism in the interpretation of animal behaviour, there was a theoretical basis for the canon. If 'higher psychical faculties' evolve from lower ones, then on evolutionary principles they must become fixed in the species as a result of environmental pressures which give them survival value to the organisms which possess them. Now, there are many activities (responding differentially to written or verbal commands to 'stop' or 'go', for example) which can be controlled by either higher or lower faculties; that is, in this case, either on the basis of linguistic competence or on that of reinforced stimulus discrimination. If we see an animal performing such an activity, we cannot tell whether the activity is being controlled by higher or by lower faculties. We can, however, judge unequivocally that the need to perform this specific activity was never, in the evolutionary history of the species, the occasion for development of the higher faculties, since *ex hypothesi* the lower ones can control it perfectly well. Development of higher faculties in this connection would consequently have been of no selective advantage to the organism; therefore, if they were to appear, they could be expected to be swamped in the genetic pool of the species. Thus, performance of such an activity, however it is governed in a specific instance, cannot serve as evidence for the existence and operation of higher faculties even on the most generous interpretation; for if the animal had not had to perform some other activity unmanageable by the lower faculties, the higher faculty would presumably never have evolved.

16 C. J. Warden, T. N. Jenkins, and L. H. Warner, *Comparative Psychology: A Comprehensive Treatise* (3 vols), New York, Ronald Press, 1935, vol. I, p. 27.

17 E. L. Thorndike, 'Animal intelligence: an experimental study of the associative processes in animals', *Psychological Review Monograph Supplement*, 1898, vol. 2, no. 8. Reprinted in E. L. Thorndike, *Animal Intelligence*, New York, Macmillan, 1911, and New York, Hafner, 1964. All page references will be to the 1964 edition.

18 *Ibid.*, p. 99.

19 *Ibid.*, p. 102.

20 Which Thorndike made explicitly (*ibid.*, p. 29). It was an assumption which Hobhouse (see below) was effectively to criticize. Justifying the assumption would require prior study of the animal's natural history. The assumption came to be replaced with the broader, more convenient, but probably false assumption that all associations can be made with equal ease. See M. E. P. Seligman, 'On the generality of the laws of learning', *Psychological Review,* 1970, vol. 77, pp. 406-18.

21 *Ibid.*, p. 26.

22 *Ibid.*, p. 123.

23 L. T. Hobhouse, *Mind in Evolution,* London, Macmillan, 1901.

24 *Ibid.*, p. 54.

25 *Ibid.*, p. 90.

26 Hobhouse receives about a dozen incidental references in the three enormous and comprehensive volumes of *Comparative Psychology* by Warden, Jenkins, and Warner *op. cit.* [note 16]. His work is not mentioned in one of the most influential texts, the *Principles of Animal Psychology,* by N. R. F. Maier and T. C. Schneirla (New York, Dover, 1964, first published, 1935), nor in most later texts. It is given one incidental reference in E. G. Boring's *History of Experimental Psychology* (New York, Century, 1929; 2nd ed, New York, Appleton-Century-Crofts, 1950).

27 Romanes, *op. cit.* [note 2], pp. 11-12.

28 Morgan, *op. cit.* [note 9], p. 53.

29 *Ibid.*, p. 29.

30 *Ibid.*, p. 358.

31 Thorndike, *op. cit.* [note 17], p. 22.

32 Hobhouse, *op. cit.* [note 23], p. 9. Orthogenic evolution is evolution toward a higher type. Hobhouse was aware of the value judgment involved.

33 R. S. Woodworth, *Contemporary Schools of Psychology,* New York, Ronald Press, 1931.

34 W. James, 'On some omissions of introspective psychology', *Mind,* 1884, vol. 9 (o.s.), pp. 1-26.

35 E. B. Titchener, 'Structural and functional psychology', *Philosophical Review,* 1899, vol. 8, pp. 290-9.

36 W. James, *The Principles of Psychology* (2 vols), New York, Holt, 1890.

37 J. R. Angell, *Psychology: An Introductory Study of the Structure and Function of Human Consciousness,* New York, Holt, 1904, p. 79.

38 J. R. Angell, 'The province of functional psychology', *Psychological Review,* 1907, vol. 14, pp. 61-91. The quotation is from p. 70.

39 There was some well-informed, although ineffective, opposition to basing functionalism on the model of consciousness dominant in introspective psychology. John Dewey (e.g., 'The reflex arc concept in psychology', *Psychological Review,* 1896, vol. 3, pp. 357-70) attempted to stress the integration of consciousness with stimulation from the environment on the one hand and with adaptive responses on the other. Experience, he maintained, could not be characterized outside the context of an individual's needs and actions; equally, 'stimulus' and 'response' could not be characterized independently of each other. Stimulus and response made up a single integrated series, while consciousness

Notes to pp. 77–86

was not something separate that did the integrating, but rather that which established the integration as unique to the requirements of a particular individual. Dewey was thus battering against the subject-object distinction basic to Western thought, by arguing that before our world-view becomes shaped by philosophical abstractions, objects are given in perception primarily in terms of their relevance or relation to the perceiver, rather than as autonomous existents. It is ironic that Dewey's 1896 paper is sometimes cited as the founding of functionalism (e.g., by Boring, *op. cit.* [note 26]). In fact, while Dewey had considerable influence on the movement, largely through his personal influence on Angell, and while his paper certainly helped to draw attention to biological factors in consciousness, his principal efforts in this paper and others to reconstitute the notions of stimulus and response had almost no systematic influence.

40 Boring, *op. cit.* [note 26], p. 556.

41 It may seem arbitrary to read Thorndike out of the functionalist camp, but in a sense it is arbitrary to put him anywhere; Watson was unwilling to count him as a behaviourist, also. Thorndike was a sufficiently individualistic thinker for it to be difficult to categorize him. Assimilating him to the British movement in comparative psychology is purely a matter of convenience, and is based on the thematic and conceptual similarities that have been discussed. Thorndike eventually came to describe himself as a 'connectionist' (*Selected Writings from a Connectionist's Psychology*, New York, Appleton-Century-Crofts, 1949), partly, it seems, because the term had not been appropriated by anybody else.

42 C. L. Hull, 'Learning: II. The factor of the conditioned reflex', in C. Murchison (ed), *A Handbook of General Experimental Psychology*, Worcester, Mass., Clark University Press, 1934.

43 W. M. Wundt, *Lectures on Human and Animal Psychology* (2nd ed), London, Scott, 1894.

44 E. B. Titchener, *A Textbook of Psychology*, New York, Macmillan, 1910.

45 M. F. Washburn, *The Animal Mind* (4th ed), New York, Macmillan, 1936.

46 W. S. Small, 'Experimental study of the mental processes of the rat', *American Journal of Psychology*, 1899-1900, vol. 11, pp. 133-65, and 1900-1, vol. 12, pp. 206-39. The quotation is from vol. 11, pp. 153-5.

47 A. J. Kinneman, 'Mental life of two *Macacus Rhesus* monkeys in captivity', *American Journal of Psychology*, 1901-1902, vol. 13, pp. 98-148; L. W. Kline, 'Suggestions toward a laboratory course in comparative psychology', *American Journal of Psychology*, 1898-1899, vol. 10, pp. 399-430; J. B. Watson, *Animal Education: The Psychical Development of the White Rat*, Chicago, University of Chicago Press, 1903 (this was Watson's doctoral thesis); J. B. Watson, 'Kinaesthetic and organic sensations: their role in the reactions of the white rat to the maze', *Psychological Review Monograph Supplement*, 1907, vol. 8, no. 2.

48 Wundt's *Lectures on Human and Animal Psychology* (*op. cit.* [note 43]) analysed the ideas and actions of animals in a way similar to Small's and, for that matter, Romanes', but much more fanciful than either. He wrote at length, for instance, on abstract reasoning processes in spiders. However, his account was not so sensationalistic as Small's, in that it made extensive use of what has been called here subjective inferences to mental operations. Unfortunately, the result was so wildly speculative that it came to be cited as a cautionary tale, illustrating the

fate of those who ignore the canon of parsimony (e.g., by Washburn, *op. cit.* [note 45]).

49 E. L. Thorndike, 'Review of W. S. Small, "Experimental study of the mental processes of the rat"', *Psychological Review*, 1901, vol. 8, pp. 643-4.

50 Watson's 1907 paper (*op. cit.* [note 47]) was the last in which he made any inferences to subjective experiences. His polemical 1913 paper ('Psychology as the behaviorist views it', *Psychological Review*, 1913, vol, 20, pp. 158-77) was based on lectures which he had delivered the previous year.

51 In particular, any kind of 'faculty psychology' was anathema in the United States, where it had been widely used as a vehicle for moral and religious training before the introduction of the introspective and experimental 'new psychology'. Watson concluded his announcement of the founding of behaviourism (1913 paper [note 50] p. 176) with the hope that behaviourism would soon be 'as far divorced from an introspective psychology as the psychology of the present time is from faculty psychology'. The viable components of the British programme of comparative psychology were, of course, similar to a kind of faculty psychology.

52 The irony would have been more pointed if the British approach had continued to stimulate progress in the field. Unfortunately, it did not, for reasons that are complex and not altogether clear. The main one seems to be that an autonomous scientific tradition of comparative psychology never developed in Britain. The writers mentioned, and others, all wrote comparative psychology as part of an overall evolutionary synthesis, or in order to propound general principles that could be applied to social philosophy, ethics, metaphysics, etc. To a surprising extent, they kept such general considerations out of their comparative psychology itself; but when the urgency of the general principles faded after the widespread acceptance of Darwinian theory they were not replaced by purely scientific considerations as a basis on which to do research in the field. The general lack of support for experimental psychology in Britain at the time is doubtless involved in the failure of an independent scientific tradition to develop specifically in comparative psychology.

53 Watson, *op. cit.* [1913 paper, note 50].
54 *Ibid.*, p. 160.
55 *Ibid.*, p. 161.
56 *Ibid.*, p. 159.
57 *Ibid.*, pp. 163-4.
58 *Ibid.*, p. 177.
59 J. B. Watson, *Behavior: An Introduction to Comparative Psychology*, New York, Holt, Rinehart, and Winston, 1967, pp. 18-19 (first published, 1914).
60 Watson, *op. cit.* [1913 paper, note 50], p. 167.
61 Behaviourism thus incorporated a kind of determinism from the beginning, but it was a determinism of environmental events, comparable to that of psychoanalysis, rather than of physical or physiological processes. The ambivalence about physiological reductive explanations in later behaviourist theorizing stems in part from this.
62 Watson, *op. cit.* [1913 paper, note 50], p. 166.
63 *Ibid.*, p. 163.
64 Of course, neither of Watson's claims stands up to examination: the physical sciences are neither so reliable, nor the introspective psychological ones so

unreliable, as he maintained. For the extent and limitations of inter-experimenter reliability in introspective psychology, see the brief discussion in Chapter I, above, and the longer one by G. Humphrey (*Thinking: An Introduction to its Experimental Psychology,* London, Methuen, 1951) on which it is based. For the quite comparable extent and limitations of inter-experimenter reliability in the physical sciences, and the *ad hominem* explanations sometimes made in its absence, see the extended discussions by T. S. Kuhn (*The Structure of Scientific Revolutions,* Chicago, University of Chicago Press, 1962) and M. Polanyi (*Personal Knowledge: Towards a Post-critical Philosophy,* Chicago, University of Chicago Press, 1958). Watson's claim on behalf of physics is, however, typical of and consistent with a methodological conception of science.

65 E.g., J. B. Watson, 'Image and affection in behavior', *Journal of Philosophy, Psychology, and Scientific Method,* 1913, vol. 10, pp. 421-8.

66 Watson, *op. cit.* [note 59], p. 321.

67 Watson's argument in this context was directed specifically against the version of the phylogenetic continuity hypothesis that sought to lift animals up (by maintaining that they have undeveloped higher faculties) rather than to pull man down (by maintaining that he has only highly developed lower faculties). The more general application of the argument to all instincts is apparent however, and was made by Watson himself (e.g., *Behaviorism,* Chicago, University of Chicago Press, 1930, Chapter 5) and, notoriously, by his student Z. Y. Kuo (e.g., 'A psychology without heredity', *Psychological Review,* 1924, vol. 31, pp. 427-48).

68 R. J. Herrnstein ('Nature as nurture: Behaviorism and the instinct doctrine', *Behaviorism,* 1972, vol. 1, pp. 23-52) has shown how the concept of 'instincts' gradually became transformed into that of 'drives' throughout the course of behaviourism.

IV IMPLICATIONS AND EFFECTS OF THE INCORPORATION OF POSITIVISM INTO BEHAVIOURIST PSYCHOLOGY

1 J. McK. Cattell, 'The conceptions and methods of psychology', *Popular Science Monthly,* 1904, vol. 66, pp. 176-86. The quotation is from pp. 179, 180, 184.

2 W. McDougall, *Introduction to Social Psychology,* London, Methuen, 1908; W. B. Pillsbury, *Essentials of Psychology,* New York, Macmillan, 1911; E. L. Thorndike, *Animal Intelligence,* New York, Macmillan, 1911; J. B. Watson, 'Psychology as the behaviorist views it', *Psychological Review,* 1913, vol. 20, pp. 158-77.

3 J. B. Watson, 'Image and affection in behavior', *Journal of Philosophy, Psychology, and Scientific Method,* 1913, vol. 10, pp. 421-8; J. B. Watson, *Behavior: An Introduction to Comparative Psychology,* New York, Holt, 1914.

4 J. B. Watson, 'The place of the conditioned reflex in psychology', *Psychological Review,* 1916, vol. 23, pp. 89-116.

5 J. B. Watson and R. Rayner, 'Conditioned emotional reactions', *Journal of Experimental Psychology,* 1920, vol. 3, pp. 1-14.

6 Z. Y. Kuo, 'A psychology without heredity', *Psychological Review,* 1924, vol. 31, pp. 427-48.

7 J. B. Watson, *Psychology from the Standpoint of a Behaviorist* (2nd ed), Philadelphia, Lippincott, 1924, p. vii.

8 S. Koch, 'Epilogue to study 1' in S. Koch (ed), *Psychology: A Study of a Science,* vol. III, New York, McGraw-Hill, 1959; S. Koch, 'Behaviorism', *Encyclopedia Britannica,* 1962; S. Koch, 'Psychology and emerging conceptions of knowledge as unitary', in T. W. Wann (ed), *Behaviorism and Phenomenology: Contrasting Bases for Modern Psychology,* Chicago, University of Chicago Press, 1964.

9 Koch, in Wann (ed), *op. cit.* [note 8], p. 9.

10 *Ibid.,* pp. 9-10.

11 *Ibid.,* p. 10.

12 G. Bergmann, *The Metaphysics of Logical Positivism,* Madison, Wisc., University of Wisconsin Press, 1954.

13 Koch, in *Encyclopedia Britannica, op. cit.* [note 8], p. 401.

14 Koch, in Wann (ed), *op. cit.* [note 8], p. 12.

15 E. C. Tolman, 'Operational behaviorism and current trends in psychology', in *Proceedings of the 25th Anniversary Celebrations of the Inauguration of Graduate Studies,* Los Angeles, University of Southern California Press, 1936. Reprinted as 'The intervening variable', in M. H. Marx (ed), *Psychological Theory: Contemporary Readings,* New York, Macmillan, 1951.

16 Significance tests and other inferential statistics are also decision procedures, of course. During the neobehaviourist period, psychologists came to rely more and more on increasingly sophisticated inferential statistics, in much the same way that they came to rely more and more on increasingly sophisticated logical techniques. The logical measures are being stressed here, to clarify the relationship with logical positivism, but it is clear that the reliance on inferential statistics to guarantee the validity of conclusions was equally a part of behaviourism's positivism. A review of the systematic limitations of inferential statistics used as decision procedures, paralleling the review which follows of the limitations of the logical techniques, is beyond the scope of this book. Such a review may be attempted subsequently. As a beginning, however, it may be mentioned that there is a wealth of evidence showing that the procedure of null-hypothesis testing is so dubious as to be practically invalid (e.g., W. W. Rozeboom, 'The fallacy of the null-hypothesis significance test', *Psychological Bulletin,* 1960, vol. 57, pp. 416-28). Variations on this procedure were the basis for most of the data analysis, including analysis of variance, reported in neobehaviourist experiments, and they continue to be widespread.

17 Koch, in Wann (ed), *op. cit.* [note 8], pp. 13-14.

18 C. L. Hull, 'Mind, mechanism, and adaptive behavior', *Psychological Review,* 1937, vol. 44, pp. 1-32. The quotation is from pp. 30-1.

19 *Ibid.,* p. 31.

20 E.g., G. Bergmann and K. W. Spence, 'Operationism and theory in psychology', *Psychological Review,* 1941, vol. 48, pp. 1-14; S. S. Stevens, 'Psychology and the science of science', *Psychological Bulletin,* 1939, vol. 36, pp. 221-63.

21 E.g., J. A. McGeoch, 'Learning as an operationally defined concept', *Psychological Bulletin,* 1935, vol. 32, p. 688 (abstract of a conference paper); S. S. Stevens, 'The operational definition of psychological concepts', *Psychological Review,* 1935, vol. 42, pp. 517-27. At a slight remove is K. MacCorquodale and P. E. Meehl, 'On a distinction between hypothetical constructs and intervening variables', *Psychological Review,* 1948, vol. 55, pp. 95-107.

22 E.g., C. L. Hull, *Principles of Behavior,* New York, Appleton-Century-Crofts,

1943; C. L. Hull, C. I. Hovland, R. T. Ross, M. Hall, D. T. Perkins, and F. B. Fitch, *Mathematico-Deductive Theory of Rote Learning: A Study in Scientific Methodology,* New Haven, Conn., Yale University Press, 1940; E. C. Tolman, *Purposive Behavior in Animals and Men,* New York, Appleton-Century-Crofts, 1932. These, however, are only the exemplars of what was significant precisely because it was becoming a general trend.

23 Koch, in Wann (ed), *op. cit.* [note 8], pp. 10-11. The reference to Hull is to C. L. Hull, 'Simple trial and error learning: A study in psychological theory', *Psychological Review,* 1930, vol. 37, pp. 241-56. The reference to Johnson is to H. M. Johnson, 'Some properties of Fechner's "Intensity of Sensation"', *Psychological Review,* 1930, vol. 37, pp. 113-23.

24 It was, of course, not just neobehaviourism that was affected, but also, by extension, other approaches to psychology as well. Kurt Lewin's attempts to construct a formal (and often hypothetico-deductive) field-theoretical account of behaviour while remaining firmly within a gestalt orientation provide the best example (K. Lewin, *Principles of Topological Psychology,* New York, McGraw-Hill, 1936, and 'The conceptual representation and the measurement of psychological forces', *Contributions to Psychological Theory,* 1938, vol. 1, pp. 1-247). But while the 'new view' of science and the hypothetico-deductive prescription had considerable influence throughout psychology, it was within neobehaviourism that they had by far their greatest influence and that their promise was most eagerly taken up. Furthermore, it was largely due to their eager promotion by neobehaviourists that these principles came to have such a widespread influence; it was mainly in this way that neobehaviourism was able to establish the standards and models for theorizing throughout psychology.

25 Koch, in Koch (ed), *op. cit.* [note 8], p. 777.

26 It is worth pointing out that the sarcasm is not justified. The logical positivist principles and techniques adopted within neobehaviourism, for the fulfilment of the scientific programme originally enunciated within classical behaviourism, were certainly highly abstract and rarefied, and had at times only a tenuous contact with actual scientific practice; but such a judgment can often be made about the theoretical and methodological apparatus, whether it works or not, of any advanced science. Even on the basis of its goals as Koch describes them, neobehaviourism can be seen as the only systematic, extensive, and detailed attempt ever made to fulfil Leibniz's dream of a universal calculus; to fulfil it, furthermore, in the context of ongoing scientific inquiry, where if accomplished it could do most good, rather than in that of the 'rational reconstruction' of an already completed theoretical structure, where in the absence of extension to just such ongoing inquiry, it could be little more than ornamentative; and to fulfil it, finally, through a sophisticated combination of logical and empirical operations and manipulations, so that it could be applied to the characterization of the world of contingent facts without impugning their contingent and independent character. Had the attempt been successful, the 'strange expectation' which Koch speaks of, that the extent to which a hypothesis was intuitively acceptable (i.e., 'plausible') was of little consequence, would have been perfectly valid. The failure of the attempt, both in practice and in principle, may quite properly stimulate a reappraisal of the limits of scientific technique; but it seems odd to take it as grounds for our scorn.

27 Thus, the logical positivist philosopher P. G. Frank (*Modern Science and its Philosophy,* New York, Braziller, 1949) judged that scholastic philosophy and the materialistic physical theories of Helmholtz and du Bois-Reymond jointly exemplified the conceptual errors which logical positivism was pledged to combat. Similarly, Hull (*op. cit.* [note 18]) castigated the early behaviourist A. P. Weiss for his faith in reductive materialism and the physicist Arthur Eddington for his faith in transcendental idealism – and both for their *faith,* as being the basis on which they each maintained adherence to their preferred positions to an extent greater than rigorous use of scientific method could justify.

28 Cf. L. Kolakowski's formulation of this requirement (*Positivist Philosophy from Hume to the Vienna Circle,* Harmondsworth, Penguin, 1972, p. 15) as the stipulation that a theoretical system which incorporates any abstractions 'must also be such that we do not forget that these abstractions are no more or less than means, human creations that serve to organise experience but that are not entitled to lay claim to any separate existence'.

29 Logical positivists, who initially tended to prefer a verificationist approach, were inclined to talk about empiricist criteria of *meaning.* Falsificationists, taking their lead from K. R. Popper (*The Logic of Scientific Discovery,* London, Hutchinson, 1959; first published in German, 1934), preferred to talk about criteria of *demarcation* between science and other forms of quite possibly meaningful discourse. The difference does not really amount to very much, however, since as already shown any empiricist criterion of meaning is stipulative and hence no more than demarcative. Popper's criterion of demarcation is thus not different in kind from logical positivist criteria of meaning; it is just more accurately named.

30 *Ibid.*

31 A. J. Ayer, *Language, Truth and Logic,* London, Gollancz, 1936.

32 A. Church, 'Review of A. J. Ayer, *Language, Truth and Logic*', *Journal of Symbolic Logic,* 1949, vol. 14, pp. 52-3.

33 E.g., C. G. Hempel, 'Problems and changes in the empiricist criterion of meaning', *Revue Internationale de Philosophie,* 1950, vol. 4; reprinted as 'The empiricist criterion of meaning' in A. J. Ayer (ed), *Logical Positivism,* New York, Free Press, 1959; C. G. Hempel, 'The concept of cognitive significance: a reconsideration', *Proceedings of the American Academy of Arts and Sciences,* 1951, vol. 80, pp. 61-77.

34 E.g., R. Carnap, 'The methodological character of theoretical concepts' and H. Feigl, 'Some major issues and developments in the philosophy of science of logical empiricism', both in H. Feigl and M. Scriven (eds), *Minnesota Studies in the Philosophy of Science, Volume I: The Foundations of Science and the Concepts of Psychology and Psychoanalysis,* Minneapolis, University of Minnesota Press, 1956.

35 *Ibid.*

36 The examples are from G. Maxwell, 'Criteria of meaning and of demarcation', in P. K. Feyerabend and G. Maxwell (eds), *Mind, Matter, and Method: Essays in Philosophy and Science in Honor of Herbert Feigl,* Minneapolis, University of Minnesota Press, 1966.

37 Maxwell [*ibid.*] argues cogently that it is not possible in principle.

38 The phrases are from W. B. Weimer and D. S. Palermo, 'Paradigms and normal science in psychology', *Science Studies,* 1973, vol. 3, pp. 211-44.

39 Hull, *op. cit.* [note 22].

40 E. C. Tolman and C. H. Honzik, '"Insight" in rats', *University of California Publications in Psychology,* 1930, vol. 4, pp. 215-32.

41 L. P. Crespi, 'Amount of reinforcement and level of performance', *Psychological Review,* 1944, vol. 51, pp. 341-57.

42 Feigl, *op. cit.* [note 34], p. 12.

43 H. Poincaré, *Science and Hypothesis,* London, Scott, 1905.

44 P. Duhem, *The Aim and Structure of Physical Theory,* New York, Atheneum, 1962 (translated from the 2nd French edition, 1914).

45 Duhem (*ibid.,* p. 218) found it necessary to appeal to the eventual 'good sense' of scientists to make a choice between theories possible: 'The day arrives when good sense comes out so clearly in favor of one of the two sides that the other side gives up the struggle even though pure logic would not forbid its continuation.'

46 Maxwell, *op. cit.* [note 36], pp. 320-21. The symbols M and P refer to the discussion of the confirmability criterion, above; they replace equivalent symbols in Maxwell's text.

47 Popper, *op. cit.* [note 29], p. 50.

48 *Ibid.,* p. 42.

49 *Ibid.,* p. 70.

50 On the contrary, if the empirical content of a theory is measured as a function of the ratio of theoretical postulates to entailed predictions (using a hypothetical calculus of infinite sets, as mentioned above), then the inclusion of any existential statement among the postulates will necessarily *decrease* the empirical content by increasing the ratio.

51 P. W. Bridgman, *The Logic of Modern Physics,* New York, Macmillan, 1927.

52 P. W. Bridgman, 'The nature of some of our physical concepts', *British Journal for the Philosophy of Science,* 1951, vol. 1, pp. 257-72. The quotation is from p. 257.

53 Bridgman, *op. cit.* [note 51], p. 24.

54 C. G. Hempel, 'A logical appraisal of operationism', in P. G. Frank (ed), *The Validation of Scientific Theories,* New York, Beacon Press, 1956.

55 Strictly speaking, what is assumed is not invariance but independence, i.e., that changes in the value of the operationally defined property or concept are independent of and unrelated to changes in the values of the undesignated 'background' variables. This qualification does not affect the argument.

56 A similar point has been elegantly made by M. E. P. Seligman ('Control group and conditioning: a comment on operationism', *Psychological Review,* 1969, vol. 76, pp. 484-91), with detailed examples from recent psychological research.

57 Poincaré, *op. cit.* [note 43].

58 This reference to operational definitions may seem to contradict what was said earlier about the subordination of operational analysis to theoretical factors in the context of construction. It is perfectly true that the choice of variables and limits with respect to which an operational analysis is carried out is no more inherent in the problem situation in the context of reconstruction than in that of construction, nor is the analysis any more able to be complete. The point here is only that the content of the old theory need not place any limitations on what variables and limits are chosen as important to emphasize in the context of reconstruction. The basis on which the choice is made is irrelevant to the

significance and import of the resulting analysis (i.e., the distinction between the traditional contexts of discovery and justification operates within the context of reconstruction, and only within that context), but the variables and limits selected can be expected to be arbitrary with respect to – not entailed by – the old theory, since otherwise they would already have been emphasized in the context of construction.

59 Cf. Planck's gloomy conclusion that 'New scientific truth does not triumph by convincing its opponents and making them see the light but rather because its opponents eventually die' (quoted by E. G. Boring, *History, Psychology, and Science: Selected Papers,* New York, Wiley, 1963, p. 247).

60 T. S. Kuhn, *The Structure of Scientific Revolutions,* Chicago, University of Chicago Press, 1962.

61 I. Lakatos, 'Falsification and the methodology of scientific research programmes', in I. Lakatos and A. Musgrave (eds), *Criticism and the Growth of Knowledge,* Cambridge University Press, 1970, p. 93.

62 *Ibid.,* p. 178.

63 S. E. Toulmin, 'Does the distinction between normal and revolutionary science hold water?', in Lakatos and Musgrave (eds), *op. cit.* [note 61], p. 47.

64 T. S. Kuhn, 'Reflections on my critics', in Lakatos and Musgrave (eds), *op. cit.* [note 61].

65 As pointed out in Chapter I, the various neobehaviourist theories each had preferred areas of application, sets of problems which they were particularly well designed to handle. It was in connection with the claims of each to generality that competition and experimental criticism arose.

66 M. Scriven, 'Views of human nature', in Wann (ed), *op. cit.* [note 8], p. 180.

67 According to the distinction between intervening variables and hypothetical constructs proposed by MacCorquodale and Meehl (*op. cit.* [note 21]), the former are no more than labels for an observed functional relationship. They are entirely specified by the independent and dependent variables in terms of which they are defined, and have no status except a descriptive one. Hypothetical constructs, by contrast, have 'excess meaning' over and above the operations involved in their specification as members of a postulate set, and thus refer to entities or processes presumed to function independently, outside the theory. The contrast is not so great as it seems, however. Whatever hypothetical constructs do outside of the theory, within the theory they are supposed to be permitted to function only in so far as their characteristics are rigorously specified in the make-up of the postulate set. Like any other theoretical terms, therefore, hypothetical constructs and intervening variables alike are required to have their theory-relevant meaning specified entirely within the theory.

68 W. K. Estes, S. Koch, K. MacCorquodale, P. E. Meehl, C. G. Mueller, W. N. Schoenfeld, and W. S. Verplanck, *Modern Learning Theory,* New York, Appleton-Century-Crofts, 1954.

69 C. L. Hull, *A Behavior System,* New Haven, Conn., Yale University Press, 1952.

70 *Ibid.,* p. 354.

71 E. C. Tolman, 'Principles of purposive behavior', in S. Koch (ed), *Psychology: A Study of a Science,* vol. II, New York, McGraw-Hill, 1959, p. 148.

72 E. R. Guthrie, 'Association by contiguity', in Koch (ed), *op. cit.* [note 71], p. 161.

73 Watson, *op. cit.* [note 2], p. 159.
74 *Ibid.*, p. 163.
75 It was on this basis that Watson declared Wundt's introspective psychology to be inescapably caught up with 'the religious mind-body problem' (see the quotation on p. 10 above).
76 The pragmatist writings of James and Dewey were not closely addressed at first to scientific questions. They could be seen as similar to explicitly positivist analyses of science only by those already engaged in the latter (as recounted by Frank, *op. cit.* [note 27]). Pierce's writings were very similar to later logical positivist analyses, but were almost completely unknown before their publication as collected papers in the 1930s.
77 Hull, *op. cit.* [note 18], p. 31.

V CONCLUSION: TOWARD A GENERAL EVALUATION OF BEHAVIOURISM

1 A. Salter, *Conditioned Reflex Therapy*, New York, Farrar, Straus, 1949.
2 J. Wolpe, 'Objective psychotherapy of the neuroses', *South African Medical Journal*, 1952, vol. 26, pp. 825-9.
3 E. Jacobson, *Progressive Relaxation*, Chicago, University of Chicago Press, 1939.
4 L. Breger and J. L. McGaugh, 'Critique and reformulation of "learning theory" approaches to psychotherapy and neurosis', *Psychological Bulletin*, 1965, vol. 63, pp. 338-58.
5 P. London, 'The end of ideology in behavior modification', *American Psychologist*, 1972, vol. 27, pp. 913-20.
6 J. B. Watson and R. Rayner, 'Conditioned emotional reactions', *Journal of Experimental Psychology*, 1920, vol. 3, pp. 1-14.
7 D. J. Freedberg, 'Behaviour therapy: a comparison between early (1890-1920) and contemporary techniques', *Canadian Psychologist*, 1973, vol. 14, pp. 225-40.
8 Skinner's version of operationism, as outlined in his contribution to the *Psychological Review* 'Symposium on operationism' (1945, vol. 52, pp. 270-7), is slightly different from both Bridgman's and Stevens'. Bridgman's original version (*The Logic of Modern Physics*, New York, Macmillan, 1927) requires a statement of the operations involved in measuring the quantity of something. Stevens' ('Psychology and the science of science', *Psychological Bulletin*, 1939, vol. 36, pp. 221-63), which is an extension of Tolman's definitional procedure for intervening variables and the version most common in neobehaviourism, requires a statement of the operations stipulated to be necessary for postulating the existence of something. Skinner's, by contrast, requires a specification of the circumstances under which the *name* of the thing is emitted or, more generally, of the situation in which a concept is employed. Skinner's operationism is thus, like his theories, more narrowly descriptive than is the case with most varieties of neobehaviourism.
9 B. F. Skinner, 'A case history in scientific method', in S. Koch (ed), *Psychology: A Study of a Science*, vol. II, New York, McGraw-Hill, 1959, p. 369.
10 It should be made clear that this statement of Skinner's assumptions is a reconstruction from his experimental practice rather than a report of his own

statements. Rendering the assumptions explicit makes it possible to understand why Skinnerians often attach great weight to the fact that Skinner carefully replicated most of his rat experiments with pigeons before claiming that he could account for human behaviour.

11 F. A. Beach, 'The snark was a boojum', *American Psychologist,* 1950, vol. 5, pp. 115-24, and 'The descent of instinct', *Psychological Review,* 1955, vol. 62, pp. 401-10.

12 M. E. P. Seligman, 'On the generality of the laws of learning', *Psychological Review,* 1970, vol. 77, pp. 406-18.

13 K. Breland and M. Breland, 'The misbehavior of organisms', *American Psychologist,* 1961, vol. 16, pp. 681-4, and *Animal Behavior,* New York, Macmillan, 1966.

14 W. Lawicka, 'The role of stimuli modality in successive discrimination and differentiation learning', *Bulletin of the Polish Academy of Sciences,* 1964, vol. 12, pp. 35-8 (cited in Seligman, *op. cit.* [note 12]).

15 The fact that the discriminated tones were vertically rather than horizontally separated rules out any easy appeal to orienting responses to account for the differential ease of discrimination.

16 B. F. Skinner, *Walden Two,* New York, Macmillan, 1948; *Science and Human Behavior,* New York, Macmillan, 1953; *Verbal Behavior,* New York, Appleton-Century-Crofts, 1957; *Beyond Freedom and Dignity,* New York, Knopf, 1971.

17 However, it is certainly true that of all the neobehaviourists, Skinner was the most uncompromising and assertive in declaring the positivist character of his psychology (in *The Behavior of Organisms,* New York, Appleton-Century-Crofts, 1938).

18 B. F. Skinner, 'Pigeons in a pelican', *American Psychologist,* 1960, vol. 15, pp. 28-37.

19 It is worth noting that research on computer simulation of learning processes (e.g., L. Uhr, *Pattern Recognition, Learning, and Thought: Computer-Programmed Models of Higher Mental Processes,* Englewood Cliffs, N.J., Prentice-Hall, 1973) has for the most part had to concentrate on pattern recognition, that is, on attempts to specify what constitutes a stimulus. The specification has by no means been fully successful, especially with 'natural' stimuli. Computers, unlike people, make no 'contribution of the observer' in perception – or if they do, it is no easier to pinpoint it in computers than in people. The phrase 'contribution of the observer' simply refers to the fact that it has not yet been found practical to characterize things that are perceived in a way that consistently eliminates reference to a potential observer who does the perceiving. The 'problem of the observer' is the problem of what this contribution consists in, and of how it varies across persons, situations, and cultures. It has been a central problem in Western philosophy (mainly because of the desire to get around it), and the discussion in this chapter makes it clear that behaviourism made no progress in resolving or avoiding it by use of purely 'objective' descriptions; on the contrary, the unspecifiable contribution of the observer turns out to be necessary for any such description, as of stimuli and responses, to be made. A related point has been made at length by H. L. Dreyfus (*What Computers Can't Do: A Critique of Artificial Reason,* New York, Harper & Row, 1972).

20 Any demonstration of how behaviourist practice has provided much of the basis

for behaviour modification does not, of course, have any implications for the systematic efficacy of behaviour modification. As in the case of Skinner described above, the question of how it is possible to make the descriptions at all is separate from the question of how valid are the systematic claims made on the basis of the descriptions. Ability to see the phenomena to be studied is in every case only the first, vitally important, step. The next is to make valid comprehensive claims; and behaviour modification is coming to follow the example of the rest of behaviourism in that the claims made on its behalf are coming increasingly under suspicion. See, for example, E. W. Russell, 'The power of behavior control: a critique of behavior modification methods', *Journal of Clinical Psychology*, 1974, vol. 30, pp. 111-36.

INDEX

191

International Library of Philosophy & Scientific Method

Editor: Ted Honderich

(*Demy 8vo*)

Allen, R. E. (Ed.), **Studies in Plato's Metaphysics** *464 pp. 1965.*
  Plato's 'Euthyphro' and the Earlier Theory of Forms *184 pp. 1970.*
Allen, R. E. and Furley, David J. (Eds.), **Studies in Presocratic Philosophy**
  Volume II *448 pp. 1975.*
Armstrong, D. M., **Perception and the Physical World** *208 pp. 1961.*
  A Materialist Theory of the Mind *376 pp. 1967.*
Bambrough, Renford (Ed.), **New Essays on Plato and Aristotle**
  184 pp. 1965.
Barry, Brian, **Political Argument** *382 pp. 1965.*
Bird, Graham, **Kant's Theory of Knowledge** *220 pp. 1962.*
Bogen, James, **Wittgenstein's Philosophy of Language** *256 pp. 1972.*
Broad, C. D., **Lectures on Psychical Research** *461 pp. 1962.*
  (*2nd Impression 1966.*)
Crombie, I. M., **An Examination of Plato's Doctrine**
  I. Plato on Man and Society *408 pp. 1962.*
  II. Plato on Knowledge and Reality *583 pp. 1963.*
Day, John Patrick, **Inductive Probability** *352 pp. 1961.*
Dennett, D. C., **Content and Consciousness** *202 pp. 1969.*
Dretske, Fred I., **Seeing and Knowing** *270 pp. 1969.*
Ducasse, C. J., **Truth, Knowledge and Causation** *263 pp. 1969.*
Edel, Abraham, **Method in Ethical Theory** *379 pp. 1963.*
Farm, K. T. (Ed.), **Symposium on J. L. Austin** *512 pp. 1969.*
Findlay, J. N., **Plato: The Written and Unwritten Doctrines** *498 pp. 1974.*
Flew, Anthony, **Hume's Philosophy of Belief** *296 pp. 1961.*
Fogelin, Robert J., **Evidence and Meaning** *200 pp. 1967.*
Franklin, R., **Freewill and Determinism** *353 pp. 1968.*
Furley, David J. and Allen, R. E. (Eds.), **Studies in Presocratic Philosophy**
  Volume I *326 pp. 1970.*
Gale, Richard, **The Language of Time** *256 pp. 1967.*
Glover, Jonathan, **Responsibility** *212 pp. 1970.*
Goldman, Lucien, **The Hidden God** *424 pp. 1964.*
Hamlyn, D. W., **Sensation and Perception** *222 pp. 1961.*
  (*3rd Impression 1967.*)
Husserl, Edmund, **Logical Investigations** *Vol. I: 456 pp. Vol. II: 464 pp.*
Kemp, J., **Reason, Action and Morality** *216 pp. 1964.*
Körner, Stephan, **Experience and Theory** *272 pp. 1966.*
Lazerowitz, Morris, **Studies in Metaphilosophy** *276 pp. 1964.*
Linsky, Leonard, **Referring** *152 pp. 1967.*
Mackenzie, Brian D., **The Origins of Behaviourism,** *1976.*
MacIntosh, J. J. and Coval, S. C. (Eds.), **Business of Reason** *280 pp. 1969.*
Meiland, Jack W., **Talking About Particulars** *192 pp. 1970.*
Merleau-Ponty, M., **Phenomenology of Perception** *487 pp. 1962.*
Naess, Arne, **Scepticism** *176 pp. 1969.*
Perelman, Chaim, **The Idea of Justice and the Problem of Argument**
  224 pp. 1963.
Rorty, A. (Ed.), **Personal Identity** *1975.*